sita returns

Modern India through Her Eyes

sita returns

Modern India through Her Eyes

CHARU WALIKHANNA

PAPER MISSILE
NIYOGI BOOKS

Published by
NIYOGI BOOKS
Block D, Building No. 77,
Okhla Industrial Area, Phase-I,
New Delhi-110 020, INDIA
Tel: 91-11-26816301, 26818960
Email: niyogibooks@gmail.com
Website: www.niyogibooksindia.com

Editor: Jyotika Mansata
Cover: Misha Oberoi
Design: Shashi Bhushan Prasad

ISBN: 978-93-86906-59-5
Publication: 2018

Printed at: Niyogi Offset Pvt. Ltd., New Delhi, India

CONTENTS

PROLOGUE

The whole world watched agape,
Sita's agnipariksha,
Her trial by fire.

As she was swearing the oath,
A miracle occurred.
The earth shook and the rocks split,
A divine lotus-shaped throne arose.
Seated on the lotus was the Earth Goddess.
Stretching out both her arms, she said, 'Come home, my child.'
Divine flowers showered from the heavens
As the throne descended back into the chasm of the earth.

Where did Sita disappear?
There was no evidence of her being,
Just the empty ground with fragments of soil.
Only heart-wrenching wails of women, beating their breasts
At the unjust fate of a faithful wife.

Years ago Sita had emerged forth,
While King Janak was furrowing the land.
This time she chose to retreat back
Into the lap of Mother Earth.

Now centuries later, the heavens opened again,
Heralding Sita's arrival.
To see what promise modern India holds for its women,
Filling them with pride and an identity so high,
Lighting the skies with brightness and hope.

INTRODUCTION

'She turns her disappointment into triumph.
Her grief into joy.
Her rejections into approvals.
If no one believes in her
It does not matter.
She believes in herself.
Nothing stops her.
No one can touch her.
She is woman'.[1]

Sita, born of the earth, raised among sages, the non-uterine daughter of King Janak of Mithila, devoted wife of Lord Ram, and single mother of twins Kush and Luv, is the central female character of the Hindu epic *Ramayana.* Sita, as an integral part of the Indian psyche, has been venerated by Valmiki in the first chapter itself,

> *Sita, the best one among ladies, a possessor of all best qualities befitting an ideal lady, the one who is as though fashioned by a divine marvel, born in*

> *Janak's family and became Dashrath's daughter-in-law, and she who is the loving wife and an ever-amiable alter ego of Ram, even she followed Ram to forests, as with Lady Rohini following the Moon ...*[2]. [sic]

A paragon of beauty, intellect, dedication, and sacrifice, Sita, the ideal woman, struggled with maintaining her dignity, her identity, and her rightful place in a patriarchal society. Worshipped throughout India, she is considered a symbol of chastity, the wife who stayed unwavering in her devotion and loyalty towards her husband Ram; like Ruth who, swearing eternal fidelity to her husband, said, 'Don't urge me to leave you or to turn back from you. Where you go I will go, and where you stay I will stay. Your people will be my people, and your God my God.'[3]

It is believed that Sita's birth preordained the elimination of evil forces, and that she was the link between the opposing forces of righteousness and evil, symbolised by Ram and Ravan respectively. Her sense of dharma or duty was superior to that of her husband, the most perfect of men, the *maryada purush* Ram, who sacrificed his conjugal life at the altar of 'higher' duties, first to fulfill the expectations of him as a son, and subsequently, that as a king. Sita's devotion and love for Ram, her firmness of purpose in upholding the truth, even at the cost of her own life, are all put to the test. Ram, her beloved husband, publicly declares that he rescued her to save his own honour, and Sita is made to prove her chastity multiple times. She passes each test and wins hands down, like the devotee who triumphs over the god he worships.

Fiercely independent, Sita dared to challenge social norms and break loose from the shackles of patriarchy, while making her own choices with courage and dignity. She did not allow her life situation to choose for her, nor did she let the abuse dishearten her. Finding strength in the knowledge of her own uniqueness—self-confident, self-disciplined, and selfless—she chose to uphold her self-respect, thereby exemplifying the power of womankind. Sita's offer of *agnipariksha* (after the battle) was not an act of self-annihilation, nor that of surrendering to the whim of an unreasonable husband. On the contrary, her emerging from the fire unscathed was proof of her defiance in challenging her husband's aspersions, showing him to be so flawed in his judgement that the gods had to come and pull up Ram for his foolishness.[4] When a pregnant Sita was abandoned deceitfully in the cruelest manner, placing her and her unborn child's life in jeopardy, she demonstrated to the world that it was possible for an abandoned single mother to not only survive, but successfully raise two outstanding and fearless sons. Sita loved her husband wholeheartedly, and sacrificed a life of luxury to be exiled with him in the forest; but when her honour was repeatedly doubted by her beloved for what he considered his kingly duty, she chose with supreme dignity to reject her husband and return to Mother Earth. Rightfully so, people perceive Sita's steadfastness as a sign of emotional strength, because she refused to forsake her dharma in upholding the truth, even though Ram forsook his dharma as a responsible husband.

Often underplayed is the fact that Sita had a mind of her own; she stood her ground and and remained determined not to give up even if the odds looked daunting. She even went to the extent of rebuking her husband that he was not man enough to take his wife along into exile. During their exile in the forest, Sita envisaged the danger in Ram's decision to eliminate the rakshasas of Dandaka forest without any provocation, and felt it was her role as a wife to remind the *maryada purush* of his dharma when she perceived he was straying from the path of righteousness. Delivering a powerful discourse on non-violence, she reminded

Ram that duty always pairs with privilege, and since he had renounced his Kshatriya powers, he should avoid involving himself in activities that run contrary to forest life and its norms. Sita, not one to be cowed down, proudly proclaimed that since she was Janak's daughter and Ram's wife, she could not refrain from free speech on observing dharma retreating. Graciously Ram responsed to her words of caution and said *'Oh, graceful Sita, you are the co-pursuer in dharma with me, hence you are loftier to me than my own life ...'*[5] When Hanuman had come to Lanka searching for her, she could have easily made her escape. But, not wanting to steal her husband's glory, she chose to wait for Ram to rescue her from Ravan's captitivty. When Ram wanted her to testify to her own innocence for the second time, instead of complying, Sita prayed to Mother Earth to take her into her recourse

Sita epitomizes the struggle of women throughout the world. Now centuries later, she felt the time was ripe to return to the mortal world, and to see with her own eyes whether or not the condition of women had transformed in 2017. Sita was curious and eager to see if any transformation had occurred in Indian society, in what was now the twenty-first century. She felt a mixture of excitement and trepidation with the many questions that arose in her mind. How were women being treated, and did they have any existence independent of their fathers or husbands? What was their relationship with nature? Did human beings follow the advice of wise ancient sages—live closer to nature and its eternal laws will protect you. Was kingship still the form of governance? Were people discriminated against on grounds of gender, race, or ethnicity, or did they live in harmony? She knew the only way to satisfy her curiosity was to return and find out for herself.

Thousands of years later, using her mystical yogic powers, Sita wanted to return to the place of her birth. The heavens opened and Sita started her descent to earth. Filled with a sense of wonder, she approached the diamond-shaped country of what is now called India—extending from the Himalayas in the north to the Indian Ocean in the south. Magnificent India, where different parts were interconnected by threads of kinship and bonding, forming a harmonious whole. Viewing the country with her intuitively perceptive gaze, Sita wanted to start her journey with the Indian woman; covering her feminine life cycle from childhood to youthful adolescence and then to a mature woman. Sita wondered if it was an exciting time for women to be alive in. What were the challenges Indian women faced? Did her own story influence their future? If yes, why and how? A plethora of questions plagued her as she was spinning downwards—another horizon, another sky, another world. But then she thought—are not women's destinies intertwined, irrespective of which world or century?

The sunlight was blinding her eyes as, tumbling wildly, Sita approached the denser layers of the earth's atmosphere. Her descent became more and more uncomfortable as she came closer to the surface of Mother Earth. Sita was unable to breathe as the intensely toxic air was choking her, and her vision was clouded by what seemed like layers of dust, smog, soil, and even lead. Closer to the earth, the air became warmer, fogging her senses, so despite intending to go to a temple in her birthplace, Sita mistakenly landed at a temple of justice. Force of habit made her turn to the scriptures for guidance, but since it was a court, someone handed her the Constitution of India. A man in a black coat informed Sita that this was the supreme law of their land. The guiding principle was in its Preamble.

> WE, the people of India, having solemnly resolved to constitute India into a Sovereign Socialist Secular Democratic

> Republic, and to secure to all it's citizens: JUSTICE, social, economic and political; LIBERTY of thought, expression, belief, faith and worship; EQUALITY of status and of opportunity; and to promote among them all FRATERNITY assuring the dignity of the individual and the unity and integrity of the Nation.

She was greatly heartened by this pledge for equality and justice.

In Sita's time, teachings were largely transmitted orally from guru to shishya or teacher to pupil. Even her sons were made to learn verbatim the 25,000 verses of the *Ramayana* by Rishi Valmiki. In the India of today, complex systems of writing seemed to have developed, and there was an abundance of written scriptures. Sita was highly stimulated by these scriptures of modern India. Reading the Constitution, she was overawed to know that its makers had enshrined in it the principles of gender equality, guaranteeing equal rights to women in every sphere. Yet she instinctively felt a sense of caution, for who knew better than her the contradiction between what is written and what is practiced. She needed to know what the condition of women in their homes, society and villages really were. Were women indeed enjoying the fairness and equality that the above Constitution claimed to bestow? Or were women victims of discrimination and gender-based violence, which undermined their health, dignity, security, and autonomy? How complicit were the family and wider community in the discrimination and violence against women? Was the condition of women in India any different from what it was centuries ago?

With the Constitution of India in her hand, Sita moved from the temple of justice to the temple of the gods. She tried walking on what appeared to be a footpath, but there were more people sleeping on it than walking. It rekindled memories of the time when she, along with Ram, had spent their first night in exile on a bed of leaves on the muddy ground. But these people sleeping in the open, exposed to the vagaries of nature, appeared to be homeless, with no one to care for them. Sita became anxious on seeing their plight, especially the troubling reality of women, who were at risk of sexual exploitation and violence. Haunting memories of her being abducted by Ravan, and the devastating consequences on her life that followed, sent a chill down her spine. Determined not to be deterred by her own memories, she continued in her quest to search for answers. She decided to go back to where it all started—the place of her birth.

Endnotes

1. 'Serena Williams pens female-power poem for fashion show'. *Samoa Observer*, September 13 2016, http://www.samoaobserver.ws/en/13_09_2016/sport/11272/Serena-Williams-pens-female-power-poem-for-fashion-show.htm Recited by Serena Williams—the only tennis player, female or male, to have won maximum singles titles—via loudspeaker as part of a female-power soundtrack for a runway show of her own Serena Williams Signature Statement collection for HSN during New York Fashion Week on 12 September 2016. In a backstage interview she explained 'I wrote it right after Wimbledon and during the Olympics, and I just was in this moment of I want to empower women. It was right around the time I was asked, "How do you feel about being the greatest female athlete?" and I was, like, they never ask men that.'
2. Desiraju Hanumanta Rao and K.M.K. Murthy, trans., *Valmiki Ramayana,* 1:1:26b, 27, 28a, https://valmikiramayan.net/utf8/baala/sarga1/bala_1_frame.htm
3. The King James Bible, The Old Testament, Ruth 1:16, https://www.bible.com/bible/1/RUT.1.kjv
4. Madhu Kishwar, 'Yes to Sita! No to Ram! The Continuing Popularity of Sita in India', *Manushi*, issue no.98 (January–February 1997), http://www.manushi-india.org/pdfs_issues/articles/Yes%20to%20Sita,%20No%20to%20Ram.pdf

5 Desiraju Hanumanta Rao and K.M.K. Murthy, trans., *Valmiki Ramayana,* 3:10:21b, c, https://valmikiramayan.net/utf8/aranya/sarga10/aranya_10_frame.htm

Birth and Childhood

After a session with his ministers
And High Priest, Satananda,
Janak set in motion the process
To get the Yaga started.

When the preliminaries were over,
On the selected morning
An hour before the sun awakes, the king
Hurried alone to the grounds.

His hands held firm the consecrated plough,
And as he made the first push
He turned the sod to cleanse the site once more
For the ancient ritual.

For Janak, King of Videhas,
It was a prayerful act,
A planted king-idea germinating
And ready for fulfillment

Poised between the infinitudes without
And within, his hands guided
The old ploughshare with an infallible
Sense of time and direction.

He had not progressed far, when suddenly
A lightning flash crossed his path;
He stopped, and his dazed eyes fell on the form
Of a wondrous golden child.

Since the vision had sprouted as it were
From the opening furrow,
The enraptured Janak cried 'Sita!'
And bent down in gratitude.[1]

The world around us is full of mysterious things and miraculous experiences, and the birth of a child is one of life's greatest miracles. Sita began reminiscing about how her birth had been mired in mystery and had always remained an enigma. The *ayonija* (non-uterine) daughter of the earth had selected her own parents, in a world where human beings are created through the process of conception, pregnancy, labour and delivery, with no power to determine who their child will be. Sita was not born of the flesh of King Janak, but love for her was suffused in his heart the moment the baby girl's tiny fingers stretched out to clasp his hand. Sita may not have had her father's eyes or her mother's smile, but she was their whole world. Special from the start, she ushered unimaginable joy into the lives of all around her. In fact, after the arrival of Sita, Janak's wife gave birth to a daughter, Urmila, and his brother's wife gave birth to two daughters, Mandavi and Shrutakirti. All four girls were adored by their fathers, who ignored taunts that that they only had daughters and no sons!

Sita, the non-uterine daughter of Queen Sunaina and King Janak of Janakpur, elder sister of Urmila and cousins Mandavi and Shrutakirti, avatar of Goddess Lakshmi[2], is known by a number of names—Seeta, Seetha, Vaidehi, Janaki, Maithili, Ayonija, Bhoomija. On returning to earth, she discovered a shrine had been erected in her memory at her birthplace in Sitamarhi, Bihar. There was a temple with a wedding hall, a Shiva temple and the Sita Kund or pond, where people claimed Sita was found by King Janak. People say the pond never goes dry, since Janak had been ploughing the fields in an act of penance during the drought facing his kingdom. Disbelievers have tried to clean the pond and dry it in vain. They even made an attempt to pour milk into the pond, but it did not mix with the water and settled down.[3]

Sita proceeded towards Jankichhati, where after her birth she had been taken to celebrate *chhati*, a ritual on the sixth day of the newborn's arrival. There, the *chhati* ceremony was being performed for a newborn baby boy. Sita became a part of the celebrations, no longer a viewer gazing down from dizzying heights. She was overjoyed to see righteous people still existing, and true believers of God praying with great devotion. She remembered how the birth of a child had always been a joyous occasion, with many festivals and ceremonies being associated with it. According to Hindu belief, the soul enters the foetus 22 days after conception. Emotions develop after four months, and the mind begins to function during the fifth month, as the foetus wakes from the sleep of subconscious existence. The intellect develops in the sixth month. Each movement of her twin babies had given Sita a thrill. Every flutter and kick made her radiant with euphoria. Her appetite increased, and she smiled more often. Repeatedly, her hand would go to her belly, as if protecting her unborn child. Her body swelled freely, and the moment of birth was approaching. Anxiously, she waited for the arrival of their child, Ram and hers. But she waited all alone.

Sita had given birth to two boys at midnight. The sons of Queen Sita and King Ram were not born in a palace. Not at Ayodhya nor Mithila. But in the middle of a forest in Valmiki's hermitage on the full moon night of Sravan Poornima.[4] *The twins had been born in the forest, and despite their being princes, there had been no celebrations. The hermit boys came in the middle of the night and gave the good news to Valmiki, urging him to go and bless the babies. He was pleased to see that the two boys were divinely beautiful. Then, with a bunch of kusa grass, splitting it from the root, he converted it into a protective charm against evil spirits. The aged women monks took the sanctified protective grass charm from Sage Valmiki's hand, and in a ceremonial rite, brushed the newborn babies with it.*

> *The eldest one brushed by the head part of the kusa grass tuft would be called Kush. Brush thereafter the younger one of the babies, by the end of the tuft. This part of the bunch is known as luv and he would be known as Luv. These twins boys will be renowned by the two names I am giving them now.*

On the advice of the sage, the women performed the purification and naming rituals, for the safety and protection of the two babies, through song and recitation. Ironically, it was the same night Shatrughana, brother of Ram, had spent in the hermitage of Valmiki, while proceeding on his way towards Madhuvana to kill the demon Lavana. He went and congratulated Sita saying, 'Oh Lady, how fortunate it is that you have become a mother.'[5]

Sita recalled how in Hindu society each important milestone is celebrated by a particular *sanskard*[6], wherein the significance of that occasion is ritualistically conveyed. A Hindu child enters into the world through ceremony and ritual, and *sanskaras* are performed to celebrate and sanctify life's crucial junctures by informing the family and community and securing their blessings. Marriage was the most important *sanskara*. Predictably, in a patriarchal society many important *sanskaras* are reserved exclusively for boys, for example the *Janeu* or investiture ceremony where the 'sacred thread' is placed over the shoulder of the boy, usually performed before he starts his education.[7] Even the *Antyeshti* or last rite of passage after the death of a person is traditionally supposed to be performed by his son or closest male relative.[8]

Sita was gratified to see that the Indian society was changing irrevocably, and in families with no sons, daughters were defiantly performing the last rites of their parents, surmounting the resentment by relatives and society. She was elated to see abundant examples in average middle-class families where daughters had become the mainstay of their parents, especially in old age and sickness—a responsibility once reserved exclusively for the son. Parents, who at one stage considered it a disgrace to even drink a glass of water in their daughter's home, now were increasingly opting to live with their daughters. Sita met Selina, who presented an unusual sight—a woman in charge of a crematorium; a Christian completely at ease with Hindu rituals. 'The mind needs to be strong. Women can do any job they want. There were times when I have cremated bodies even at 3 am. I have never felt scared,' she says. To keep her family afloat, Selina started taking up odd jobs, mostly as a daily-wage construction worker, until she 'grabbed' the job of a helper at the crematorium. 'An acquaintance, who was then the caretaker, taught me the basics. For the first four years, I worked under him, assisting him in cremating bodies,' she says. 'My daughters never objected to my work, but my brother initially tried to stop me. I said, "Ok, will you take care of my expenses? Will you repay my debts?" Then he stopped,"[9] she said to Sita.

While on the surface things seemed to have improved, the deeper she delved, the more disturbing revelations came to light. Sita was confronted with the harsh reality that even after almost 70 years of being a modern-day democratic republic, the birth of a girl child in India was still looked upon as a curse. She was appalled to see advanced medical technologies being rampantly misused to determine the sex of the foetus, and abort it if it was a female. Adding to the prejudice, the girl child was discriminated against even after birth. Not breast-fed for long, the girl child was being deprived of basic nutrition, healthcare, education and the right to make informed choices in her life.

From Blessing to Burden—Female Infanticide

Baby Sita's gentle touch and her sweet cry had a soothing effect on King Janak. A child wants to be held close and touched affectionately from the very first day of life. Touch is a strong communicator of emotions, and bonds the child with a parent. To a newborn, a parent's nurturing closeness is as important as milk. Sita, on observing other parents, found that rather than clasping the infant girl to their bosom, their actions were calculated to produce her death instead. In India, while people prayed to female deities and looked up to them as embodiments of strength, courage, wealth and education, yet a deep-rooted preference for a male child still prevailed, leading to a skewed sex ratio. Sita, wanting to know the population of women in India, and the ratio of women to men, read the Census of India 2011. It stated that Kerala, the state with the highest literacy rate (93.91 per cent) led the country with the highest sex ratio with 1084 females per 1000 males, which was higher than the national average (940); while Haryana featured the lowest sex ratio in India with just 877 women per 1000 males. Interestingly, the ratio favoured women in the comparatively remote backward states of Manipur (985), Meghalaya (989), Mizoram (976) and Andhra Pradesh (993).[10] Like the sex composition of the total population, the sex composition by age group is vital for studying the demographic trends of the young population, its future patterns, and particularly, the status of the girl child. In the 2001 Census, the sex ratio of the population in the age group 0–6 years has been registered as 927, declining from 945 in 1991 and 962 in 1981. The decreasing sex ratio in this age group has had a cascading effect on population over a period of time, leading to a diminishing sex ratio in the country. The imbalance that has emerged in this early age group is difficult to be removed and will remain to haunt the population for a long time to come.

The problem is better understood if one considers the fact that the child sex ratio (CSR) is primarily influenced by the sex ratio at birth (SRB) and mortality rates in early childhood. The natural sex ratio at birth usually has a higher number of female births. It ranges between 943 and 954. But the advantage of a higher SRB is neutralized due to higher female infant mortality rates in the normal population. Prior to 2001, the child sex ratio was close to the SRB but due to rapid decline, this has fallen even below the natural SRB in the 2001 Census. This paints a grim picture of the status of the girl child in the country and a majority of the states. As per the 2011 Census, the child sex ratio (0–6 years) has shown a further decline from 927 females per 1000 males in 2001 to 919 females per thousand males in 2011.[11] The magnitude of the decline can be seen by the fact that more than half of the States/Union Territories have registered a decline in child sex ratio during 2011. Alarming trends are discernable in some of the major states like Jammu and Kashmir, Madhya Pradesh, and Andhra Pradesh. While Punjab, Haryana, and Kerala continued to show an increase, Lakshadweep, which had shown an increasing trend from 1991–2001,[12] noted a decrease in 2011.

Sita was astonished that discrimination against a girl child started even before she is born, when she is killed as a foetus. If she manages to see the light of day, then she is killed as an infant. She heard the radio address 'Mann ki Baat', by the Prime Minister of India, where he expressed concern about the declining child sex ratio in the country, which had been on the decline and was currently the worst it had been since Independence. The preference for sons had taken an ugly turn. The barbarous practice of female infanticide prevailed, and methods included stuffing the newborn's mouth with black salt, lacing the milk she drinks with either pesticide, toothpaste, sedatives, the juice of the poisonous oleander berry or the grains of paddy husk that can slit the tender gullet.[13] Sita even heard accounts of female infants being suffocated with either a wet towel or a bag of sand, or being drowned in a basin of milk. Disquieting was the story of a woman, depressed since the birth of her third daughter, who strangled her one-month-old baby before committing suicide.[14] The most unbelievable story was of a mother who, annoyed at giving birth to a girl child instead of a male, murdered the three-month-old baby and hid her body inside a washing machine.[15]

Sita, having spent a long time amongst intimidating rakshasis, thought she was immune to being horrified, but almost let out a scream on hearing the hair-raising story of a mother who refused to nurse her baby girl; to silence the infant's famished cries, village women squeezed milky sap from a coriander shrub, and after mixing it with castor oil, thrust the poisonous potion down the newborn's throat. The baby died a painful death.[16] Sita was aghast at how human beings had become so inhuman that they could murder helpless innocent babies without a thought. Even the rakshasis had left her untouched, only making empty threats while saying, *'Squeeze the neck of this cruel woman. Why do we delay? We will divide her in equal pieces and dance afterwards propitiating Nikumbila.'*[17] Now these rakshasis appeared to be angels compared to the cruel mothers of the India of today.

On the one hand, Sita read with glee about how revolutionary changes were taking place in India—from wrestling to business, women were excelling in fields that were until recently completely dominated by men. While on the other hand, Sita was repelled on reading reports of the prevalence of female infanticide in twenty-first century India. North, south, east, west—no region remained untouched. Horrific stories from Tamil Nadu, Bihar, Orissa, Rajasthan, and Maharashtra, chilled her blood. In Tamil Nadu there was a recognized 'female infanticide belt' that started from Madurai, extending across the districts of Dindigul, Karur, Erode, Salem, Dharmampuri and North Arcot.[18] While the government of Tamil Nadu was patting itself on the back for eradicating female infanticide, a shallow grave of a female infant was found at Narasingapuram in Vickramangalam block, Madurai District.[19] Sita was also alarmed to see a tiny body with 17 stab wounds. The culprit, her mother, was upset about having a second daughter.[20] A survey conducted by the Social Action Forum for Manav Adhikar (SAFMA)[21] in New Delhi revealed that 8.2 per cent of the respondents knew someone who had indulged in infanticide.[22] While this figure on its own may seem low, and likely under-reported, the mere existence of such a crime, in the very capital of India, was indicative of its prevalence.

Parents who did not have the heart to directly slaughter their baby girls simply neglected them or abandoned them, allowing them to die for want of timely and proper medical assistance. The Minister of Women and Child Development admitted in an interview, 'You have 2,000 girls who are killed in the womb every day ... Some are born and have pillows on their faces choking them.'[23]

Sita was terrified to imagine that a baby, growing in her mother's womb, may already be in danger because her parents might choose to end her life if she is born female. Sita's eyes fell on a study[24] conducted in Uttar Pradesh, a state for which she had special love since she had gone to Ayodhya as a young bride. The report contained responses to the question as to whom the respondents would rather give birth to—a daughter or a son. 50 per cent of the rural men and 64 per cent of the rural women stated that they would prefer a son; while 72 per cent of the urban men and 78 per cent of the urban women said they had a penchant for a daughter. The organisation conducting the survey suspected that the urban respondents had probably given this response because they knew the purpose of the study and, being qualified educated professionals, wanted to look good. Their hypocrisy was exposed when they were queried as to why they wanted a boy. Not denying the desire for a son, they gave a number of reasons in justification, which included the belief that a person can only get moksha if he is cremated by his son, and the notion that a son is a support in one's old age.

Most women in India are socialised to believe that their status depends upon how many sons they have. The study revealed that mothers, depending on their access to resources, usually see two options. In rural areas the option is having many pregnancies in order to have sons (according to the study, 34 per cent of the women had five to nine pregnancies and 16 per cent had over 10 pregnancies, with one woman even having 15 pregnancies); and in urban areas women consider having pre-birth gender testing and ending a pregnancy if the foetus is a girl (though none admitted to having an abortion). The respondents (both male and female) who were a part of the sample in the urban area of Agra were highly educated, ranging from graduates to holders of doctorates. All denied ever having undergone a sex-determination test. Strangely enough, the facts mirrored a different position since almost all had one son and one daughter, which leads one to presume that there may have perhaps been some sex determination intervention to arrive at such a perfect family combination! The study also revealed the tremendous social and cultural pressure to bear sons. If the woman has only daughters she is cursed for it and the husband's family even goes to the extent of threatening remarriage, not taking into account that the husband is solely responsible for the sex of the child.

She glanced through a range of statistics which narrated a grim story of female foeticide, girl child discrimination and gender bias.

- 60 per cent of girls receive full immunization, against 62 per cent of boys. (Ministry of Statistics and Programme Implementation, 2012).
- Girls in India have a 61 per cent higher mortality than boys aged 1–4 years (National Family Health Survey III).
- 56 per cent of adolescent girls (15–19 years) in India are anaemic, as against 30 per cent of adolescent boys (National Family Health Survey III).
- The school dropout rate amongst adolescent girls in India is as high as 63.5 per cent (Ministry of Statistics and Programme Implementation, 2012).

Sita had heard that in India every year, during the 10 days of Dussehra, a dramatic folk re-enactment takes place of her rescue from Ravan's captivity in Lanka, marking the victory of good over evil. She found women taking the art of theatre one step ahead and watched the play, 'Muthi Bandho Behna', performed by women on a mission to prevent infanticide in Madhya Pradesh's Chambal area, which is infamous for being infested by bandits. Clutching her infant daughter, the actor, a simple village woman, dramatically announces to her family that she would not let them kill her baby, and looks at the audience for support. There is no response, only a collective hush. Suddenly, the silence is pierced by a shout: *mutthi bandho behna* (clench your fist, sisters), and tears of guilt roll down the faces of the mothers in the audience who, in the past, had failed to save their daughters from infanticide.[25]

How did the blessing of a child come to be seen as a burden? Sita wanted to give a high-pitched shout—wasn't it time to assert that each woman and girl was a unique and valuable human, entitled to equal opportunities and universally-adopted human rights? It was time for a world where the girl child was celebrated with equal pomp and festivity as that of a boy child. A world in which she had access to equal opportunities to study, to grow and to prosper as her male counterpart. Could anyone hear her voice? Every cloud has a silver lining, and Sita's silent cry motivated a woman to challenge the system. She hailed from a village in Jaisalmer, Rajasthan—a popular international tourist destination, where there were only 12 girls in a village with a population of 2,000. Supported by her husband, this bold mother initiated change by literally gifting life to her female baby, while everybody else around her was killing their daughters.[26]

Female Foeticide

Motherhood is considered to bring a woman joy and fulfillment. The maternal instinct is nature's purest, most tender and powerful tie. Yet, in India, one of the crudest forms of discrimination was taking place subtly, sanctioned in the name of culture. Girls were socialised to believe that they were less important than boys, less deserving of basic human rights in life. They were treated as inferior and were socialized to put themselves last, thus undermining their self-esteem. Some of these retrograde notions in the guise of culture had been so deeply internalized by women that they frequently endorsed their own second-class status, leading to a bias for male children and their disdain for female children.

Sita was dumbfounded to see mothers nurturing their unborn babies for nine months in the womb, only to commit the cruel act of abandoning girl children on being born. Sita thought back to the day Laxman had abandoned her in the forest on Ram's instructions. She had wanted to commit suicide, but the thought of the unborn children in her womb kept her going. Sita scanned frequent media reports of female foetuses being found abandoned in fields, gutters, sewage canals and even dustbins. Illegal sex-selective abortions were being practiced with impunity, and secret brews to abort were given to pregnant women. She found it difficult to comprehend what instigated or provoked a mother, driving her to take such a heart-wrenching decision to kill or abandon her child. A mother, who had her second daughter killed, said, 'Abortion is costly… and you have to rest at home. So instead of spending money and losing income, we prefer to deliver the child and kill it.'[27]

No one knows what went through the mind of Mandodari, Ravan's wife, when she tied a stone around her baby girl's neck and threw her into the river. According to legend,[28] Sita's horoscope revealed that she would cause Ravan's death,[29] so his wife, Mandodari, tied a stone round the child's neck and threw her into a river. The child, not fated to die or join the category of 'Missing Girl Child'[30], was washed ashore, and discovered by King Janak, who accepted her as his daughter.

Drawing parallels between ancient India and modern India, Sita found that social pressure to have a male child, and stigma associated with the birth of a girl child, still prevailed today, as it did centuries ago. Bewildered at how the gods in the Hindu pantheon all have male sons except for Riddhi-Siddhi? Every man was not like King Janak, who did not get provoked by people's jibes. Unlike King Dashrath who, yearning for a son, married again and again, when he already had a child, his daughter Shanta.

> *Mocking King Janak, people had said, 'Four daughters and no sons! Why don't you take the assistance of Rishyashringa, like King Dashrath, the father of Lord Ram, did to beget sons.' In response the King proudly proclaimed, 'The earth grants Janak what he deserves. The fire grants Dashrath what he wants. I choose the destiny of daughters. He submits to the desire of sons'.*[31]

Sita, frequently referring to her non-uterine birth, and having been discovered in a furrow by King Janak, narrates the story of her birth to Anasuya and Lopamudra. Sita told Anasuya:

> *The King Janak, who was absorbed in scattering handfuls of seeds, was surprised to see me, with all my limbs covered with dust. It is said that a voice resembling that of a human being in the air above me rang out, saying: 'O, King! Let it be so. This divine child*[32] *without a match is a daughter to you, rightly.'*[33]

Popular sentiment and Mathili folklore treat Sita as the daughter of every household in Mithila, for they believe that if King Janak had not gone to plough the fields on that particular day, then by chance some other resident of Mithila may have found her. Sita's adopted status never came in the way of her happiness and growth, and she grew up to be as happy and healthy as her sisters. Secure in her relationship with her adoptive family, she led a well-adjusted life. In fact, King Janak seemed to have offered her more advantages and opportunities than her sisters. Today, centuries later, she was compelled to think of herself as an abandoned child, equating herself to the missing girl child referred to by Amartya Sen.[34] Almost 30 years ago, he documented that 100 million girls and women were 'missing' from the global population as a consequence of neglect, infanticide, and inequalities in care. Concerned, Sita inquired further into the issue, only to detect that 'missing daughters', was a matter of grave concern. She was astounded to know that the share of girls in the under-six age group, was declining faster than that of boys in the same age group, leading to nearly three million girl children being categorized as missing.[35] According to the economic survey tabled in Parliament, the desire of Indian parents for sons has created an estimated 21 million unwanted girls because couples keep having children until they produce a boy. It recommended that India must confront the societal meta-preference for a son, observing that the adverse sex ratio of females to males has led to 63 million 'missing' women.[36]

Sita gathered from a United Nations Children's Fund (UNICEF) Report—'The Situation of Children in India',[37] that the drop in the child sex ratio had largely been attributed to sex-selective abortions. India contributed to more than 20 per cent of child deaths in the world, and 682,000 female foetuses had been destroyed between 2001 and 2005. The report stressed that the extent of female infanticide had reached crisis proportion, with 1800–1900 female foetuses being butchered daily.[38] The popular adage in vogue was 'Abort your daughter now, save dowry later'. The report also disclosed some alarming figures which have been disputed by the Government of India. It stated that in India, 25 million children under five years are wasted and 61 million are stunted.[39]

Sita was horror-struck at how an inclination for male children seemed to have been 'sanctified by technology'. The focus of the use of technology to detect genetic or chromosomal abnormalities was slowly moving towards using technology for sex-determination tests. Consequently, every 12 seconds, a baby girl was being aborted in India. Simply put, about 7,000 girls were killed every day in India, just because of their gender.[40] Most shameful was the active involvement of the medical fraternity. Ethics had been completely bypassed, especially in the fields of gynecology and infertility. Doctors wanting to wash their hands from responsibility emphasise that they are only responding to a need, even if the solution is illegal. In an apparent display of misplaced empathy, principles are buried under the easy money they gain. Consequently, they are closing their eyes to the fact that the increase in population of men has led to a steady rise in the instances of gender-based violence. Sita reviewed the basic criminal law of the country, the Indian Penal Code (IPC), which made 'induced abortion' an offence under Sections 312 to 316. However, termination of pregnancy in order to protect the life of the mother was permitted.

Despite the law, Sita was startled to see abortions being rampantly conducted by illegal and untrained persons under highly unhygienic conditions, frequently leading to the death of the woman. According to a research paper published in 'The Lancet Global Health' medical journal, about 15.6 million (1.56 crore) abortions took place across India in 2015, against the figure of 7 hundred thousand (7 lakh) that the Centre has been putting out every year for the last 15 years. The study stated that 81 per cent of women took medicines at home instead of going to a hospital; 2.2 million (14 per cent) underwent surgical abortions, while 0.8 million (5 per cent) abortions were through other methods, most probably unsafe.[41] What was worrying was the fact that sex-selective abortion was higher among the better-off, educated and predominantly urban community, although Amartya Sen points out that the better educated are more likely to take care of their daughters once they are born. Resultantly, the urban and the prosperous segments of the society were emerging as they 'epi-centres' of female deficit. Being 'role models' for the rural and the poorer segments, they reinforce the misconception that 'a girl is a liability'. What inititally started as an urban phenomenon spread like wild fire in the rural areas. Greedy and unscrupulous medical practitioners, to increase their practice and make profits soar, started targeting clients from remote rural areas by providing them with door-to-door mobile services of sonography machines.

When questioned about the dismal sex ratios at birth, more than 80 private hospitals in New Delhi cited divine intervention, blaming God and luck for delivering mostly boys.[42] Sita brooded, thinking to herself that God did not cause all our misfortunes, some are caused by bad people. Why then were humans misusing God's name to conceal their cruel actions?

Confused, Sita leafed through the National Crime Records Bureau (NCRB) Crimes in India 2016 Statistics[43], which revealed a completely contradictory scenario. The state of Uttar Pradesh, followed by Maharashtra and Madhya Pradesh, recorded the highest number of crimes against children in 2016. However, only 93 cases of 'infanticide' were recorded under IPC Section 315, 144 cases of 'foeticide' under IPC Section 316, and 815 cases of 'exposure and abandonment' under IPC Section 317.[44] This clearly supports the argument of child activists that the data does not reflect reality, and that the true figures may be much higher as most cases do not get reported and instead are recorded as natural deaths, to conceal what is in actual fact, murder.

Sita heard a hue and cry being raised in Gorakhpur because of the death of infants due to the termination of the liquid oxygen supply at the hospital. Over 70 children had died in just five days in the hospital, and questions were being asked and fingers pointed about the cause of death. On enquiring, she was told that Gorakhpur was a part of the famous kingdom of Koshal, one of 16 mahajanpadas in the sixth century BC, where the earliest known monarch, Iksvaku, ruled with his capital at Ayodhya, Sita's matrimonial home. Now this fell in the state of Uttar Pradesh, which had the worst infant mortality rate in the country.[45] If the data available from the hospital was to be believed, of the first 30 deaths that occurred on two consequentive days, only five deaths were due to acute encephalitis syndrome or AES; one was due to hepatic encephalopathy, which is related to AES. The other deaths were of terminally-ill newborns.[46] Some of them suffered from diseases such as pneumonia, sepsis, and swine flu, while others were pre-term babies in critical conditions. As per the list, all the other babies were newborns who were apparently in need of expert emergency care services. Was it possible that parents neglect the girl child until she becomes terminally ill and then, in a show of false concern for the girl child, bring her to the hospital when there are limited chances of her treatment and survival? Sita felt a little relieved on knowing that remedial actions were being taken in the form of a pilot project[47] in which the deaths would be examined through minimally invasive autopsies[48] to ascertain the exact cause of death, benefitting districts like Gorakhpur, where child deaths were high.

Sita continued in her quest to understand the reality for girls. Alarmed at the high child mortality rate in India,[49] she noted that among the biological factors affecting foetal and neo-natal infant mortality rates, the important factors were those relating to the mother: the age of the mother, birth order, period of spacing between births, pre-maturity, weight at birth and mothers health, along with additional factors such as faulty feeding practices, poor hygiene and malnutrition, which were further aggravated by social, cultural, economic and environmental constraints. Curious to know the extent of discrimination against the girl child, she read the National Study on Child Abuse.[50] Major findings alluded to a failure to provide for the girl child's basic needs, domination of girls by their brothers in play activities, being physically teased and punished by their brothers in day-to-day activities with parents usually taking the side of the brother, and parents giving more love and attention, as well as larger amounts of food, to the brother. In addition, a large majority of the girls were asked to do household work as well as to look after their younger siblings. Their brothers, on the other hand, were not given any such responsibilities, thereby impeding the girl child's legitimate right to education, health, recreation and development. The study has also revealed variations on data among different age groups, gender variations, state variations and variations within evidence groups. The group of younger children (5–12 years of age) reported higher levels of abuse than the other age groups. What was more odious was that persons in positions of trust and authority turned out to be the major abusers; out of those children physically abused in family situations, 88.6 per cent were physically abused by parents.

Legal Challenge

Sita was confounded. On one hand, the Constitution guaranteed right to life; yet on the other, the law was being breached, with sex-determination tests and sex-selective abortions posing serious challenges to the legal system. It was unclear to her as to how the law would ever be enforced, considering the fact that in Indian society a predilection for sons manifested itself, irrespective of religion, caste or class. The ramification of sex-selective abortion, especially in states like Haryana where the imbalance was most acute, is that a very large population of young men are unable to find wives, which has led to a proliferation of trafficking and other forms of gender-based violence.

The skewed sex ratio in Haryana, Punjab and western Uttar Pradesh has led to a flourishing trade in women from Assam, West Bengal, Jharkhand and Odisha. Bought for as little as Rs 5000 ($76.60), they are known in the local language as *paro* or *molki*, which literally means 'one who has a price'.[51] Whether the woman serves as a bonded labourer, a sex slave, a house maid, or will be accorded the status of a wife, all depends on the inclination and circumstance of her buyer. Less than two hours away by road from the capital of India, and close to Gurugram (an IT hub and host to many automobile manufacturing units), lies Mewat, with an imbalanced sex ratio of 907 women for every 1,000 men against the national average of 927. The *paro*s, who are usually promised marriage, end up in Mewat, where middlemen sell them to men who cannot find local women. Cut off from their native states, they are often confined and forced to work as bonded labour or are pushed into forced marriages or prostitution. Sita found it loathsome when people openly said that it was impossible to find a *paro*'s grave, since she was passed on from man to man and didn't stay in one place for long. A field study by the NGO, Drishti Stree Adhyayan Prabodhan Kendra revealed that out of the 10,000 households they surveyed in Haryana, over 9,000 married women were bought from other states. 'Families here don't give their daughters to men who are older than twenty, poor, handicapped or widowed. If you belong to any of these categories, you will have to buy a bride,' said Zakir Hussain, the sarpanch of Luhinga Khurd village. A trafficked survivor and a member of a district legal aid authority revealed that, on average, a girl is sold between two to five times. 'You will never find a *paro* staying with the man who brings her to Haryana or to a neighbouring state,' she said. Poor people from states such as West Bengal and Assam find it difficult to get their daughters married as they cannot afford the dowry. If they send their girls to Haryana, they don't have to give any dowry. Additionally, the parents and guardians of the girl get money in exchange for the girl. On the other hand, men in Haryana find it difficult to get a local bride, so the system works for both parties.

Sita heard the horror story of Razia, a Muslim woman, who was not sure about the number of times she has been sold. Bestowed with the name of a queen, she had been cursed with a fortune worse than a slave. It began when she was brought, at age fourteen, from Bihar's Bhagalpur district to Rajasthan by a middleman. 'He was the first to rape me. It continued for three days. Then he sent me to some other place where I lived maybe for a month,' she said. There, again, she was violated by at least five men. Finally, the broker then dumped her with a man who was already married as well as a father of six children. When she was three months pregnant with her second child, he left her with a family in a neighbouring village saying she had to help them at a family wedding. When she did not hear from him for a month, she got suspicious. That was when she learnt that she had been sold for Rs 25,000. The husband was made to take her back at the Panchayat's intervention. However, no police complaint was lodged. Razia's hardships did not end. Her husband and his first wife both died, and she was pushed out of the family by her stepsons.

Sita interacted with another survivor, Lakshmi, a Hindu girl who was twelve years old when she woke up one day in Haryana. After floods wreaked havoc in her home state of Assam, a man approached her father and asked him to send both his daughters to Delhi for a better future. He showed them a picture of the prospective groom, and gave her father Rs 12,000 for the two sisters. Lakshmi was brought to Haryana's Mewat district and handed over to a man in his late fifties. He was the uncle of the boy whose picture had been shown to Lakshmi's father. No marriage was performed and she had to live with the man. When she objected, she was repeatedly beaten by the broker. After a year and numerous pleas, the middlemen took her back to Assam where she narrated her woes to her father. 'But the only way my father could get me back was by returning the Rs 6,000 he had been paid for me. He didn't have it,' she said. So once again, the broker showed Lakshmi's father a photograph of a man and assured him that, this time, she would certainly be married. Life did not turn out to be as rosy as the young girl dreamed, for her new husband abused her sexually and physically. She had no option but to stay on, for in case she resisted, she ran the risk of being sold again for Rs 5,000. 'This is the worth of a *paro*. Even a buffalo costs more.'

The government of India has initiated a campaign 'Beti Bachao', an awareness campaign to 'Save the Girl Child', involving many actors and forms of media. The famous film star Aamir Khan's reality show on social problems, 'Satyamev Jayate' (the opening episode discussed female foeticide), may have been be the critical first step in highlighting this issue. Acting on the proposition is the next step,[52] but it is one that is fraught with difficulty, especially since sex-selection experts argue it is an expression of a woman's reproductive rights, and a misuse of the family-planning ethos.

The first legal response to this challenge came in the form of the Pre-Natal Diagnostic Techniques (Regulation and Prevention of Misuse) Act 1994 (Act No. 57 of 1994), the title of which was substituted[53] by the Pre-Conception and Pre-Natal Diagnostic Techniques (Regulation and Prevention of Misuse) (PCPNDT) Act in 2004. The Act prohibits sex selection, before or after conception, and regulates pre-natal diagnostic techniques for the purposes of detecting genetic abnormalities, metabolic disorders, chromosomal abnormalities, certain congenital malformations or sex-linked disorders, and for the prevention of their misuse for sex determination leading to female foeticide. To summarise: the preliminary object of the Act is to put a check on female foeticide.

It is simple to satisfy the mandatory provisions of the Act. The few basic requirements comprise: registration under Section 18 of the PCPNDT Act, written consent of the pregnant woman, prohibition of communicating the sex of the foetus under Section 5 of the Act, maintenance of records as provided under Section 29 of the Act, and creating awareness among the public at large by placing a prohibition on sex determination. The Act penalises all the errants, either involved in sex determination or non-maintenance of records, and no doubt is draconic from the perspective of its effect on radiologists and sonologists, against whom stringent action can be taken on violation of the Act. The Act is legislated with the specific objective of being a deterrent for those indulging in sex-determination tests, and mandates compulsory registration of all diagnostic laboratories, all genetic counselling centres, genetic laboratories, genetic clinics and ultrasound clinics.

It is notable that in a patriarchal society like India, even the husband of the pregnant woman is prohibited from seeking or encouraging the performance of any pre-natal diagnostic techniques on her.[54] Most importantly, the court shall presume, unless the contrary is proved, that the pregnant woman was compelled by her husband or any other relative, to undergo pre-natal diagnostic techniques[55] for sex-selective abortions. The drastic decline in the male-female sex ratio brought in the need to take stringent legislative measures, which include suspension of registration, filing of criminal cases and sealing of machines. Besides, criminal prosecution will also bring in suspension and cancellation of registrations granted by the State Medical Council. Sita thought that if the radiologists and sonologists followed simple precautionary measures in maintaining records scrupulously, filling Form-F, as provided in the Act, accurately and correctly, and submitting the records to the appropriate authority within the stipulated time, then there would be nothing to worry about. The Act also prohibits any person from advertising pre-natal and pre-conception sex-determination facilities. Any person advertising in the form of a notice, circular, label, wrapper or any document, through media in electronic or print form, or engaging in any visible representation by means of hoarding, wall painting, signal, light, sound, smoke or gas, is liable for imprisonment for up to three years and a fine. Remedies are also provided, i.e. filing an appeal before the appellate authority and getting the machine released from the court of law, but all these remedial measures are time-consuming and bring the career of an individual to a standstill.

Far from being repentant, doctors justified their actions, and Sita was stunned to find the Act not only being flagrantly violated but also ineffectively enforced. It was an inefficient deterrent in the misuse of advanced medical technology, for in spite of the Act having been in force for over a decade, the natural sex ratio in India continued to be distorted, leading to a gender imbalance—a fact which was evident from the poor rate of conviction of offenders. According to the written reply provided by the former union health minister Ghulam Nabi Azad to the Rajya Sabha in 2013, only 143 people have been punished for conducting sex determination tests, and the medical licenses of only 65 doctors in the entire country have been suspended since the enforcement of the PCPNDT Act.[56] Had the law been enforced effectively, the child sex ratio should have improved; on the contrary it has reached its lowest level as per the 2011 census data. This clearly shows the gap in the formulation and the implementation of the PCPNDT Act. The Supreme Court of India, in a writ petition,[57] has directed the government to publish information by way of advertisements, as well as on electronic media, for the effective implementation of the Act. This process should be continued till there is public awareness that there should not be any discrimination between male and female children; and quarterly reports by the appropriate authority, which are submitted to the Supervisory Board, should be consolidated and published annually for educating the public at large. Additionally, as provided under Rule 17(3), the public should have access to the records maintained by the different bodies constituted under the Act.

The courts have been taking a stern approach, and in a case from Haryana,[58] a doctor was convicted for conducting tests that were in violation of Section 4(1), 4(2) and 4(3) of the Act, and also for failing to maintain proper records of the ultrasound centre. On his behalf on the point of the quantum of the sentence, it was argued that he was the sole breadwinner of the family and had an old mother and small children to look after. He was a doctor by profession and had never been convicted previously, and therefore a lenient view should be taken. The Court opined that the accused did not deserve leniency for, due to the illegal acts of such persons, the sex ratio was declining day by day in the country and in the state, and that the day was not far when there would be no girl children around. Sita was flabbergasted at how the accused had conveyed the sex of the foetus to the patients, by ingenuously working out their own sex-determination code. 'If the doctor tells us to come and get the report on Monday, we know it's a boy. Friday means a girl,' says Sarla, a proud mother of three strapping boys in Karnal's Chonchda village. Her neighbour's doctor adopted a slightly different modus operandi—his signature in red ink indicated a girl and blue indicated a boy. 'No words are exchanged. It's an unspoken thing and one doesn't even have to ask.' she said. 'If the doctor doesn't oblige, some tout does'. The Court held that both the accused had been indulging in a very serious crime. To kill a person who may have the opportunity to defend himself was a very serious offence, but even more serious was the offence where a person kills someone who is not even at a stage to defend himself. The determination of sex by persons like the accused led to the above reality where, on determining the sex of the foetus as female, the same is killed in a cruel manner. The act of the accused was to be condemned, and the punishment to be awarded should act as a deterrent to other persons, so that no one indulged in such heinous crimes.

In a case before the the High Court of Bombay,[59] a married couple sought to challenge the constitutional validity of the Act. The challenge, in a nutshell, was that the personal liberty of a citizen of India includes the liberty of choosing the sex of the offspring. The High Court clarified that the enactment does not bring about a total prohibition of tests. It only intends to prohibit indiscriminate use of such tests to determine the sex at the pre-conception or post-conception stage. Section 4 (2) carves out an exception and provides that no prenatal diagnostic techniques can be conducted, except for the purposes of detection of (1) chromosomal abnormalities, (2) genetic metabolic diseases, (3) haeamoglobinopathies, (4) sex-linked genetic diseases, (5) congenital anomalies and (6) any other abnormalities or diseases as may be specified by the Central Supervisory Board. Thus, the enactment permits such tests if they are necessary to avoid an abnormal child coming into existence. Apart from that, such cases are permitted as mentioned in section 4(3) where certain dangers to the pregnant woman are noticed. The High Court held that the right to life or personal liberty cannot be expanded to include the personal liberty to determine the sex of a child which may come into existence. The conception of a foetus is a physical phenomena. It need not take place on the copulation of every capable male and female. Even if both are competent and healthy enough to give birth to a child, conception need not necessarily follow. With that being a factual medical position, claiming the right to choose the sex of a child which has come into existence cannot be called a right. The right to personal liberty cannot expand, by any stretch of the imagination, to the liberty to prohibit the coming into existence of a female or male foetus, as that was for nature to decide. To claim a right to determine the existence of such a foetus or the possibile existence of such a foetus is claiming a right which may never exist. The right to bring into existence a life in the future with a choice to determine the sex of that life cannot in itself be a right. The High Court finally concluded that the petition did not make even a prima facie case for violation of Article 21 of the Constitution of India, and hence dismissed it.

In 2008, a concerned citizen[60] filed a group interest writ petition seeking directives from the Supreme Court of India for the implementation of the PCPNDT Act. Internet companies[61] were asked to respond to certain questions, including the need to block 'auto-complete' failure for 'key-word' searches which related to pre-conception and/or pre-natal determination of sex or sex selection. Almost ten years have passed, yet the Supreme Court has still to adjudicate on the legal question of whether the companies can take shelter in free access or choose to be catalysts in the depletion of the sex ratio. The petitioner counsel has had submitted that the respondents, namely, Microsoft, Google India and Yahoo! India are bound to scrupulously follow what is stated in Section 22[62] of the PCPNDT Act, which specifically prohibits advertisements relating to pre-natal determination of sex and provides punishment for contravention. In all fairness to the respondents, their counsels contended that they did not intend to take an adversarial position with the petitioner, but on the contrary, they would play a participative and co-operative role so that the law made by the Parliament of India to control sex selection and to enhance the sex ratio is respected. It was further accepted by them that if the Nodal Officer of the Union of India communicates to any of the respondents about any offensive material that contravenes Section 22, they will block it. Needless to say, the intimation has to be given to the respondents.

With women even being denied the right to be born, Sita was perplexed at how the country would fulfil the dream of a 'New India' where women were empowered, strong and equal partners in the nation's overall development. India was 'moving from women development to women-led development' emphasised the Prime Minister, quoting Swami Vivekananda's saying that the idea of a perfect womanhood was perfect independence.[63]

Child Trafficking

The girl who somehow manages to survive foeticide or infanticide runs the risk of being sold by her parents or guardian and passed on to another person, turning a blind eye to the fact that she may be trafficked. This is done for financial gain, and for what is considered 'preventing the girl from being a burden on the family'. Unsurprisingly, India has been included in a list of the world's most dangerous countries in which to be born a woman.[64] While Afghanistan has been ranked first on the list, the Democratic Republic of Congo (DRC), Pakistan, India and Somalia feature in descending order after Afghanistan in the list.

Sita almost fainted while reading the Global Slavery Index 2016, according to which one in four victims of modern slavery are children.[65] India had the world's largest number of modern slaves, at 18.3 million, with 1.4 per cent of the population living in slavery-like conditions.[66] Despite the government discrediting the data, one cannot overlook the fact that in spite of India having made tremendous progress on the economic front, the country still lags behind in gender equity, with it's disproportionately skewed sex-ratio, rampant incidents of infanticide, foeticide, sex-selective abortion, neglect and abandonment of the girl child, and sex trafficking. To a large extent in India, trafficking continues to be synonymous with commercial sexual exploitation, and as a result, there exists no reliable data on the buying and selling of children for labour, organ trade, marriage, adoption, entertainment, begging, and drugs.

How did these monsters who exploit children procure them? Were they kidnapped or were the innocent children sold by their own parents? Sita was appalled to hear that the cyber crime wing of the Kerala Police had busted a child porn racket run by a highly educated postgraduate from Malappuram, and had seized hundreds of photos and videos involving minors.[67]

Pornographic material collected from social media and other sources was being traded under various names on Telegram, an instant-messaging system. According to the police, the offensive clips were being broadcast to more than one lakh subscribers everyday. The videos were not for the faint-hearted since some of them involved children between the ages of two and five years. Unfortunately, even the NCRB Crimes in India 2016 Statistics Report, in Chapter 4A entitled 'Crimes Against Children', does not portray the actual condition, for it records a mere 3.7 per cent of cases of kidnapping and abduction of girls to compel them into marriage (Section 366 IPC),[68] and 0.6 per cent of procuration of minor girls (Section 366A IPC).[69] What is most surprising is that it records nil percent for the importation of girls from foreign countries (Section 366B IPC),[70] when it is a known fact that girls from Nepal are smuggled across the border. UNICEF reports that as many as 7000 women and girls are trafficked out of Nepal to India every year, and around 200,000 are now working in brothels in India.[71] The NCRB data is also found to be flawed since, according to a news report,[72] the Sashastra Seema Bal[73], in its anti-human trafficking operations on the Indo–Nepal border, rescued minors in the age group of 11–16 years at the railway station in Raxaul, out of which six came from Nepal. Raxual is situated on the India–Nepal border opposite Birgunj, Nepal, and is an entry point to Nepal by road and rail. The ages from 11–14 years are often referred to as early adolescence, and is the period when the child is most 'at risk', since varied and rapid physical changes are taking place, making the child confused and vulnerable to manipulation. According to the data about New Delhi, children between the ages of 12–16 are most vulnerable to abduction or kidnapping.[74] In more than 40 per cent of kidnapping and abduction cases in New Delhi in

2016, the victims were aged between 12–16 years, and within this age group more girls were abducted than boys.

The tendency of children to be docile and easily controlled makes them the preferred choice of traffickers. Girl children from Nepal, as young as eight years, are trafficked into India, being desirable not only for their fair complexion but also to satisfy the myth that having sex with a virgin can cure AIDS. A young girl of twelve years said she was forced to have sex with 'all kinds of men from 13-year-olds to old men with no teeth'.[75] Sita wanted to throw up as she read that children are not necessarily at the higher end of the price range as they are not exotic or hard to find. Often, they are the cheapest to procure. They are sought out by the poor and marginalized as something they can have power over. They do not know the price of their own sexuality and will sell themselves for a cigarette. The attraction of children (for the very poor) may simply be that they are social failures and that the child's social status and small size provides a means of exercising power which is otherwise not available to them.[76] This phenomenon explains instances of brothers and cousins raping their younger sisters. A twelve-year-old girl, raped by her cousin brother, moved the court to terminate her pregnancy, but it was too late and she had to give birth through c-section.[77] One dreads to imagine the future of the survivor who has lost her childhood, and of the infant, if it survives.

Sita was exasperated that child trafficking was a misunderstood and badly-defined phenomenon, when it was imperative to fathom the extent and nature of the problem so as to formulate meaningful policy decisions and interventions. A simplistic schema can be actively damaging as it hijacks 'attention away from structural, underlying causes that give rise to exploitation, and structural violence.'[78] A clear international definition was agreed upon and set out in the UN Protocol to Prevent, Suppress and Punish Trafficking, Especially Women and Children[79] (also known as the Palermo Protocol). Through the ratification of the Protocol, there exists significant international agreement that trafficking is a serious form of organized crime that governments need to combat. The Protocol states '(c) The recruitment, transportation, transfer, harbouring or receipt of a child for the purpose of exploitation shall be considered "trafficking in persons" even if this does not involve any of the means set forth in subparagraph (a)[80] of this article.'

The United Nations Convention on the Rights of the Child[81] and the Optional Protocol on the Sale of Children, Child Prostitution and Child Pornography[82] both emphasize that the child is a victim of exploitation and emphasise the sexual exploitation of the girl child. The Optional Protocol recognizes that a number of particularly vulnerable groups, including girl children, are at greater risk of sexual exploitation and that girl children are disproportionately represented among the sexually exploited.

The Worst Forms of Child Labour Convention, 1999 (Convention No. 182) of the International Labour Organization (ILO) states that the worst form of child labour comprises 'the use, procuring or offering of a child for prostitution'.[83] According to the ILO, the prostitution of children and child pornography are the two primary forms of child sexual exploitation, which often overlap. The former is sometimes used to describe the wider concept of commercial sexual exploitation of children (CSEC). It excludes other identifiable manifestations of CSEC, such as commercial sexual exploitation through child marriage, domestic child labour and the trafficking of children for sexual purposes.[84]

The number of trafficked persons is difficult to determine due to the secrecy and clandestine nature of the crime. Sita was horrified at the frightening revelations of studies and surveys sponsored by the Ministry of Women and Child Development, under the Government of India, which estimated that 40 percent of the (approximately) three million prostitutes in the country were children, as there is a growing demand for very young girls to be inducted into prostitution on account of customer preferences.[85] According to the NCRB statistics, major crime heads under 'Crime Against Children' during 2016 were kidnapping and abduction (52.3 per cent) and cases under the Protection of Children from Sexual Offences Act, 2012 (34.4 per cent) including child rape. The maximum number of cases under 'Crime Against Children' have been reported in Uttar Pradesh, Maharashtra and Madhya Pradesh. The maximum number of children missing in 2016 were reported from the state of West Bengal, followed by New Delhi, and Madhya Pradesh—only about half have been traced, while the rest remained untraced, most probably in the grips of traffickers. A city-wise comparison revealed that the maximum cases of crimes against children were reported in New Delhi, followed by Mumbai, the commercial capital of the country, and Bengaluru, the IT hub of the country. As Sita was sieving through this data, someone informed her that the Central Bureau of Investigation (CBI) had arrested the main administrator and kingpin of a WhatsApp group named 'KidsXXX'. Cases had been registered against the members, who were spread globally across countries like the USA, Pakistan, China, and Sri Lanka, for uploading and circulating child pornography videos. The CBI recovered computers, hard disks, phones and incriminating videos and photos of children being sexually abused.[86]

Sita was jittery, and thought that she was going crazy on this full-moon night of Poornima. Yearning for some sanity, Sita went to a temple to meditate and to share her anguish with the Mother Goddess. In a country like India where women were victims of violence, it was possible that in the future even the goddesses prayed to would not be spared. What she saw in the temple made her skin crawl—a small six-year-old girl, overloaded with jewellery, was sitting terrified in front of a priest who was immersed in the chanting of hymns. Sita asked what was happening and was informed that the girl was being dedicated to God through an initiation rite in which she was being married to the presiding deity at the local temple. Sita froze, her eyes fixed with terror. She opened her mouth to scream but no sound came out as she witnessed the barbaric practice of a young child being branded with a hot iron on both her shoulders and her breasts. Some people whispered in subdued tones that the girl's virginity would be auctioned off, before she reached her age of menarche.

Religious prostitution under the guise of dedicating girls to temples or to gods was still in practice in many parts of the subcontinent. This system, known by different names such as *Venkatasani*, *Jogini*, *Nailis*, *Muralis*, *Theradiyan* and Devadasi, was prevalent in temple towns where young girls were dedicated to deities such as Yellamma, Meenakshi, Jagannath and Hanuman. The term 'devadasi' literally means 'female slave to God', and is mainly prevalent in Karnataka, Andhra Pradesh and Maharashtra, and is widely extensive among the Beriya and Nat communities. The reasons for this, which play a major role in legitimizing the system, include the rite as a substitute for human sacrifice, to appease and secure blessings for the community as a whole, to ensure the fertility of the land and the increase of the human and animal population, and to create a custom to exploit lower-caste people by the upper castes.[87]

A number of reports reiterate that 'religious beliefs', 'the caste system', 'male domination' and 'economic stress' play an important role in stimulating the phenomenon. Temple priests, traditionally pawns in the hands of powerful upper-caste landlords, try to convince parents to consecrate their daughters to the divinity, and carry out the instructions of upper-caste men who have bribed them. It is possible that a man from a higher caste, who fancies a lower-caste girl, may order the priest to ask an old devadasi to go into a trance during a religious festival and indicate the name of that girl. As the dedicated girl attains puberty, another ceremony, '*Uditumbuvadu*' is conducted, which effectively completes the process of her dedication. In this second ceremony, the priest 'marries' the girl, dressed as a bride in a ceremonial red sari, to the deity. After the ceremony, the young virgin is forced to spend her 'wedding' night with a village elder who invariably belongs to a higher caste, and thereafter she cannot refuse sexual services to any member of the village. In the past, the priest of the local temple, who normally belonged to the caste of Brahmins, enjoyed the right of de-flowering devadasis after had attained puberty. In fact, priests claimed that as representatives of the gods on earth (*bhudevas*), they should have the first claim to a girl's virginity.

Child rights activists contended that state governments were not strictly enforcing the laws legislated to eradicate the demeaning devadasi system.[88] Further, the funds allotted for the rehabilitation of girls were not being properly utilized which is the reason why the devadasi system continues in the southern states of India—Karnataka, Maharashtra, Andhra Pradesh and Tamil Nadu, while also being prevalent in some other states such as Gujarat, Goa, Assam and Orissa.

Sita was disappointed that little action had been taken by the National Commission for Protection of Child Rights, a statutory body set up in March 2007, to protect, promote and defend child rights in the country. The functions of the Commission are as follows: to examine and review the safeguards provided by or under any law for the protection of child rights and recommend measures for their effective implementation; to examine all factors that inhibit the enjoyment of rights of children and recommend appropriate remedial measures; to look into the matters relating to children in distress, marginalized and disadvantaged children without family and children of prisoners and recommend appropriate remedial measures; to spread child rights literacy among various sections of the society and promote awareness of the safeguards available for protection of these rights; and to inquire into the violation of child rights and recommend initiation of proceedings in such cases. The state governments also had such institutional mechanisms, but to what extent they were functional was debatable.

Sita was stirred by the intervention of the courts, who have consistently upheld gender justice. A socially conscious organization filed a writ petion before the Supreme Court[89], challenging the unhealthy practice of forcing young girls to serve as devadasis. After making detailed reference to the age-old undesired practice of the devadasi system, a specific plea was made to deal with devadasi dedication, which was to be held on 13 February 2014 at the Uttangi Mala Durga Temple in Karnataka. Among the relief sought was urgent action to rehabilitate the girl children who fell prey to such practices by providing education as well as other basic facilities. The Union of India, in its affidavit, pointed out that it had issued an advisory, dated 22 December 2015, to all the states as well as union territories to stop such illegal practices as well as carry out the following: (i) ensure the strict implementation of existing laws (ii) any instances/cases of devadasis should be dealt with strictly and without exception as per extant law (iii) initiate a special drive to identify all such victims and suitably rehabilitate them by providing proper counselling, medical treatment, guidance, support and motivation to lead a dignified life. In another case[90], where the exception clause to the heinous offence of rape, which allowed a man to have sex with his wife (as long as she was above the age of 15), was challenged, the Supreme Court referred to the Report of the Convention on the Rights of the Child (CRC) in which certain recommendations had been made. Specifically recommended was that the State party take necessary measures to combat the inhuman practice of devadasis by conducting awareness-raising programmes and campaigns with a view to change attitudes.

Home to one-fifth of the world's children, India ratified the CRC in 1992, embracing standards in health care, education, legal, civil and social services. India has reiterated its commitment to prevent and combat trafficking by being a signatory to the UN Protocol to Prevent, Suppress and Punish Trafficking in Persons, Especially Women and Children, supplementing the United Nations Convention against Transnational Organized Crime. It has also ratified other related conventions such as the SAARC Convention on Preventing and Combating Trafficking in Women and Children for Prostitution.

Sita was cognizant of the fact that widespread and entrenched exploitation, gender discrimination and caste bias in India cannot be wished away overnight, but a beginning has to be made somewhere. 'We are all aware that rights can be declared and policies formulated, but unless the life of the child in the family and community is improved, all our efforts are meaningless.'[91] The rights spelled out in the convention must become a reality for each and every child in this great nation. The problem of sex pre-selection, sex-selective abortions, and debasement of the girl child (consequently resulting in her being trafficked), is a manifestation of the devalued status of women in society. Unless that is addressed, females will continue to be aborted, neglected, deprived, and trafficked, and the 'Don't stop till you get a boy' phenomenon will persist. Sita felt that she was truly lucky to have been adopted by parents who had provided her with a loving home, education and a promising future—unlike the over-20 million homeless or abandoned helpless children in today's world, who are exposed to disease, malnutrition and death, and the risk of abduction, trafficking and sexual exploitation. Even centuries ago, abandoning an innocent infant was considered a transgression against divine law, with local folklore blaming Ravan and his abandonment of Sita as the cause of his family's ruin.[92] Thankfully, today in India there are many couples like King Janak and Queen Sunaina, who are willing to love unconditionally and make adoption[93] a life-changing experience for both parents and children, thus creating positive futures for the children.

Sita, considered to be the manifestation of primordial nature or *mahaprakriti*, embodied the message: 'I, a girl child, will survive and fulfill my full potential.'

Endnotes

1. K.R. Srinivas Iyengar, *Sitayana: Epic of the Earth-born* (Madras: Samata Books, 1987), p.29.
2. Sita is believed to be an avatar of Goddess Lakshmi, the consort of Lord Vishnu and the goddess of wealth, prosperity, light, wisdom, fortune, fertility, generosity, and courage.
3 Santosh Singh, 'A Day in the Life of "Birthplace" of Sita: Looking for Sita in Sitamarhi', *The Indian Express,* May 7, 2017, http://indianexpress.com/article/india/a-day-in-the-life-of-the-birthplace-of-sita-looking-for-sita-in-sitamarhi-4644113/
4. July-August.
5. Bharadvaja Sarma, *Valmiki's Ramayanam,* 7:18:65–66 (New Delhi: Supernova Publishers & Distrobuters Pvt. Ltd, 2015), p.520.
6. *Sanskaras* are considered important rites of passage in the life of a Hindu. Detailed mention of the *sanskaras* has been made in the ancient Hindu scriptures - the Smritis and Grihasutras.
7. Wearing the sacred thread or the *Janeu* is one of the most important *sanskaras* for male Hindus and is usually performed at the age of seven years when the boy is ready for schooling. This ceremony of wearing the sacred thread or the *Yagnopavitra* is also known as *Upanayanam* and is generally associated with the so-called higher caste Hindus. The thread is a reminder to the child to remain committed to learning and education. During the *Upanayanam* the child receives his first lesson of reciting the Gayatri Mantra from his father who becomes his first guru or teacher.

   A bachelor is supposed to wear only one thread, a married man should wear two threads and if the married man has a child then he wears three threads. The three strands of the thread symbolize the three debts of man, ie the debt to one's teacher, parents and ancestors. The three strands also symbolise the three Goddesses, Parvati, Lakshmi and Saraswati, signifying that a person becomes complete only with the help of these three deities of strength, wealth and knowledge, respectively.
8. The *Garuda Purana* details the importance of the eldest son or male relative performing the last rites.
9. Vishnu Varma, 'This Woman Does the Final Rites at Kochi Crematorium', *The Indian Express,* February 8, 2018, http://indianexpress.com/article/gender/this-woman-does-the-final-rites-at-kochi-crematorium-5032061/
10. Census of India, Office of the Registrar General and Census Commissioner (Ministry of Home Affairs), 2011, http://www.census2011.co.in/states.php
11. 'Decline in Child Sex Ratio', press release by the Ministry of Health and Family Welfare, 11 February, 2014, http://pib.nic.in/newsite/PrintRelease.aspx?relid=103437

12. Census of India, Office of the Registrar General and Census Commissioner (Ministry of Home Affairs), 2001, http://censusindia.gov.in/Census_And_You/gender_composition.aspx
13. Charu WaliKhanna, *Law on Violence Against Women* (New Delhi: Serials Publication, 2009), p.29.
14. 'Woman Kills Infant Daughter, Hangs Self', *The Hindu,* January 27, 2018, http://www.thehindu.com/news/cities/Delhi/woman-kills-infant-daughter-hangs-self/article22531664.ece
15. Peeyush Khandelwal, 'Mother Kills Infant Daughter, Hides Body in Washing Machine', *Hindustan Times,* December 4, 2017, https://www.pressreader.com/india/hindustan-times-delhi/20171204/281694025107719
16. Charu WaliKhanna, *Law on Violence Against Women* (New Delhi: Serials Publication, 2009), p.29.
17. Desiraju Hanumanta Rao and K.M.K. Murthy, trans., *Valmiki Ramayana,* 5:24:42,44,47, https://valmikiramayan.net/
18. Sheela Rani Chunkath and V.B. Athreya, 'Female Infanticide in Tamil Nadu—Some Evidence', *Economic and Political Weekly* 32, issue no. 17 (1997), p.22.
19. Sneh Lata Tandon and Renu Sharma, 'Female Foeticide and Infanticide in India: An Analysis of Crimes against Girl Children', *International Journal for Criminal Justice Science* 1, issue no. 1 (January 2006), http://www.sascv.org/ijcjs/snehlata.pdf
20. Harsha Kumari Singh, 'Obsessed About Having Son, Mother Allegedly Stabbed Baby Girl 17 Times', *New Delhi Television Limited (NDTV),* September 9, 2016, http://everylifecounts.ndtv.com/obsessed-about-having-son-jaipur-mother-stabbed-baby-girl-17-times-4811
21. Social Action Forum for Manav Adhikar (SAFMA) is an NGO with Special Consultative Status of the Economic and Social Council of the United Nations, comprising lawyers, professionals and people committed to the protection of human rights. The philosophy of SAFMA is reflected in its name, for 'Manav', the Hindi word for human being, stands not only for human values (life) but also for humanism (life with dignity). And 'Adhikar', the Hindi word for rights, stands not only for protection but also for empowerment.
22. Charu WaliKhanna, *Law on Violence Against Women* (New Delhi: Serials Publication, 2009), p.29.
23. Rishi Iyengar, 'Indian Minister Says 2,000 Girls Are Killed Across the Country Every Day', *Time Magazine,* April 22, 2015, World section, http://time.com/3830874/2000-girls-killed-every-day-india-minister/
24. 'Discrimination of the Girl Child in Uttar Pradesh', Study conducted by the Social Action Forum for Manav Adhikar (SAFMA), New Delhi, India,http://ncw.nic.in/pdfreports/discrimination_of_the_girl_child_in_uttar_pradesh.pdf
25. Shruti Tomar, 'The Power of Art: Chambal Women Take to Theatre to Save the Girl Child', *Hindustan Times,* January 12, 2018, https://www.hindustantimes.com/art-and-culture/the-power-of-art-chambal-women-take-to-theatre-to-save-the-girl-child/story-R9agjdhCBYvxbMX2KMRfEP.html

26. Palak Nandi, 'In 10 Years, No Baraat at Devda', *The Times of India*, May 6, 2008, https://timesofindia.indiatimes.com/india/In-10-years-no-baraat-at-Devda/articleshow/3013283.cms
27. Ruth Macklin, 'The Ethics of Sex Selection', *Indian Journal of Medical Ethics 3,* no. 4 (1995), http://ijme.in/articles/the-ethics-of-sex-selection/?galley=html
28. In Sanghadaṣa Jaina's version (5th century AD) Sita, called Vasudevahindi, is born as Ravan's daughter. According to this version, when Vidyadhara Maya offered his daughter Mandodari to Ravan in marriage, astrologers predicted that his first child would destroy Ravan's lineage. Nevertheless, Ravan, enamoured with Mandodari, marries her on the understanding that her first child shall be abandoned. When Mandodari gives birth, Ravan orders the infant to be placed in an urn and buried in a distant land. This view is reiterated in the Kashmiri version of *Ramavataracarita* composed by Divakara Prakasa Bhatta (18th century AD) according to which, since the child's horoscope reveals that she will cause Ravan's death, his wife Mandodari ties a stone round the child's neck and throws her into a river.
29. S. Singaravelu, 'Sita's Birth and Parentage in the Rama Story', *Journal of Asian Ethnology 41* (published by the Nanzan Institute for Religion and Culture), no. 2, (1982), https://nirc.nanzan-u.ac.jp/nfile/1178
30. Dr Amartya Sen, 1998 Nobel Prize winner for his contributions to welfare economics, warns about the depleting sex ratio and of discrimination against the girl child in his book *More Than 100 Million Women Are Missing.*
31. Devdutt Pattanaik, *Sita: An Illustrated Retelling of the Ramayana* (New Delhi: Penguin Books, 2013), p.17.
32. *Divyajanma* = divine birth.
33. Desiraju Hanumanta Rao and K.M.K. Murthy, trans., *Valmiki Ramayana,* 2:118:29,31, https://valmikiramayan.net/utf8/ayodhya/sarga118/ayodhya118_frame.htm
34. Amartya Sen, 1998 Nobel Prize winner for his contributions to welfare economics, warned in 1990 about a new form of sex discrimination leading to lower numbers of females than males, in *More Than 100 Million Women Are Missing.*
35 'Children in India: A Statistical Approach', Study published by the Ministry of Statistics and Programme Implementation, 2012, p.7, http://mospi.nic.in/sites/default/files/publication_reports/Children_in_India_2012-rev.pdf
    Though, the overall sex ratio of the country is showing a trend of improvement, the child sex ratio is showing a declining trend, which is a matter of concern. During the period 1991–2011, the child sex ratio declined from 945 to 914, whereas the overall sex ratio showed an improvement from 927 to 940. Compared to 2001, only five States/Union Territories showed a decline in overall sex ratio in 2011, while 27 States/UTs showed a decline in child sex ratio during this period. This opposite direction in the movement of sex ratios of children aged 0–6 years compared to the overall sex ratio suggests a shift in the demographic

composition of the population. The decadal decline in child sex ratio (number of girl children per 1000 male children in the age group 0-6 years) however, is less steep from that of the previous decade (1991 to 2001). In 1991, it was 945 and fell to 927 in 2001, a fall of 18 points (1.9 per cent). In 2011, it has fallen to 914, a fall of 13 points (1.4 per cent).

36. 'India has 21 Million "Unwanted" Girls, Says Economic Survey as it Turns "Pink"', *Hindustan Times,* January 29, 2018, https://www.hindustantimes.com/business-news/economic-survey-turns-pink-asks-indians-to-confront-son-preference/story-6ul0cq6kzle9WclSysBUSM.html
37. 'The Situation of Children in India: A Profile', A study published by the United Nations Children's Fund (UNICEF), New Delhi, India, 2011, http://www.unicef.org/sitan/files/SitAn_India_May_2011.pdf
38. Ibid, 110n, p.102.
39. National Family Health Survey (NFHS) India Factsheet: For studying the trends in underweight children, the National Center for Health Statistics (NCHS) reference population has been used and children under age three have been considered. Data for wasting and stunting is not available for NFHS 1. The UNICEF report titled 'Tracking Progress on Child and Maternal Nutrition—A survival and development priority' released in November 2009, has recalculated the underweight rate for children under age 5 (MDG 1 indicator on hunger) with NCHS reference population. According to the recalculation, the underweight rates for the years 1992–93, 1998–99 and 2005–06 are 54, 49 and 48 per cent respectively.
40. Barkha Dutt, 'The Place of Women in India', *Outlook India,* January 18, 2016, https://www.outlookindia.com/website/story/the-place-of-women-in-india/296427
41. Malathy Iyer, '1.6 Crore Abortions a Year in India, 81% at Home: Study', *The Times of India,* December 12, 2017, https://timesofindia.indiatimes.com/india/1-6-crore-abortions-a-year-in-india-81-at-home-study/articleshow/62030066.cms
42. Anonna Dutt, 'Low Sex Ratio? Hospitals in Delhi Blame God, Luck, Poverty, Weather', *Hindustan Times,* Agust 7, 2016, https://www.hindustantimes.com/low-sex-ratio-delhi-hospitals-blame-god-luck-poverty/story-bccnfplrRUQw6ARVimmokN.html
43. Report published by National Crime Records Bureau (NCRB), Chapter 4A – Crime against Children, Ministry of Home Affairs, 2016,http://ncrb.gov.in/
44. **Section 315.** Act done with intent to prevent child being born alive or to cause it to die after birth.—Whoever before the birth of any child does any act with the intention of thereby preventing that child from being born alive or causing it to die after its birth, and does by such act prevent that child from being born alive, or causes it to die after its birth, shall, if such act be not caused in good faith for the purpose of saving the life of the mother, be punished with imprisonment of either description for a term which may extend to ten years, or with fine, or with both.

Section 316. Causing death of quick unborn child by act amounting to culpable homicide.—Whoever does any act under such circumstances, that if he thereby caused death he would be guilty of culpable homicide, and does by such act cause the death of a quick unborn child, shall be punished with imprisonment of either description for a term which may extend to ten years, and shall also be liable to fine. Illustration A, knowing that he is likely to cause the death of a pregnant woman, does an act which, if it caused the death of the woman, would amount to culpable homicide. The woman is injured, but does not die; but the death of an unborn quick child with which she is pregnant is thereby caused. A is guilty of the offence defined in this section.

Section 317. Exposure and abandonment of child under twelve years, by parent or person having care of it.—Whoever being the father or mother of a child under the age of twelve years, or having the care of such child, shall expose or leave such child in any place with the intention of wholly abandoning such child, shall be punished with imprisonment of either description for a term which may extend to seven years, or with fine, or with both.

Explanation.—This section is not intended to prevent the trial of the offender for murder or culpable homicide, as the case may be, if the child dies in consequence of the exposure.

45. National Family Health Survey-IV (2015–16). Uttar Pradesh has an infant mortality rate of 78 per 1,000 live births against the national average of 41.
46. Neetu Chandra Sharma, 'Gorakhpur Tragedy: Most Children's Deaths Not Due To Encephalitis, Hospital Records Show', *Livemint.com,* August 16, 2017, http://www.livemint.com/Politics/XspLuS7RqCId9KRuqDNu4O/Gorakhpur-tragedy-Most-children-deaths-not-due-to-encephali.html
47. The pilot project, to begin in January 2018 at New Delhi's Safdarjung Hospital, is a part of the global CHAMPS—Child Health and Mortality Prevention Surveillance project, wherein biopsies of the brain, liver, spleen and other tissues are taken in a minimally invasive way.
48. Rhythma Kaul, 'India to Begin Minimally Invasive Autopsies in Case of Child Deaths', *Hindustan Times,* December 2, 2017, http://www.hindustantimes.com/health/india-to-begin-minimally-invasive-autopsies-in-cases-of-child-deaths/story-SAHVmY85Kt5SUXts3L2jPL.html
49. 'Children in India: A Statistical Appraisal', Study published by the Ministry of Statistics and Programme Implementation, 2012, http://mospi.nic.in/sites/default/files/publication_reports/Children_in_India_2012-rev.pdf

    Neo-natal deaths refer to the deaths of infants less than 29 days of age. In 2010, the percentage of neo-natal deaths to total infant deaths was 69.3 per cent at a national level, varying from 61.9 per cent in urban areas to 70.6 per cent in rural areas. The conflict ridden state of Jammu and Kashmir (82.1 per cent) registered the highest percentage of neo-natal deaths to infant deaths and the lowest was registered in Kerala (53.2 per cent).

50 'National Study on Child Abuse,' study conducted by Prayas in collaboration with the Ministry of Women and Child Development, supported by UNICEF and Save the Children Fund, UK, 2007

Girl Child Neglect-29. Neglect is the failure to provide for the child's basic needs. Neglect can be physical, developmental, educational or emotional. In the Indian scenario, the girl child is often seen as victim of this neglect.

30. Nearly one half (45.3 per cent) of the girl child respondents who had brothers (N=4138), stated that they were dominated by their brothers in play activities, 40.6 per cent were physically teased and punished in day to day activities by their brothers, and in 48.4 per cent cases the parents took side of the brothers. What is significant here is not that brothers are teasing their sisters (which is a socio-cultural phenomenon almost the world over), but that parents in India are still favouring their sons over their daughters in any given situation.

31. Almost one-third of the girls (32 per cent) who had brothers, reported that their parents gave more love and attention to their brothers. The data also revealed that, compared to their brothers, the girls were not given the same amount of food (27.3 per cent).

32. A large majority of the girls were asked to do household work (70.4 per cent) as well as to look after their younger siblings (48.7 per cent) while their brothers were not given any such responsibilities. The above is a clear indication of the fact that a sizeable proportion of the girls were expected to perform a variety of functions associated with housekeeping. Evidently if these activities hamper the child's legitimate right to education, health, recreation and development, it can be construed as abuse.

33. 45.7 per cent of the young girl adults reported that looking after the younger sibling was a full- time job.

34. 44.8 per cent of the girl respondents felt it was an advantage being a girl, though almost half of the total girl child respondents (N = 5981) still wished they were a boy. At the same time, practically one-fifth of the respondents felt that it was disadvantageous to be a girl while 35.8 per cent indicated that they did not have any idea about this issue. This indicates that children at this age are not particularly concerned with such issues and clearly, it is not an indicator of abuse in this case.

51 Danish Raza, 'When Women Come Cheaper Than Cattle', *Hindustan Times,* March 23, 2014, http://www.hindustantimes.com/india/when-women-come-cheaper-than-cattle/story-EJD38cJ4kaTGVn03LJzUkJ.html

52. Ranjini Iyer Mohanty, 'Trash Bin Babies: India's Female Infanticide Crisis', *The Atlantic,* May 25, 2012, http://www.theatlantic.com/international/archive/2012/05/trash-bin-babies-indias-female-infanticide-crisis/257672/

The abandonment of babies is not just a third-world problem. Although with less severity, developed nations—such as the USA, UK, and several European countries—are also facing this issue. As in India, babies have been found abandoned in a variety of places: on roadsides and in alleyways, outside temples and churches, in shopping malls and public bathrooms, and inside garbage cans. A baby hatch is basically a safe place—maybe a crib or a room, often attached to a health center—where a parent can leave their child without fear of prosecution. These children are then looked after by the government and, if possible, placed with an adoptive family. There is a special term for such children—not orphans because they have living parents—but foundlings: they have been found. Since the eighteenth century, variations of the baby hatch concept have existed in much of central Europe, where they have sometimes been called 'foundling wheels'.

Many American states now have 'safe haven' laws, designated safe drop-off locations where parents can leave unwanted babies. These are usually hospitals, police stations, or fire stations. In France, a woman is allowed to deliver her baby in a hospital and, if she doesn't want to keep it, leave it behind—no questions asked. Many countries have set up their own systems of baby hatches: Italy, Hungary, Poland, Russia, Japan, the Philippines, and South Africa, to name a few. Canada installed its first baby hatch at a hospital in Vancouver. Einsiedeln, a small town in Switzerland, has had a baby hatch for 10 years, and even though they've received only two babies in that time, they still feel it worthwhile to keep it open. As *The Economist* reports, 'Now Germany has around 200 places where a mother can either leave her baby—heated 'baby hatches', usually with an alarm to summon a carer—or where she can give birth anonymously.' In Pakistan, the Edhi Foundation accepts abandoned babies at its numerous welfare centers throughout the country. In China some officials are testing what they call 'safe islands for babies', and Australia is considering its own safe-haven law.

Since 2007, the idea of a baby hatch has been slowly resurrected in India. There are already some baby hatches operating in India, in the state of Tamil Nadu. A United Nations Population Fund report explains, 'Instead of resorting to female infanticide, parents who were unwilling to bring up their female babies could place them anonymously in cradles located in noon meal centres, PHCs, selected orphanages and NGOs. Subsequent to their placement in cradles, babies were to be placed for adoption.' Since the program's inception in 1992 in selected districts, some 390 boys and 2400 girls have been safely left, according to the Tamil Nadu government's directorate of social welfare.

53. The Pre-Natal Diagnostic Techniques (Regulation and Prevention of Misuse) Amendment Act, 2002 Act No. 14 of 2003 (with effect from 14 February 2003) Section 3. Amendment of section 1.-In section 1 of the principal Act, in sub-section (1), for the words and brackets 'the Pre-natal Diagnostic Techniques (Regulation and Prevention of Misuse)', the words and brackets 'the Pre-conception and Pre-natal Diagnostic Techniques (Prohibition of Sex Selection)' shall be substituted.

54. Section 4(4). No person including a relative or husband of the pregnant woman shall seek or encourage the conduct of any pre-natal diagnostic techniques on her except for the purposes specified in clause (2);

Section 4(5). No person including a relative or husband of a woman shall seek or encourage the conduct of any sex selection technique on her or him or both.

55. Section 24. Presumption in the case of conduct of pre-natal diagnostic techniques.—Notwithstanding anything contained in the Indian Evidence Act, 1872 (1 of 1872), the court shall presume unless the contrary is proved that the pregnant woman was compelled by her husband or any other relative, as the case may be, to undergo pre-natal diagnostic technique for the purposes other than those specified in sub-section (2) of section 4 and such person shall be liable for abetment of offence under sub-section (3) of section 23 and shall be punishable for the offence specified under that section.
56. Inian, 'Gender Inequality in India', *IOSR Journal of Humanities and Social Sciences 21*, issue 7, version 3 (2017), pp. 18–25, http://www.iosrjournals.org/iosr-jhss/papers/Vol.%2022%20Issue7/Version-3/D2207031825.pdf
57. Centre for Enquiry into Health and Allied Themes (CEHAT) and Others vs Union of India and Others, Writ Petition (Civil) 301 of 2000, http://pndt.gov.in/writereaddata/mainlinkfile/File44.pdf
58. State through District Appropriate Authority-cum-Civil Surgeon vs Dr Anil Sabhani and Others, Case No.295/2 of 2001, http://pndt.gov.in/writereaddata/mainlinkfile/File42.pdf
59. Vinod Soni and Anr. vs Union of India, Criminal Writ Petiton 945 and Criminal Application No.3647 of 2005, http://pndt.gov.in/writereaddata/mainlinkfile/File43.pdf
60. Dr Sabu Matthew George vs Union of India and Others, Writ Petition (Civil) No.341 of 2008.
61. Google India Private Limited, Yahoo! India and Microsoft Corporation (I) Pvt. Ltd.
62. Section 22. Prohibition of advertisement relating to pre-natal determination of sex and punishment for contravention.
    1. No person, organization, Genetic Counselling Centre, Genetic Laboratory or Genetic Clinic, including clinic, laboratory or centre having ultrasound machine or imaging machine or scanner or any other technology capable of undertaking determination of sex of foetus or sex selection shall issue, publish, distribute, communicate or cause to be issued, published, distributed or communicated any advertisement, in any form, including internet, regarding facilities of pre-natal determination of sex or sex selection before conception available at such centre, laboratory, clinic or at any other place.
    2. No person or organization including Genetic Counselling Centre, Genetic Laboratory or Genetic Clinic shall issue, publish, distribute, communicate or cause to be issued, published, distributed or communicated any advertisement in any manner regarding pre-natal determination or preconception selection of sex by any means whatsoever, scientific or otherwise.
    3. Any person who contravenes the provisions of sub-section (1) or sub-section (2) shall be punishable with imprisonment for a term which may extend to three years and with fine which may extend to ten thousand rupees.

Explanation.—For the purposes of this section, 'advertisement' includes any notice, circular, label, wrapper or any other document including advertisement through internet or any other media in electronic or print form and also includes any visible representation made by means of any hoarding, wall-painting, signal, light, sound, smoke or gas.

63. 'Moving From Women-Development to Women-Led Development: Emphasizes Modi in "Mann ki Baat"', *News18.com,* February 25, 2018, https://www.news18.com/news/india/moving-from-women-development-to-women-led-development-emphasises-pm-modi-in-mann-ki-baat-1671983.html

64. The survey has been compiled by the Thomson Reuters Foundation to mark the launch of a website, TrustLaw Woman, which aims at providing free legal advice for women's groups around the world. The survey ranked India the fourth most dangerous country. 'India's Central Bureau of Investigation estimated that in 2009 about 90 per cent of trafficking took place within the country and that there were some 3 million prostitutes, of which about 40 per cent were children,' the survey found.

65. 'Forced Labour, Modern Slavery and Human Trafficking', International Labour Organization (Source: Global Estimates of Modern Slavery: Forced Labour and Forced Marriage), Geneva, September 2017, http://www.ilo.org/global/topics/forced-labour/lang--en/index.htm

66. 'Over 40 Million People Living in Slavery Worldwide: ILO', *The Hindu,* September 21, 2017, http://www.thehindu.com/data/over-40-million-people-living-in-slavery-worldwide-ilo/article19725918.ece

67. Ramesh Babu, 'Child Porn Racket Busted in Kerala, MCA Graduate Arrested for Circulating Clips', *Hindustan Times,* December 23, 2017, http://www.hindustantimes.com/india-news/child-porn-racket-busted-in-kerala-mca-graduate-arrested-for-circulating-clips/story-fmOGKVTJa2g9tpOdUSLvwK.html

68. Section 366. Kidnapping, abducting or inducing woman to compel her for marriage, etc. Whoever kidnaps or abducts any woman with intent that she may be compelled, or knowing it to be likely that she will be compelled, to marry any person against her will, or in order that she may be forced or seduced to illicit intercourse, or knowing it to be likely that she will be forced or seduced to illicit intercourse, shall be punished with imprisonment of either description for a term which may extend to ten years, and shall also be liable to fine; [and whoever, by means of criminal intimidation as defined in this Code or of abuse of authority or any other method of compulsion, induces any woman to go from any place with intent that she may be, or knowing that it is likely that she will be, forced or seduced to illicit intercourse with another person shall be punishable as aforesaid].

69. Section 366A. Procuration of minor girl. -Whoever, by any means whatsoever, induces any minor girl under the age of eighteen years to go from any place or to do any act with intent that such girl may be, or knowing that it is likely that she will be, forced or seduced to illicit intercourse with another person shall be punishable with imprisonment which may extend to ten years, and shall also be liable to fine.

70. Section 366B. Importation of girl from foreign country. -Whoever imports into India from any country outside India or from the State of Jammu and Kashmir any girl under the age of twenty-one years with intent that she may be, or knowing it to be likely that she will be, forced or seduced to illicit intercourse with another person, shall be punishable with imprisonment which may extend to ten years and shall also be liable to fine.
71. Katie Orlinsky, 'Women, Bought and Sold in Nepal', *The New York Times,* August 31, 2013, http://www.nytimes.com/2013/09/01/opinion/sunday/women-bought-and-sold-in-nepal.html
72. 'SSB Rescues 15 Children From Human Trafficking Cartel', *Hindustan Times,* December 5, 2017, p.24.
73. The Special Service Bureau (SSB) was declared as a Border Guarding Force on 15th January, 2001 under the Ministry of Home Affairs, Govt of India and renamed the 'Sashastra Seema Bal' (SSB) on 15th December, 2003. On 19 June, 2001 the SSB was given the mandate to guard the Indo–Nepal Border (1751 km) and was declared the Lead Intelligence Agency for that area. The added responsibility of guarding the Indo–Bhutan Border was given to the SSB on 12th March, 2004, along with being declared the Lead Intelligence Agency for that border.
The SSB is now spread along the international border across Uttarakhand, UP, Bihar, West Bengal, Sikkim, Assam and Arunachal Pradesh. The SSB's present charter of duties is to safeguard the security of assigned borders of India and promote a sense of security among the people living in border areas; Prevent trans-border crimes, smuggling and any other illegal activities; Prevent unauthorized entry into or exit from the territory of India; Carry out civic action programme in the area of responsibility and perform any other duty assigned by the Central Government. (The SSB is used for maintaining law and order, counter-insurgency operations, and election duty).
The challenges of manning the open border are more daunting than securing a closed border. The 2450 kms long Indo- Nepal and Indo-Bhutan border is more challenging because the open border not only provides alluring encouragement to traffickers and smugglers, but also offers huge opportunities for militants/ANEs trained on foreign soil to infiltrate and pose a serious threat to national security.
74. Shubhomoy Sikdar, 'Delhi: Victims in Over 40% Kidnapping Cases are 12-16 Years Old', *Hindustan Times,* December 4, 2017, http://www.hindustantimes.com/delhi-news/delhi-victims-in-over-40-kidnapping-cases-are-12-16-years-old/story-JBisEy8AmcAiINJ7NTj1UK.html
75. 'Prostitution in India Hurts Nepal', *Taipei Times,* June 10, 2003, http://www.taipeitimes.com/News/feat/archives/2003/06/10/2003054750
76. K.J. Lalor, 'Victimisation of Street Children in Addis Ababa: Factors of Resilience and Susceptibility' (PhD diss., University College Cork, 1997), p. 214.
77. 'Child Survivor Dumps Baby Born of Rape', *The Times of India,* November 27, 2017, https://www.pressreader.com/india/the-times-of-india-new-delhi-edition/20171127/282175061429531

78. Heather Montgomery, 'Defining Child Trafficking and Child Prostitution: The Case of Thailand', *Thailand Journal of Law and Policy 15*, issue 1 (2012), http://www.thailawforum.com/articles/child-trafficking-and-child-prostitution-thailand-2.html#13
79. G.A. Res. 55/25, Annex II, U.N. Doc. A/Res/55/25 (Jan. 8, 2001), [hereinafter Palermo Protocol]. This Protocol supplemented the Convention for the Suppression of the Traffic in Persons and of the Exploitation of the Prostitution of Others, Mar. 21, 1950, 96 U.N.T.S. 271, and gave added protections to those discussed in the Convention on the Elimination of All Forms of Discrimination Against Women, Dec. 18, 1979, 1249 U.N.T.S. 13.
80. (a) 'Trafficking in persons' shall mean the recruitment, transportation, transfer, harbouring or receipt of persons, by means of the threat or use of force or other forms of coercion, of abduction, of fraud, of deception, of the abuse of power or of a position of vulnerability or of the giving or receiving of payments or benefits to achieve the consent of a person having control over another person, for the purpose of exploitation;
81. **Article 19.** 1. States Parties shall take all appropriate legislative, administrative, social and educational measures to protect the child from all forms of physical or mental violence, injury or abuse, neglect or negligent treatment, maltreatment or exploitation, including sexual abuse, while in the care of parent(s), legal guardian(s) or any other person who has the care of the child.

    2. Such protective measures should, as appropriate, include effective procedures for the establishment of social programmes to provide necessary support for the child and for those who have the care of the child, as well as for other forms of prevention and for identification, reporting, referral, investigation, treatment and follow-up of instances of child maltreatment described heretofore, and, as appropriate, for judicial involvement.

    Article 34. States Parties undertake to protect the child from all forms of sexual exploitation and sexual abuse. For these purposes, States Parties shall in particular take all appropriate national, bilateral and multilateral measures to prevent:

    (a) The inducement or coercion of a child to engage in any unlawful sexual activity;

    (b) The exploitative use of children in prostitution or other unlawful sexual practices;

    (c) The exploitative use of children in pornographic performances and materials.
82. **Article 2.** For the purposes of the present Protocol:

    (a) Sale of children means any act or transaction whereby a child is transferred by any person or group of persons to another for remuneration or any other consideration;

    (b) Child prostitution means the use of a child in sexual activities for remuneration or any other form of consideration;

    (c) Child pornography means any representation, by whatever means, of a child engaged in real or simulated explicit sexual activities or any representation of the sexual parts of a child for primarily sexual purposes.

Article 3. 1. Each State Party shall ensure that, as a minimum, the following acts and activities are fully covered under its criminal or penal law, whether such offences are committed domestically or transnationally or on an individual or organized basis:
(a) In the context of sale of children as defined in Article 2:
(i) Offering, delivering or accepting, by whatever means, a child for the purpose of:
a. Sexual exploitation of the child;
b. Transfer of organs of the child for profit;
c. Engagement of the child in forced labour;
(ii) Improperly inducing consent, as an intermediary, for the adoption of a child in violation of applicable international legal instruments on adoption;
(b) Offering, obtaining, procuring or providing a child for child prostitution, as defined in Article 2;
(c) Producing, distributing, disseminating, importing, exporting, offering, selling or possessing for the above purposes child pornography as defined in Article 2.
2. Subject to the provisions of the national law of a State Party, the same shall apply to an attempt to commit any of the said acts and to complicity or participation in any of the said acts.
3. Each State Party shall make such offences punishable by appropriate penalties that take into account their grave nature.
4. Subject to the provisions of its national law, each State Party shall take measures, where appropriate, to establish the liability of legal persons for offences established in paragraph 1 of the present article. Subject to the legal principles of the State Party, such liability of legal persons may be criminal, civil or administrative.
5. States Parties shall take all appropriate legal and administrative measures to ensure that all persons involved in the adoption of a child act in conformity with applicable international legal instruments.

83. Worst Forms of Child Labour Convention, (Convention No. 182), International Labour Organization, June 17, 1999.
Article 3. For the purposes of this Convention, the term the worst forms of child labour comprises:
(a) all forms of slavery or practices similar to slavery, such as the sale and trafficking of children, debt bondage and serfdom and forced or compulsory labour, including forced or compulsory recruitment of children for use in armed conflict;
(b) the use, procuring or offering of a child for prostitution, for the production of pornography or for pornographic performances;
(c) the use, procuring or offering of a child for illicit activities, in particular for the production and trafficking of drugs as defined in the relevant international treaties;
(d) work which, by its nature or the circumstances in which it is carried out, is likely to harm the health, safety or morals of children.

84. O.P. Narayan, *Harnessing Child Development: Children and the Culture of Human Rights*, Vol.1 (New Delhi: Gyan Publishing House, 2005).

85. 'India Country Report: To Prevent and Combat Trafficking and Commercial Sexual Exploitation of Children and Women', Report undertaken by the World Congress III Against Exploitation of Children and Adolescents, Rio de Janeiro, Brazil, November 2008, Published by the United Nations Office on Drugs and Crime and the Ministry of Women and Child Development, https://www.unodc.org/pdf/india/publications/India%20Country%20Report.pdf
86. Neeraj Chauhani, 'CBI Arrests Main Admin of WhatsApp Group Sharing Child Pornography', *The Times of India,* February 22, 2018, https://timesofindia.indiatimes.com/india/cbi-arrests-main-admin-of-whatsapp-group-sharing-child-pornography/articleshow/63031019.cms
87. V. Bharathi Harishankar and M. Priyamvadha, 'Exploitation of Women as Devdasis and its Associated Evils' (Vol.1), Report conducted for and published by the National Commission for Women, 2016, http://ncw.nic.in/pdfReports/Exploitation_of_Women_as_Devadasis_and_its_Associated_Evils_Report.pdf
88. Nash Colundalur, 'Devdasis are a Cursed Community', *The Guardian,* January 21, 2011, https://www.theguardian.com/lifeandstyle/2011/jan/21/devadasi-india-sex-work-religion
89. S.L. Foundation through its President vs Union of India and Others, Writ petition (Civil) No. 127 of 2014.
90. Independent Thought vs Union of India and Another Supreme Court Writ Petition (Civil) No.382 of 2003, http://supremecourtofindia.nic.in/supremecourt/2013/17790/17790_2013_Judgement_11-Oct-2017.pdf
91. Shanta Sinha and Karin Hulsoff, 'Twenty Years of the Convention on the Rights of the Child', press release published by UNICEF India, http://unicef.in/PressReleases/141/Twenty-Years-of-The-Convention-on-the-Rights-of-the-Child
92. S. Singaravelu, 'Sita's Birth and Parentage in the Rama Story', *Journal of Asian Ethnology 41* (published by the Nanzan Institute for Religion and Culture), issue 2 (1982), p.240, https://nirc.nanzan-u.ac.jp/nfile/1178
93. Himanshi Dhawan, 'Maharashtra Leads Again in Domestic Adoptions', *The Times of India,* August 8, *2016,* http://timesofindia.indiatimes.com/india/Maharashtra-leads-again-in-domestic-adoptions/articleshow/53590781.cms

Adolescence

The same youthful, almost boyish archer
With the lure of sapphire blue
Who haunted her lately in her dreams,
Now paired with his fair brother!

This was beyond all anticipation,
Surmise or coincidence;
And Maithili recalled Maitreyi's words,
And sensed coming fulfillment.

For Sita it was an instantaneous
Canter of recognition:
Wasn't Vishwamitra the Grace Paraclete,
And Ram the ordained goal?

Perhaps, she mused, Ram's wandering eyes,
As they swept the space across,
Sought her alone, and at last happily
Rested in deep contentment!

It was a moment prefigured, unique,
When two infinities met
And felt in their reservoir of Spirit
Their two-in-one destiny.

Ram carried with him still the aura
Of Ahalya's ascesis,
For her penitence had transfigured her
As Beauty of Holiness.

But Sita's was beauty of innocence,
Freshness, self sufficence,
The perfect fusion of all perfections,
The exemplum of feminine.[1]

Adolescence is an important developmental stage when a girl begins her transition from childhood towards young adulthood. It is a time of exploration and discovery, but also of vulnerability and the need for guidance and support from family and elders. For this period is marked by rapid physical and neuro-psychological changes and growth—including that of puberty and sexual awareness. With adolescence comes a youthful desire for freedom, to experience excitement, unrestrained exploration, and push against boundaries imposed by society. Sita felt fortunate that King Janak had been a man of wisdom and provided her and her sisters with all the learning opportunities possible, and had not held them back because they were girls.

If Sita was the ideal woman, it was because she had an ideal, loving and supportive father. King Janak took a personal interest in her upbringing, despite the fact that she was not his own blood and he had another natural-born daughter. Sita was well provided for and was in no way lacking in resources. This goes to prove that if a girl child's father is affectionate, supportive, and involved, he can contribute greatly to her cognitive and social development, academic achievement, sense of well-being and self-esteem. Research indicates that fathers are as important as mothers in their respective roles as caregivers, protectors, financial supporters, and most importantly, models for social and emotional behavior. A fathers' support for a girl child's autonomy has been found to be strongly correlated with higher levels of reading and mathematical achievement. Although gender commonly tends to be the primary factor in a fathers' decreased involvement with his children's education, King Janak did not conform to this. He regularly interacted and intellectually engaged with his daughters, thus greatly enhancing their academic skills and social behaviour.

Education: Asset or Threat?

King Janak, a man of great wisdom, provided his daughters with a multitude of learning opportunities, so that they gained proficiency in a variety of subjects, enabling Sita to grow up to be the able, independent and confident woman she eventually became. As Jean Jacques Rousseau said in *Emile, or On Education*, 'Everything we do not have at our birth and which we need when we are grown is given us by education', and Videha, with its rich and stimulating environment, was an exemplary academy for the young girls. Sita, having mastered the use of words, was proficient in the range, power, complexity and sophisticated subtleties of language. Due to her interaction with different seers and sages, she could comprehend many languages, including the language of the rakshasas. It is said, 'Words are, of course, the most powerful drug used by mankind.'[2] They can paint amazing images, inspire and intoxicate. It was this quality of Sita, her skills with words and proficiency in articulating her thoughts, which gave her the grit to challenge even Ram on several occasions.

Sita noted that unfortunately, the current prejudice that prevailed in India was that if the girl is educated it would be difficult to find her a husband, and hence families considered it a waste to commit resources towards a daughter's education. Sita saw that girls were being socialized to put themselves last, which in turn undermined their self-esteem and ability to reach their full potential as human beings. Amartya Sen[3] identifies that in addition to survival and natal inequality, females tend to be further disadvantaged by 'unequal facilities', in the form of lack of access to higher levels of education and technical training. Sita was disappointed to see that in 2017 young girls were still deprived, and subjected to neglect and discrimination and that 'achieving universal primary education'[4] appeared to be a distant dream for India. Adequate knowledge regarding social responsibilities would help women face challenges in life without feeling inferior or underqualified. About 8 per cent of India's population is tribal, but according to the 2011 census, the overall literacy rate among the Scheduled Tribes is 58 per cent, making it lag behind not only the general population, but also far behind the Scheduled Caste community in terms of literacy and education attainment. Experts state that these averages mask the diversity among the tribal-dominated states. Strangely enough, the predominantly tribal state of Mizoram was among the top five literate states, while Jharkhand was among the bottom five. Sita felt that the educational experience of tribal girls could be enriched by incorporating the local culture, poetry, and songs into the curriculum. In addition, the learning outcomes of tribal girls could be radically transformed by engaging the community and the teachers with mediums of instruction that were familiar to them.

Sita recalled how her education had commenced under the supervision of Mithila's high priest, Sage Satananda[5], and at a young age the sisters engaged in intellectual discourse with erudite genius seers.

Sage Satananda was not an ordinary instructor, and encouraged discussion and reasoning, as a strategy for enhancing his student's motivation and fostering their intellectual acuity. Debate and curiosity were encouraged. Discussions were enriched with the search for truth and understanding, with the belief that reason, thoughtfulness and critical inquiry are gifts from God; and it is only after undergoing this process can one become acquainted with one's true self. Sometimes, at the end of the discourse, it became uncertain who felt more rewarded, the pupil or the teacher. The receptive sisters were offered an unparalleled opportunity to deliberate and debate on topics, and the most trivial affairs of life became the subject of conversation and lessons of existence. The level of discussion exceeded all standards when Yajnavalkya was present and wise King Janak presided over the discourse, for Janak was not only renowned as a great king, but also a great philosopher, and his court comprised many eminent intellectuals and scholars, including the 'navratna'[6] or the nine gems. Sita had a quest for knowledge and during conversations with court intellectuals, she proved to be a silent learner. Despite being a shy person, these debates enhanced Sita's self confidence, and made her fearless in speaking her mind. She learned the skills of how to develop a strong argument and the power of persuasion, in order to convince others to take appropriate action—a skill often apparent during her discussions with Ram.

Satananda delighted the sisters with Vedic lore and narrated, with meticulous details, the saga of Savitri's rescue of her husband Satyavan, from the noose of death. He also imparted knowledge of the four Vedas[7], the vast body of spiritual and esoteric knowledge. The sisters gained understanding of the *Rig Veda*, relating to cosmology and veneration of deities, the *Sama Veda*, for appreciation of the fine arts, music and dance, the *Yajur Veda*, for comprehension of the rituals, and *Atharva Veda* for know-how on medicine, healing and principles of construction and architecture.

Her experience of education had been totally in contrast with the Indian educational system where the emphasis was on rote learning, rather than augmenting a higher order of critical thinking and problem solving. Why did India still follow the system put in place by the British during the colonial rule which had the intention to suppress critical thinking? Wasn't education supposed to be about learning and understanding? Instead of focusing on analysing literature, or describing scientific phenomena, it seemed like a child's entire future pivoted on how much she could memorize. How could Sita convince people that good grades did not necessarily equate to proper learning. She suspected that the purpose of education was being defeated and students were not developing the ability to think rationally. Nor was education being able to nourish a wide range of capabilities in a child, such as the creative and literary abilities or a potential to bond with nature. Sita was ill at ease, for students had low sensitivity levels on issues of ecology, gender equality, or religious and cultural diversity. Was not one of the major goals of education to produce active citizens who could make informed decisions and solve problems in a changing world? Sita mused at how students could find a quality learning environment in schools when there were teachers like the biology teacher from Chattisgarh who, instead of concentrating on teaching the subject, gave blatantly sexist discourses.[8] She accused women of inviting rape and molestation through revealing attire and denounced girls who wore jeans and used lipstick. She claimed that they were 'shamelessly' inviting the attention of boys. Sita heard the audio clip made by some students as evidence of her outrageous comments, where she said that when boys see girls 'doing it' with one person they assume the girl would 'do it' with others as well.

Sita visited a school and was puzzled at how so many girls could be crammed into a crude one-room school run by a single person, and how it could provide a safe learning space. It was a madrasa or religious school, being run by a cleric from his shanty. The neighbours were whispering in hushed tones that he had raped his nine-year-old student, and possibly even others. The girl's neighbour first noticed the blood stains on her clothes when she was helping her package incense sticks. At first she too afraid to give a clear reply, but eventually the nine-year-old broke down and tearfully said that she had tried to stop the bleeding for two days but hadn't been able to.[9]

Pointing the way out of the gloom were shining beacons like Savitribai Phule, a pioneer in womens education, and social reformer, who went house to house begging people to send their daughters to school. She strongly spoke against the discriminatory boundaries imposed on women which led to their oppression, and encouraged parents to educate their daughters to make them capable of independent thought; insisting that 'education should give one the ability to choose between right and wrong and between truth and untruth in life.'[10] She and her husband believed that an industrial department should be attached to the schools where children could learn useful trades and crafts and be able to manage their lives. Enthused by her contribution, even the technology giant Google honoured Savitribai Phule on the occasion of her birth anniversary.

Success stories like that of Poonam brightened Sita's day. Sheer hard work and perseverance saw the daughter of an auto rickshaw driver topping the Provincial Civil Services (PCS-judicial) examinations. She achieved the feat on her third attempt, saying that perseverance is the key to success: 'One should not get disheartened by failures, these examinations are [the] ultimate test of knowledge and endurance.' Her father, to whom she was beholden for her success, sounded like King Janak. She proudly exclaimed,

> My father always told me not to give up and asked me to take the examination again. My teachers and friends too were a source of help as they had full faith in my abilities . . . I hail from a poor family. As my father is an auto rickshaw driver, education is the only means by which I could improve the lot of my family. People give a lot of respect to judges, they are seen as upholder of justice.[11]

Janak had provided Sita with an ideal learning environment. It was not only intellectually stimulating, but also safe; a place in which studying was interesting, fun, challenging, and seemed worth every minute; a place of change and growth brought about by learning. Sita imbibed a vast ocean of knowledge due to which she ingeniously devised the plan to help Ram cross the ocean and reach Lanka. She remembered asking Hanuman to communicate her message to Ram.

Hanuman, quoting Sita verbatim said, 'O Ram! I have narrated to you whatever has occurred, in its entirety. Let a bridge be constructed, by all means, across the waters of the ocean.'[12]

Sita's attainments, learning and chastity had led her to acquire special powers. There prevails a belief that chaste women have special yogic powers, and their words come true if uttered with a certain concentration. If she wanted to, Sita could have said to Ravan *hato bhava* or 'dead, you are' but she did not say so. Why? Because she wanted her husband to get the credit since Ram had promised the saints and sages that he would eliminate evil on earth—and the pledge had to be fulfilled by Ram alone! Like a dutiful devoted wife she did not want to steal his glory.

When Hanuman, after meeting Sita in the Ashoka Grove in Lanka, and wrecking the royal pleasure garden attached to the gynaecium, was taken captive by Indrajit, he had proudly professed being a messenger of Ram. Adding that although he was incapable of being bound even by a missile presided over by Brahma, he had surrendered only to see Ravan in person. Celebrating the glory of Ram, Hanuman warned Ravan that if he wished to survive, he should return Sita or be prepared for annihilation. Hearing this, Ravan was incensed and ordered the rakshasas to set Hanuman's tail on fire. Hanuman was ablaze literally and physically. His face resembled the fierce rising sun, and his mind was smouldering and inflamed with anger and impatience. Striking and throwing down the rakshasas, Hanuman started to set the whole city of Lanka on fire, as he moved from the rooftop of one house to another with his burning tail (barring the abode of Vibhishana). The fire spread with the wind, its flames shooting up and escalating with great speed and intensity. It blazed with such a fury as if to destroy the world. Lanka appeared to be afflicted by a curse. Enveloped in flames, its distinguished heroes were killed and its warriors retreated.

A miracle took place.

The fire scorched the whole of Lanka, but did not burn Hanuman. He had been saved by the kindness and prayers of Sita, who had come to know of his fierce act. At the time Hanuman's tail was burning, Sita had been praying 'Let the fire on the tail of that monkey be coolant to Hanuman.'[13] *And that is exactly what happened. The burning tail scalded the whole of Lanka, without having any effect on Hanuman.*[14]

Sita remembered how eagerly she had accompanied her father to visit the hermitages to gain proficiency in spiritual knowledge. In those sacred abodes, she heard of wise and learned female sages such as Anasuya and Lopamudra, but her favourite was Gargi Vachaknavi,[15] a *brahmavadini,* who she followed with close attention. Sita was impressed by the boundless curiosity of Gargi and her spirit of questioning everything, much to the displeasure of the sages who reprimanded her and said, 'If you ask so many questions your head will fall off.' Gargi was invited to attend an assembly of scholars to discuss philosophical matters, in a conference convened by King Janak, almost 3000 years ago.[16] She not only attended the conference, but also challenged the most revered philosopher of those days, Yajnavalkya. Sita asked around to know if women of such brilliance and erudition existed in the India of today. She found no answers, but stumbled upon a convention by The International Astronomical Union, where craters on Venus were being named after women who had made fundamental and outstanding contributions to their fields. Three such craters were named after the Indian women—Ramabai Medhavi, a women's rights activist; Anandibai Joshi, the first female Indian physician; and Jerusha Jhirad, a transformative physician.[17]

Having an analytical mind, Sita often introspected on the vagaries of gods, demons and men, and found herself perplexed by providence. She had been taught that introspection and questioning of one's own and others' motives and actions were the only route to personal growth. She was stupefied at why the gods were so free in granting favours to men without thinking of the consequences.

Just before her swayamvara when Sita heard the news of Ahalya's[18] resurrection by Ram, a number of questions on special privileges given to gods and not humans, troubled her, which made her ponder on society's discriminatory treatment against women. She asked herself, 'Gods and demons seemed to persist in their respective perversities or egoisms—no repentance, no change, no transformation for them! Sita had heard that Indra, 'God of gods', as he was brazenly known, author of many an aberration, had shown no remorse at all. It was left to Ahlaya alone, first born of the Feminine, frail, flawed, human and more sinned against than sinning, to pay for her transgression! And Sita wondered whether Ahalya, now transfigured in rebirth, wasn't the chaster and holier paragon, excelling the gods themselves?[19]

Sita was speculating on how the education needs of girls from tribal and marginalized groups were being fulfilled, when she read information given by the Union Minister for Tribal Affairs in a written reply in the Rajya Sabha.[20] To bridge the gap in the literacy rate of Scheduled Tribe (ST) children, the government had been implementing a number of schemes, namely the Scheme of Girls & Boys Hostels for STs, and the Scheme of Ashram Schools in Tribal Areas. The Scheme for Strengthening Education among ST Girls in Low Literacy Districts was impressive, which aimed to bridge the gap in literacy levels between the general female population and tribal girls through facilitating 100 per cent enrolment of tribal girls in schools, especially in Naxal-affected areas and in areas inhabited by Primitive Tribal Groups (PTGs), and by reducing dropouts at the elementary level by creating the required ambience for education. The Right of Children to Free and Compulsory Education (RTE) Act, 2009 under Section 29 states that, wherever practicable, children should be taught in their mother tongue, and accordingly, in the last few years several states had taken initiatives to help the transition of children from tribal groups, who speak a different language at home, to the languages used in school. Teacher training under the Sarva Shiksha Abhiyan (SSA) has sessions on sensitizing teachers to actively dispel traditional perceptions regarding gender or caste roles, take measures which would help girls and children from disadvantaged groups and weaker sections of society pursue education which is equitable and free of anxiety. Further, the revision of syllabi, textbooks and supplementary learning material was done to address the issues of gender and social inclusion.

Sita had the exceptional ability to perceive the emotional state of another person, which included a desire to alleviate their suffering. Renowned for her compassion, she genuinely believed that suffering is not necessarily due to an individual's own culpable action—for dreadful things happen to good people even though they are faultless—but due to their past karma. Sita was well aware of her non-uterine birth, but chose not to unnecessarily dwell upon it too much. Living neither in the past nor future, she was interested only in the present, cultivating self-mastery, and wisdom. It is said that having a strong male influence is important in a young boy's life, but in the case of girls it is equally important. A positive father-daughter relationship can have a huge impact on a young girl's life, and King Janak's influence in his daughter's life shaped her self-esteem and confidence. Sita's spirit was invigorated to know that there was another father as supportive as hers.

Ziauddin Yousafzai, on being questioned about how his daughter Malala[21] was so courageous, passionate and poised answered, 'Don't ask me what I did. Ask me what I did not do. I did not clip her wings and that's all.'[22] He proudly stated that in a society where fathers are usually known by their sons, he was one of the few fathers known by his daughter.

Sita wondered why people did not consider the obvious—that a community's development could be measured by the level of women's education or status. Were women's chances of healthier and happier lives not reason enough for promoting girls' education? Not only the woman, but the family and ultimately society benefitted as a whole. Why then was education seen as a threat rather than an asset? An educated woman could gain the prowess, information and self-confidence needed to be a better parent, worker and citizen.[23] Early in the morning throughout rural India, Sita could see young giggly girls in uniforms walking to school. She wanted to talk to them, to gauge their confidence and curiosity levels; she wanted to know whether education nurtured their creativity and sense of imagination. Did they ask unusual questions, had they learnt to think independently like she had, and did education help them garner courage to challenge societal conventions and assumptions? Despite a large number of girls attending school, Sita descried the implicit social expectation that a girl's sole purpose of education was to bide time until her true calling—that of becoming a wife. She read a study that looked at skills beyond foundational reading and arithmetic, focusing on the four A's—activity (what they were doing), ability (level of basic skills), awareness (their access to media, traditional and new) and aspirations. The Annual Status of Education Report (ASER) 2017 revealed that currently school education in India is not equipping youngsters for life outside school. It was not surprising that two minor girls, aged seven and ten years, who were suspected of being trafficked, did not know the basic details of their residence or the name of their village. All they knew was that their parents were very poor and had sold them.[24]

The survey also found a glaring gender divide, with boys outperforming girls in almost every task assigned to them, such as counting money and adding weights, and on many other parameters such as access to digital media. It also found that 89 per cent of females were engaged in household chores as against

77 per cent of males. The Report revealed that most fourteen to eighteen-year-olds could use cellphones but could not read basic text. More rural teens were staying back in school but struggled with reading and mathematics; girls were even worse off. Sita spoke to the CEO of the NGO Pratham, who told her, 'Our education system is currently designed to get you to class 10, 11 and college. But these academic skills don't seem to get transferred to life skills or everyday skills. It's time to connect the dots. It probably involves a relook at the curriculum. What the survey tell us is that this is a group that is not confident to engage, doesn't know math, doesn't want to stick their necks out. These skills that they are lacking are important not just in terms of work but broader life itself.'[25]

Child marriage was proving to be the biggest hurdle to the development and growth of girls in India. There prevails a misapprehension that educating girls causes excessive independence, with education being misconstrued as a hindrance to the girl participating in family life, i.e. household responsibilities. Sita was disheartened to find minor girls dropping out of school to take care of a sick parent or sibling. In spite of all these obstacles young girls were struggling to be educated. Sita was impressed with the single-minded determination of a group of 100 girls, who had made the state government succumb to their demands for the upgradation of the village school.[26] It was reported that the girls had gone on an indefinite strike, since they allegedly faced harassment and even molestation while travelling to the senior secondary school about three kilometres away. A principal was deputed to the government high school in the village and the admission process commenced—all due to the efforts and persistence of the girls.

Sita also commended the efforts of a young girl, whose classroom notes had been turned into a book. Shruti, finding herself struggling with physics, chemistry and biology, started making her own notes in Hindi, which have now been compiled into a book titled *Science Sense.* Her book launched on Amazon and Flipkart, and was displayed in the World Book Fair in New Delhi. After she topped her school in class 10, Shruti's teachers encouraged her to publish her notes so that other students could benefit from them. 'When I saw her notes, I realized that they were very simple and anyone could easily understand several complex theories by reading them. That is why I was one of the many teachers who encouraged Shruti to get her work published,' said BD Shukla, Shruti's school teacher.[27]

Sita glanced through the National Family Health Survey,[28] according to which nearly 11.8 per cent of children between the ages of 5–14 years worked either for their own household or for somebody else. Notably, at all ages, girls were more likely than boys to be doing chores. The disturbing figures in the Report, 'Children in India 2012'[29] reflected discrimination not only at the primary level but also in the field of higher education. About 40 per cent of girls were not allowed to pursue higher studies due to conservative familial ideologies. The safety of girls, travelling alone to school was a major concern in rural India, especially in the context of recent events of violence. Furthermore, there was a reluctance on the part of parents to send a girl to school after she reached puberty, mainly due to the lack of infrastructure, safety and functioning toilets for girls. One could not really blame the parents for worrying about the lack of safety and toilets, as both created barriers in the education of the girl child. It is not unusual to come across reports of sexual abuse of minors by teachers. For example, the case of a chess trainer in a private school who was arrested by the Ludhiana police for allegedly molesting a class two student inside the school premises.[30]

The parents also alleged that despite the complaint, the school had not taken any action against him. The teacher would apparently tempt the girl by giving her candies and chips, and used to molest her. The parents of the girl caught their six-year-old daughter bringing home packets of chips, chocolates and candies from school, and became suspicious since they did not give her money to buy it. Other classmates of the girl had also been molested by the teacher, but the parents were afraid of filing a complaint. According to a study last December by the NGO ActionAid India, one in every three public toilets in the capital city of India did not have separate sections for women. Of the 229 toilets in the city surveyed by them, 28 per cent did not even have doors. Another 45 per cent that did have doors could not be locked from the inside. In underprivileged neighbourhoods, the toilets are considered so dangerous, even women prefer defecating in the open. 'Local youths use the toilets for taking drugs and strew the premises with used injections', said the caretaker. When he objected, they approached him menacingly with a syringe in their hand. Often, there are men in toilets meant for women, compelling women to urinate in a dark part of a park instead of in the public toilet. A woman complainant visiting the office of a Deputy Commissioner of Police in south Delhi recently nearly ran out in panic when she found a policeman using toilets meant for women.[31]

Sita's education and knowledge were the source of her inner harmony and endurance throughout her ordeals, whether in exile with her husband, during her abduction and captivity by Ravan, or when she was abandoned and banished by Ram and compelled to raise her children alone as a single mother. She strongly felt that a lack of education denied the girl child the knowledge and expertise needed to advance her status, to realize her full potential, to think, question and judge independently, to be a wise decision-maker, and to be self-reliant, free from exploitation, and an actively-contributing citizen. This made her all the more impressed with the Dongria Kondh girls, who were breaking the gender barrier in order to study. Overcoming their mundane, humdrum existence in the remote Railima village in the foothills of Odisha's Niyamgiri Hills, 14 girls made history by becoming the first from their backward community to clear the class 10 examinations. Their success, though a tiny dot compared to the nationwide figure—in 2017, 92.5 per cent of female students who appeared for the class 10 Central Board of Secondary Education (CBSE) exams across the country, passed it—has left a mark on the community, egging many families to overcome their age-old beliefs and apprehensions against sending their daughters to school. This motivated another small-time subsistence farmer to persuade his wife to send their eight-year-old daughter to the village primary school. This was a crucial decision, for nobody in the family, leave alone a girl, had been to school before. The Dongria Kondhs are one of Odisha's most primitive and backward tribal communities. As per the 2011 census, the Scheduled Tribe community has a population of about 8000, with just a 10 per cent literacy rate, and a dismal three per cent female literacy rate. Most of the 14 achievers were the alumnae of the residential school started by the Dongria Kondh Development Authority (DKDA), a state government agency set up to mainstream the community through development activities such as skill training and education. In a community where girls are merely seen as helping hands at home and on the field, or are married off at a young age, the achievement of these girls is no mean feat, says Guha Poonam Tapaskumar, Rayagada's collector. '... a silent revolution is underway in the lives of these tribal community. It is encouraging, especially as the district has a history of high infant and maternal mortality rate propelled largely by illiteracy, early marriage, poor hygiene and superstitious beliefs,' he adds.

However, the path to education is still strewn with challenges. It's not easy to convince parents to send their children to school. 'Many of them have never stepped out of their village. For them, sending their kids to a residential school is unthinkable. Language poses another big challenge. The children, when they come here know only the local dialect called Kui. We have to make them learn Odia,' said Anjali Nachika, in charge of the Kansur educational complex.[32]

Sita remembered how she would sit beside Ram and take an interest in the welfare of Ayodhya, and wondered what action the administration in India was taking considering that children between 0–14 years comprised one-third of the total population in the country. It was the duty of the king or state to provide every child with a conducive and enabling environment so that they could blossom to their maximum capability. Sita had read that the Constitution of India guaranteed free and compulsory education to all children as a Fundamental Right.[33] She was consequently informed that the RTE Act, 2009, was legislated with the aim to give every child an elementary education of a satisfactory and equitable quality in a formal school. She was also updated about the various government schemes, such as the mid-day meal programme, and the construction of toilets for girls—an initiative benefitting thousands of girls, which was succeeding in achieving the desired increase in enrolment[34] and decreasing the drop-out rate of girls on attaining puberty. Sita was referred to an example that helped promote girls' rights. 'Meena' was a communication initiative coordinated by the United Nations Children's Fund (UNICEF), developed in cooperation with Bangladesh, India, Nepal and Pakistan, in which a cartoon character called Meena was used as a role model for girls. The series provoked discussion on gender discrimination in childhood and touched on such issues as the unfair treatment of girls in the family, and their reduced access to education and health services.

Ziauddin Yousafzai, father of Malala, said:

> When a girl is born … she is not welcomed, neither by father nor by mother. At the age of five, when she should be going to school, she stays at home … When she turns 13, she is forbidden to leave her home without a male escort … She becomes the so-called honour of her father, brothers and her family. If she transgresses the code of that so-called honour, she could be killed.[35]

Sita perked up while reading the National Charter for Children (NCC), 2003, which highlighted the constitutional provisions towards protection of children's interests, and the responsibility of the wider society, communities and families in fulfilling children's basic needs. The well-being of special groups such as children of below-poverty-line families, street children, girl children, child-care programmes, and educational programmes for prevention from exploitation find special mention in the NCC. It secures for every child the inherent right to be a child and enjoy a healthy and happy childhood, to address the root causes that negate the healthy growth and development of children, and to awaken the conscience of the community in the wider societal context to protect children from all forms of abuse, while strengthening the family, society and the nation. For empowering adolescents, the Charter stated that the state and community shall take all steps to provide the necessary education and skills to adolescent children so as to equip them to become economically productive citizens.

Sita felt admiration for the government for adopting The National Plan of Action for Children (NPA), 2005, which had as its goal the complete abolition of female foeticide, female infanticide and child marriage, and ensuring the survival, development and protection of the girl child. She scrutinised the important schemes for the well-being of children which included among others—the Integrated Child Development Service Scheme; the Integrated Child Protection Scheme; Balika Samriddhi Yojna; the Nutrition Programme For Adolescent Girls; Early Childhood Education for 3–6 Age Group Children; Welfare of Working Children in Need of Care and Protection; Childline services; the Rajiv Gandhi National Creche Scheme for Children of Working Mothers; Ujjawala: A Comprehensive Scheme for Prevention of Trafficking and Rescue, Rehabilitation and Re-integration of Victims of Trafficking and Commercial Sexual Exploitation; the Rajiv Gandhi Scheme for Empowerment of Adolescent Girls (RGSEAG) Sabla; Dhanalakshami–Conditional Cash Transfer for Girl Child with Insurance Cover; and the National Commission for Protection of Child Rights.

Sita couldn't help but wonder if the State was taking over the role of a father or a mother, and if it could really make up for what the child should have be getting from her parents. But the practical side of her acknowledged that sometimes the powers that be needed to step in, as sadly not all fathers were as able or willing to support their daughters as hers had been.

Health

Sita was impressed to know that the Constitution of India empowered the State to make special provisions for children,[36] ensure that they are given facilities to develop in a healthy manner, and guarantee protection of childhood.[37]

Not all parents were concerned, like her father, King Janak, or aware of the basics of keeping children healthy. He provided Sita and her sisters with proper nutrition, rest and safety, and was cognizant of the fact that in early childhood, the first six years were the most crucial as the foundation was laid for the cognitive, social and physical development of the child. This was especially vital since newborns upto three years of age were most vulnerable to the vicious cycle of malnutrition, disease, infection and resultant disability.

Nutrition is among any human's fundamental needs, and Sita remembered that in her childhood, she and her sisters had been pampered with the choicest of foods. She was discouraged to know that nearly half of all deaths of children under five years of age in India could be attributed to under-nutrition.[38] Poor nutrition in the first 1,000 days of a child's life also leads to stunted growth, which is irreversible, and is associated with impaired cognitive ability and reduced school and work performance. She scanned the malnutrition figures, which presented abysmally high levels of underweight and stunted children.[39] Malnutrition being labelled a 'national shame,' incited civil society to make a collective appeal to policymakers to 'declare malnutrition a medical emergency to save India's children from dying of hunger.'[40] The critical window of opportunity, when nutritional interventions offer children the best chance for survival and development to their full potential, is during adolescence, a woman's pregnancy, and a child's first two years of life. After the age of two, this window begins to close and the future outlook for the child starts to drastically diminish.[41]

Sita was disturbed to know that in spite of statistical indicators showing progress in the health sector, the situation was not adequate enough to ensure a bright future for the children of India. This multi-faceted problem was directly linked, to a large extent, to the mother's health, unsafe delivery conditions, the socio-economic conditions of the family, and the country's healthcare system. Sita read the findings of the Global Nutrition Report 2017, which placed India at the bottom of the table with the maximum number of women in the world impacted by anaemia, followed by China, Pakistan, Nigeria and Indonesia. In India, more than half or 51 per cent of all women of reproductive age have anaemia, while this number was nearly 48 per cent in 2016.[42] Low awareness, illiteracy and the practice of putting the family before self when it comes to care are factors that often deter women in India from taking proper nutrition and care for themselves, which leads to anaemia, says Dr Taneja. 'The impact can be severe at times, especially when it happens in the child-bearing age,' she said. Anaemia among women in the reproductive age often leads to health issues in the mother as well as the child. While such women are prone to infection and may need blood transfusions during pregnancy, children born of such women often remain under-developed with poor immunity. Stunted children who are too short for their age due to a lack of nutrients, suffer irreversible damage to their brain capacity. Anaemia, caused by an iron deficiency in the body, mostly affects women, primarily because a majority of women in India do not have a balanced and nutritious diet. An iron deficiency may also increase due to deficiencies in folic acid, vitamin C, vitamin A or vitamin B12, since women in India tend to put their dietary and health needs secondary to family. In addition, pregnancy and blood loss due to menstruation causes iron deficiency, resulting in the woman giving birth to a gravely anaemic child. Undoubtedly, over the years, despite a number of child-centered programmes having been implemented, much remains to be done to guarantee better health conditions for the girl child.

Sita was impressed by the proactive measures taken by the Government of India, which launched the National Nutrition Mission (NNM),[43] a humongous programme of convergence between the Ministry of Women and Child Development and the Ministry of Health and Family Welfare, in the fight against malnutrition. The programme, which will be driven by technology to monitor the growth of children, will also check for the pilferage of food rations provided at *anganwadis*.[44] Commencing in 315 high-burden districts, it is to be implemented over three years, covering all districts by 2019–20. By 2020, an estimated 10 crore people will benefit from this programme for which the Cabinet had approved a budget of Rs 9046.17 crore. The mission has a target to reduce undernutrition and low birth weight in children by 2 per cent per annum. It also aims to bring down anaemia among young children, women and adolescent girls by 3 per cent per annum until 2020. The government will also strive to reduce the prevalence of stunting from the current level of 38.4 per cent (as per the NFHS IV) to 25 per cent by 2022. At the heart of the mission is the use of information communication technology for real-time monitoring of the services delivered by *anganwadi* workers, frontline community health workers or ASHAs (accredited social health activists) and auxiliary nurse midwives (ANMs). The growth chart plotted by the software will provide the daily progress of the child and when the graph indicates adverse results an SMS alert is sent to the parents. The pilot project has helped identify 12,000 severely malnourished children and has made subsequent interventions. This project has a six-tier real-time reporting system, which includes an *anganwadi* worker, an *anganwadi* supervisor, a child development project officer, a district official, an official appointed by the chief secretary at the state level, and officials at the Centre.

Sita wished the government success in its mission, for the irony did not escape her that the consequences of maternal undernourishment or depriving a girl child of nutrition tended to be far reaching, and not restricted just to that particular girl or woman. This would eventually affect males as well, as they would one day be borne out of this neglect and deprivation. Female inequality has a way of affecting multiple generations and both genders, ultimately permeating the core of a nation.

Physical Ability and Sport

Sita had learnt that play is necessary to help children develop social skills, so that they learn to get along with others, take turns and share. Sita was no different and, like all children, she liked to play, be active and have fun. Pretending, or imaginative play, is one of the cornerstones of a young child's world. Almost anything could spur young Sita's imagination, stretching it to unlimited possibilities. Imaginative play gave her a sense of control as she interpreted the dramas of everyday life and practiced the rules of social behavior. Supported by a father who encouraged her to be who she was, Sita defied any gender stereotyping. She was fond of both outdoor and indoor games, and loved to play ball. Beneath the quiet and seemingly submissive exterior was a woman of great underlying physical strength and power. It was while playing with her friends that their ball rolled under the casket that carried the Shiv *dhanush,*[45] or mighty bow of Shiv. Innocently, the young child took a close look under the box and raised it a little with her left hand, while retrieving the ball with her right hand. King Janak happened to enter the room just then, and was astonished to see the heavy bow, which could not be lifted or handled by anyone except

Lord Shiv himself (or Parshuram, incarnation of Lord Vishnu), being lifted by young Sita.

Sita felt sad to see that today even play spaces had become gendered, with marketing and consumerism reinforcing gender roles. Athletics had become primarily male dominated, characterized by masculine qualities such as strength, aggression, and competition, whereas girls stayed at home playing with dolls, when and if they had free time from domestic chores. Gendered expectations were being played out in everyday life, as it was considered normal for a girl to be gifted a doll and a boy to receive a cricket bat or ball. Disappointed, Sita felt that she should have been an inspiration for girls, since she had proved her superior physical strength in effortlessly lifting the divine bow of Shiv. But due to long-standing gender norms, women today still faced multiple challenges when pursuing their athletic desires.

In ancient India, women of the Kshatriya (warrior) caste received martial arts coaching and arms training. The *Adbhuta Ramayana*[46] elucidates upon Sita's physical prowess and dexterity in the martial arts. According to this version of the *Ramayana*, she slays Ravan, engaging him first in combat and then assuming the terrifying and destructive form of the Goddess Kali.[47] In a patriarchal society can a woman be in the spotlight instead of her husband? No; she has to play the femininity game and give her husband all the glory. It is possible that this was the reason why, when Hanuman offered to help her escape, Sita politely declined the offer. She wanted her husband to take the credit for eliminating the evil Ravan. She said, '*Therefore, you act in such a way that the high-souled Ram, valiant in battle, may exhibit prowess worthy of him.*'[48]

What may look like mere child's play is in fact a critical part of learning and brain development—problem solving, skill building, and overcoming physical and mental challenges.

At a young age Sita often played chess with her sisters, with their rival armies battling in the black and white squares. While playing, she analyzed why she lost or won, and the game increased her levels of mental strength and self-confidence much beyond the chess board. Playing chess with her sisters stimulated deep concentration and calm, helping her to learn to relax, while experiencing different degrees of anxiety. Playing helped her work through her emotions. Sita also had a fascination for the game of Snakes and Ladders and felt hypnotized by the squares, in which ladders ascended, symbolizing virtue, and squares with a head of a snake, representing evil, forced you to descend. With every rise there lurked a fall. The punishments and promotions, taught her lessons of humility and hope. The monstrous mouth of the snake made her realize that the fear of suffering is worse than the suffering itself, and that with great risks come great rewards.[49]

Sita felt optimistic upon hearing that, centuries later, another father had been born who nurtured his daughters like King Janak, defying social norms and breaking gender stereotypes that girls are weak and cannot participate in sports like wrestling, which are perceived as overtly masculine. Mahavir Singh Phogat, a wrestler and senior Olympics coach from Haryana, a state where every mother probably wants to give birth to a son, trained his daughters as wrestlers. Overcoming the resentment and opposition of society, he communicated the message that it's 'cool for girls to be strong', saying *'Mahari chorian choron se kum nahin*—my girls are no less than boys ... The gold medal does not recognize gender, it does not differentiate between boy or girl but only incomparable performance.'[50] When Mahavir Singh's eldest daughter, Geeta, took on the local boys in a wrestling bout, she made history by being the first girl to enter a strictly male arena, with people speculating whether they were girls or boys.

> I was not worried about the outcome of the fight or the fact that my opponent would be a boy ... But the fact that I was

> going to fight in front of such a big crowd full of men for the first time gave me a strange feeling. I was shy, but it took me only two–three *dangals* to get used to the atmosphere and I soon began to enjoy myself … We were the ones to start the trend of wrestling with boys in India. They were scared of fighting with us as people would make fun of them if they lost or if we gave them a close fight. *Ladkiyon se harna kisko pasand hai?* (Who likes to lose to girls after all?) People would taunt …'*Tu is chori se haar gaya*' (You lost to this girl). And we would enjoy the attention. We would hear people talk about us when we passed by: '*Yeh Balali wali ladkiyan hain*' (These are the girls from Balali). Some would say, '*Yeh ladkiyan hain ya ladke?*' (Are they girls or boys?)[51]

Geeta not only overpowered her male opponent in her first public fight, but went from victory to victory, winning India's first ever gold medal in wrestling at the Commonwealth Games in 2010.

> As Mahavir stood amid the cheering crowd that day, his gaze locked in on his daughter with pride, the cold winter morning of 1988 flashed before his eyes. That was the day when he had held her in his arms and emphatically proclaimed one day she will make her family proud.[52]

Not only in India, but female athletes the world over, who do not necessarily represent the hegemonic feminine ideal, such as Venus and Serena Williams, Mia Hamm, and mixed-martial arts fighter Gina Carano, encounter more difficulties in their careers as they attempt to balance a feminine image with the masculine qualities associated with their sports.[53] Women who participate in highly differentiated sports that are 'gender-inappropriate', like boxing, wrestling or weight lifting, most often experience negative consequences, such as being labeled 'manly' or having comments like 'Who will marry her?' made about them. Sportswomen in India who are redefining hegemonic femininity continue to persevere and work through various gender constraints. With role models like Sakshi Malik—2016 Summer Olympics wrestling bronze medal-winner, and Mary Kom—five-time World Amateur Boxing champion, they inspire women to believe that they too can break societal barriers and gender prejudices that surround them, and bring home medals or gain recognition. Another example is that of Razia Shabnam, who wanted freedom from the gender stereotype that women, especially those who belong to the Muslim community, cannot box. Her family was publicly abused and told that what she was doing was un-Islamic.[54] Supported by her family, she remained undeterred and took to the boxing ring in 1998 to become one of the first women boxing coaches in India, and the first female international boxing referee and judge. The disparity in what successful female athletes are paid compared to the millions received by male athletes is well known around the world. In yet another clear case of gender bias, Sita read a letter written to the Sports Minister by the National Commission for Women (NCW) after the Board of Control for Cricket in India (BCCI) made a payment of about 12.5 million US dollars from the Indian Premier League's profits to former male cricket players for their previous contribution to the game. The NCW demanded that former female cricket players should also get a share of the payment for their contribution as well.[55]

In a nation obsessed by cricket, there are few takers for women's cricket in India. This is despite the Mithali Raj-led Indian team giving a brilliant performance to outclass hosts South Africa in the first One Day International (ODI) of the

International Cricket Council (ICC) Women's Championship in 2017. Enthusiastically, Sita expressed a desire to watch the match on a device the modern world called 'television', but was disheartened on being told that the match would not be broadcast. In fact, the BCCI, the national governing body for cricket in India did not even deem it tweet-worthy.[56] Not even one post was devoted to the match on the BCCI's main Twitter handle. It came as a big shock to Sita since the teams were ranked third and fourth in the ICC rankings. On the other hand, the Indian men's team was also in South Africa and all their matches were being broadcast live. The emphasis in college on 'superstar' male athletes ignores the health and well-being of all students in favour of creating a few profitable athletes. In addition, male athletes in certain sports are taught to de-humanize and degrade women as part of their sports training.[57] This in turn can lead to increased violence against women by these male athletes. The need of the hour is to create an environment in which sports and fitness is for everyone, not just a few, and in which everyone's abilities are tested and respected.

Dronacharya, Indian mythology's greatest coach, banished an aspiring and brilliant low-caste archer from his camp, to ensure that Arjuna, his favourite student, would not be upstaged. Today, Indian sportswomen are akin to the lowest caste in the field of sports. They are shunned, objectified and treated badly by the men who dominate the field and the bureaucracy that controls it.[58] Sania Mirza, the Indian professional tennis player who was formerly ranked No.1 in women's doubles, and United Nations Women's Goodwill Ambassador for the South Asian region, expressed her anguish to Sita and said, 'Women face discrimination. They are treated like animals and it is not right. The thinking needs to be changed. Mentality needs to be changed. Men must understand that women also go out to do their work just as they do. But even women have to realise their own worth.'[59] The media is also at blame for sensationalizing the personal lives of sportswomen and creating controversies about their breakups or marriages. If that was not enough, even religious clerics jump into the fray, deciding what costumes they should wear, what the length of their skirts should be or how their t-shirts should not be so tight. The finest sportswomen in India have faced discrimination at some level in their sports career, be it at the hands of authorities, selection teams, coaches, governments, or even their own families. P.T. Usha, India's former sprint queen, broke down in front of the media regarding the discrimination meted out to her. Sita felt that while the nation was rooting for some female athletes, it also needed to push for equal opportunities.

In the 2016 Olympic Games in Rio de Janeiro, India fielded it's largest-ever contingent, with a number of girls participating in fields ranging from archery, athletics, badminton, golf, gymnastics, swimming, table tennis, and tennis to shooting, boxing, weight lifting and wrestling.

For the first time in history an Indian woman–

- Won an Olympic silver medal, worth it's weight in gold – P.V. Sindhu.
- Won a bronze medal in wrestling, considered a male preserve – Sakshi Malik.
- Came fourth in the Olympic individual vault final – Dipa Karmakar.
- Became the first Indian golfer to qualify for the Olympics – Aditi Ashok.
- Became the first Indian woman to reach the Olympic final in steeple chase—Lalita Babar.

- And the Indian women hockey team qualified for the Olympics after 36 years.

In the 2016 Summer Olympics it was two women who saved the honor of the nation. Dipa Karmarkar, a gymnast from Tripura, who missed the bronze by a whisker, was among the top trending stories of 2016.[60] The young girl and her coach knew that if she had to make a mark in the field of gymnastics, she would have to master the Produnova, the vault of death. Dipa's relentless effort and determination took her agonizingly close to landing a medal in the Olympics, making her a source of inspiration for aspiring young girls to believe that they can 'hit the mark' with proper training and a well-managed balanced diet. What is notable is the fact that all countries in the top ten medal table in Rio, led by the USA, were those listed in the 'Very High Human Development'[61] category in the United Nations Development Programme's (UNDP) Human Development Index, proving that health, literacy and standard of living are important factors.

Sita was saddened to know that many of these women athletes, who were role models as inspirational players, were not even able to afford a square meal due to abject poverty. Sita was dismayed to see the plight of her namesake, another Sita, a fifteen-year-old wonder[62] who did India proud by winning two bronze medals at the 2011 Athens Special Olympics, but was then compelled to drop out of school and work to sustain her family. The Olympian's mother lamented that she could not afford milk or fruits to feed her children. Another example was the former archery champ, Nisha Rani Dutta, who was forced to sell her bow to fix her house after it collapsed in the rains. Her trainer had gifted her the bow, which was worth about Rs 4 lakh. One could also look at the case of Rashmita Patra—

the acclaimed Oriya footballer—who was born in a daily wage labourer's family and represented India in the Asian Football Confederation (AFC) for the under-sixteen women's qualifier at Kuala Lumpur in 2008. She is now compelled to run a betel nut shop in her village.

India abounds with out-of-the-box stories of young girls who were stepping out of the shadows. Behind India's record haul of five gold medals at the International Boxing Association (AIBA) World Women's Youth Boxing Championships are stories of grit from the homes of five girls—from a mother who lived her life behind a veil but taught her daughter to step out, to a father who almost left his government job to support his child.[63] For example, Jyoti Guliya, the seventeen-year-old girl who, after winning a gold medal at the Women's Youth World Boxing Championship, is back working in the buffalo shed in her everyday modest life. She uses a wooden spade to scoop the animal refuse into an iron pan, hauls it around on her head and empties its contents into a pile of dung nearby. When Jyoti wanted to join the boxing academy that had recently come up in her village, her father objected. But her mother put her foot down and said, '*Main hi iske pita se ladti thi ke main toh bhejjungi boxing mein. Hum toh aise reh gaye, par meri beti aise nahi rehni chahiye.*' (I fought with her father and said I will definitely send her to the boxing academy. I couldn't do much, but I wouldn't let my daughter end up like me). As usual Jyoti's father's biggest fear then was, 'What would the villagers say?' Just as Ram gave priority to what other people thought, similarly even today parents are more concerned about false notions of honour and what society and people will say, rather than giving priority to the happiness of their own daughter. Jyoti's father argued that if they as parents allowed her to box, then after her marriage she would get into the habit of hitting her husband and the panchayat would have to intervene to resolve their fights. When the gold medal came with a cash prize of Rs 20 lakh, their fellow villagers became supportive. A similar story is that of Shashi Chopra, whose mother barely went to school herself, but gently nudged her four children towards education, encouraging them to blossom in whatever field they chose. Now every time Shashi returns home after winning a bout, she follows a ritual of putting the medal around her mother's neck.

Sita firmly believed that if India was to progress, it must ensure respect for women players. Gender inequality can be addressed when more fathers emerge to support the girl child's survival, development and protection. King Janak provided his daughter with not only a conducive environment for education but also the opportunity to engage in sporting activities, so that Sita could excel in whatever she chose, and be no less than any man.

Yet, on the other hand she was dismayed to note that in spite of several focused initiatives, statistics presented a dismal picture and much more was needed to be done to improve the condition in all realms for the girl child. The plight of millions of women would be different if all fathers had been like King Janak, Ziauddin Yousafzai or Mahavir Singh, for behind every independent girl there is an open-minded father who trusted her and encouraged her to soar to new heights. Every girl child's unrealized potential translates into an unrealized growth potential for the country. Our girls still have a long way to go on the road to fairness and equality.

Sexuality and Youth

Sita remembered, as a young girl she had been overcome with a heady mixture of feelings when she first set eyes on Ram. Her mind and body reeled with intense love, attraction and exhilaration. As if struck by lightning, she had been inexplicably overcome by the breath-stopping feeling of passionate love for Ram. It was a feeling like she had never felt before. She was transported into a bygone era when she had gone to the temple of Gauri. As soon as she had finished praying, astonishingly, one of her friends disappeared to see the flowers in the garden.

While wandering around admiring the garden, the young maiden spotted the two brothers. Totally mesmerized, her heart was overcome with love. When she returned her friends noticed her euphoric state, and eyes brimming with tears of joy. Did they reprimand her for her misdemeanour, or threaten to complain to the queen mother about her playing truant? No, instead they all entreated her to disclose the reason for her ecstasy. All the friends, forgetting her dereliction of duty, curiously in gentle affectionate tones asked her what gladdened her heart.

Destiny had given this unnamed girl the honor of announcing Ram's presence to Sita. She said, 'Two princes have come to see the garden, both of tender age and altogether charming, one dark and the other fair; how can I describe them? For speech is sightless and the eyes are mute!' The young maiden was so moved by the profound experience that she found words inadequate to describe the beauty that touched the core of her heart so deeply. Having glimpsed Ram, the girl articulated the limitations of her senses. Although her eyes had the pleasure of seeing him, her tongue must describe what it had not seen. One of Sita's friends, trying to be helpful, suggested:

> *They must be the two princes, my dear, who, I was told, arrived yesterday with the sage (Vishwamitra), and who have captivated the hearts of men and women of the city by casting the spell of their entrancing beauty. All are talking of their loveliness here, there and everywhere. We must see them, for they are worth seeing!*

Sita was filled with excitement on listening to the account of her friend. Her eyes were restless to see Ram. Shocked at her own response, Sita wondered why she was feeling this way. She was bewildered that she, a king's daughter, whose destiny was bound by the outcome of the Dhanush yajna, was restless to meet a total stranger. Then, recollecting the words of Narada,[64] *she was relieved of her guilt. This intense attraction for an unknown man was not born out of lust, but was predestined. Sita knew that Ram was an incarnation of Vishnu, and she herself was an incarnation of Lakshmi, which created between them an ageless and eternal bond.*[65]

Love is a strange propelling force, which makes one break all the rules and decorum of society. Sita was aware that social propriety required a princess to lead, and the rest of her entourage of friends to follow. But since the unnamed friend had seen the brothers, she was asked to lead. Sita was confident that she would lead them to the exact spot where Ram would be. The friend may have been leading the way, but Sita's heart and eyes were racing ahead, and her feet were finding it difficult to keep pace with her racing heart.

Sita's tinkling bangles and anklets revealed her impatience. In her lovelorn state and enthusiasm she tried to cover two–three steps in one stride. Ram was close by and was struck by Cupid's arrow on hearing the tinkling of Sita's bangles, the small bells tied round her waist and anklets. He had only heard the sound of her ornaments, but suddenly he felt alive and his heart was filled with love. He was yet to see Sita, but the tinkling of her ornaments spurred incomprehensible emotions within him, creating an uncontrollable excitement and desire.

Ram was mesmerised by Sita's beauty. Tongue-tied, words failed him. It was as if in the creation of Sita, God's eternal existence was being revealed. His invisible creative attributes, his eternal power and divine nature.[66] *'She lends charm to charm itself and looks as if a flame of light is burning in the house of loveliness.' Ram, spellbound, was drowning in a sea of emotion and felt that all the similes used by poets were stale and prosaic, and wondered to whom he should compare the daughter of Videha. Overwhelmed by his thoughts, he feared uttering something inappropriate. Calming his spirit, he tried to regain his composure and draw himself out of this state of ecstasy. Ram was conscious of the fact that, being a 'maryada purush', his speech should always be appropriate to the occasion. Being of impeccable character, he himself was surprised as to how and why his heart was attracted to this young girl! Pretending to act normal, and using words which did not reveal his inner conflict, Ram said innocently to Laxman, 'Dear brother, this is no other than the Janaka's daughter, to win whom the contest of the bow is being held. She has been escorted by her girl-companions to worship Gauri and is moving about in the garden diffusing light all about her.'*[67]

Love can be very confusing, and it is difficult to bottle up one's feeling. Sooner or later what ever is in one's heart is going to come out of the mouth. And Ram nervously blurted out his inner thoughts to Laxman. He said:

> *My heart which is by nature pure, is agitated by the sight of her divine beauty—God alone knows why! But I tell you, brother, the throbbing of my lucky (right) side betokens good fortune. Men of the house of Raghu never even in set their heart on evil course; that is their nature. As for myself, I am fully confident of my mind, which has looked on another's wife even in a dream. Rare in this world are those honourable men who turn not their back on the foe in battle, nor give their heart to or cast an amorous glance on another's wife, and from whom no beggar meets with a rebuff.*

For the first time his heart has been so stirred by just looking at a woman. Why? Only God knows!

Ram could see Sita, but she yet had to catch a glimpse of him, and was timidly searching for him. Looking all round the garden, Sita speculated about where the princes could have gone. Wherever the fawn-eyed princess cast her glance, a continuous stream of white lotuses, the purest among flowers, seemed to suddenly blossom. Just then, her companions pointed out to the two brothers who were standing behind a fence of creepers—one dark and the other fair of hue.

A unique moment transpired when two infinities met and there occurred a fusion of body, spirit and soul. As if they were one. Sita was overcome with a heady mixture of feelings on first setting eyes on Ram. Her mind and body reeled with intense love, attraction and exhilaration, as if struck by a bolt of lightning. Energised, an inner sparkle heralding romantic love was overtaking her senses. A feeling like she had never felt before.

Beholding the beauty of the two princes, Sita's eyes were filled with greed and rejoiced, as if they had discovered a long-lost treasure. Her eyes became transfixed at the sight of Ram, and her eyelids forgot to blink. Swooning in a state of ecstasy, she felt as if her body had lost consciousness. She was inexplicably overcome by a breath-stopping feeling of passionate love for this man. It seemed as if a Cakora bird was gazing at the autumnal moon. Receiving Ram into her heart through the passage of her eyes, she cleverly captured him by closing her eyelids.

On finding Sita in the throes of love, oblivious to her surroundings, her friends were too abashed to question her. Holding their peace, none uttered a single word. Not wanting to break the spell, they waited patiently for Sita to open her eyes. At that very moment the two brothers emerged from a bower, like a pair of spotless moons had shone forth, tearing the veil off a cloud. Sita froze on the spot, mesmerized by the chance encounter.[68]

While leaving, Sita turned around again and again, pretending to look at a deer, bird or tree, and each time she gazed at the incomparable beauty of Ram, the hero of Raghu's race. With every glance her love only increased, instead of waning with separation. Modesty made it unbecoming for her to conspicuously turn around and stare boldly at Ram, so she repeatedly stole quick, sideways glances and then looked away. The distance between them was slowly widening, yet their hearts continued to come closer. But the unyielding bow of Shiv loomed over them like the sword of Damocles. Sita's heart drooped at its thought, putting her in the throes of a dilemma. Time had caught her off guard. She did not know what the future held, but she certainly knew who held her future. Ram, and only Ram—the man she loved and wanted to marry. She did not know if she would get another chance to see her beloved so closely. All she knew was that this chance encounter had changed her life. Sita, forcing her body to move mechanically, returned home with her friends, but her heart remained focused on Ram.[69]

The fire had been lit on both ends. Having been struck by the arrow of Kamdeva,[70] Ram's condition was no different. He was talking to Laxman and physically walking by his side, but his heart was fixated on Sita. When he saw *'Janaka's daughter going, that fountain of bliss, affection, grace and virtue—then with the gentle ink of supreme love he traced her infinite beauty on the tablet of his soul.'*[71] But there was a difference in their circumstances. Ram was the master of his fate. He was free of any constraint, nor under any pressure or social custom. He was in a position to make every possible effort to gain Sita's hand. But Sita's fate was tied to Shiv's bow and her freedom of choice was restricted. If it was a normal *swayamvara*, she would have garlanded Ram, the man of her choice, without any hesitation. But, in spite of having selected her life partner, she was not in a position to do as she wanted, for her father had tied her marriage to the outcome of the bow contest. Being dependent on her father, she did not have the authority to take any decision on her own. She needed her father's seal of approval. Sadly, even today in India if, in defiance of societal norms, a girl independently exercises her choice to marry, she may face reprisals, ranging from being ostracized to being severely punished, including being killed.

True love has the potential to take us to the heights of happiness and into the depths of pain. Although Sita craved for a union with Ram, yet a multitude of questions arose in her mind and her love turned into fear; a fear which made it impossible for her to concentrate on anything, for worry and fear are the two great enemies of concentration. Her fear made her doubt Ram's ability to lift and string the mighty bow of Shiv. Had she not seen him perspiring in the garden simply by collecting flowers? Sita's heart swung between love and fear like a pendulum. At that moment she remembered that while praying to Goddess Gauri, she had unambiguously beseeched her for a suitable husband, and immediately afterwards she had met Ram. This convinced Sita that the Goddess had heard her prayers. Had her marriage not been predestined to be with this stranger, then would they have entered the garden at the same time?

While we, as humans, may to some extent romanticize love, scientific research shows clear evidence that there is indeed a unique neurochemistry to the elixir of love, which is responsible for making our cheeks flush, our palms sweat and our hearts race. The brain functions very differently when in love, and its three phases include lust, attraction and attachment.[72] The worst is the disease called 'lust' that turns the afflicted into their own enemies. Sita shuddered at the thought of the 14,000 warriors whose lives had been expended due to Surpanakha being inflamed with lust. Nor did their wasteful deaths deter her from repeatedly inciting Ravan—who, enslaved by his evil passions, forgot all ties of kinship and shut his eyes to his own impending disaster. The dilemma of love and lust is that there is a very thin line between the two. Love is a beautiful emotion filled with tenderness and affection, while the crude passions of lust and violence need to be curbed. Love in a relationship can keep two people together, while lust can keep the relationship alive. However, lust often leads to objectification, in which the uppermost thought in one's mind is a desire for sex and not about caring for your partner's feelings.

So what exactly is love? Is it a mysterious mix of sentiment and sex? Or a combination of infatuation and companionship? Or is there more than that? It is said that sexual desire in females is both more complex and more fragile than it is in males, as in the former it is less linked to biology, and more to psychology. It is generally related to how they feel about themselves, and what is happening in their lives. The beautiful transition from childhood to adulthood includes not only a physical but also a psychological transformation. In this period, if a teenager gets mixed signals from society, it may result in the confused youth indulging in risk-taking behaviour. However, awareness regarding sexual health can help prepare young people to have a responsible attitude towards several aspects of sexuality. Sita was astonished to detect that the issue of sex and sexuality remained a taboo in Indian society and was off limits in everyday life. While India had given the world the *Kamasutra*, and the ancient temples of Khajuraho boldly illustrated sexual pleasures, yet the modern-day youth was socialized to consider such desires as being sinful or debased. This was so much so that the government had restricted the telecast of advertisements relating to safe-sex awareness and condoms to between 10 pm and 6 am. The reasons given for this were that these advertisements were 'indecent especially for children' and could 'create unhealthy practices'. It was strange that sex could sell everything, except sex! Sita was astonished at this hypocrisy, which was contradicted in the advertisements of products, ranging from cars to mango juice, which showed both lip-biting sensuality and contained covert innuendoes. A glaring example was the cement brand commercial which showed a woman emerging from the water in a swimsuit for no reason, and was being aired every 20 minutes during cricket matches. The larger problem—that of low market penetration—was being pushed under the carpet. 'Only five per cent of Indian men buy condoms as of now,' an expert said. 'So even a Sunny Leone couldn't get enough men to buy them.'[73] Since the development of sexual desires and interest is a natural (and biologically-programmed) aspect of being human, such stigmatization and denial serves neither gender well, and becomes a cause of deep-rooted social problems. This make sit all the more important to educate youngsters about their bodies and bodily processes. Surprisingly, in India, most adolescent girls are not sufficiently prepared to cope with critical biological and psychological changes, such as the onset of menstruation, the development of secondary sexual characteristics, and sexual urges. The vicious cycle of ignorance continues; for in a country which considers sex education forbidden, how do parents who are uneducated about sex or menstruation, initiate a conversation with their children?

Menstruation, the most natural part of the reproductive cycle, is surrounded by secrecy and taboo, and excludes girls from many aspects of social and cultural life. It is not uncommon for girls/women to be barred from entering temples or participating in spiritual ceremonies while menstruating. Girls are frequently told 'Don't enter the kitchen, don't touch any utensils, don't serve food, don't go to the temple, don't touch the water' and many more 'do nots'. These taboos prevail even in cities and upper class families, although some concessions have been given to the women. She can go to the temple, but not make offerings or touch the deity. She can sleep on the bed instead of the floor, but not change the bed sheet! According to the National Family Health Survey NFHS-4 (2015–16)[74], 77.5 per cent of urban women between the ages of 15–24 years used hygienic methods of protection, like locally prepared napkins or tampons, during their menstrual period, as against a mere 48.2 per cent in the rural areas. Government data was contradicted by another report, which revealed that only 12 per cent of India's 355 million menstruating women used sanitary napkins.[75] Alternatives included using old newspapers, rags, sawdust and even ash, making women vulnerable to severe infection. To distract herself from these innumerable problems, Sita was advised to go and watch a film, a form of modern entertainment. She went to a theatre and bought a ticket for the current show. Interestingly, the film not only relaxed her, but also assisted her in releasing her pent-up emotions. It was inspired by the life of Arunachalam Muruganantham, a caring husband, who went about creating affordable sanitary towels after discovering that his wife, Shanthi, had been using dirty rags during her periods.[76] 'I wouldn't use that cloth to clean my vehicle,' said Muruganantham. He continued:

> When I asked her why, she said we would have to cut half of our milk budget to buy sanitary pads. I went to the pharmacy to buy her the pads as a gift. The shop assistant wrapped it in newspaper like it was a smuggled item. It was only 10 grams of cotton, but cost 40 times its worth. I thought of how most women in rural areas couldn't afford them. I wanted to change my wife from unhygienic to hygienic practices during menstruation. Everything started from my wife and now it's gone global.

Instead of encouraging Arunachalam, the community thought he was a pervert and was possessed by demons. He narrated a humiliating episode about when he was trying his prototype pad, and had made an artificial uterus from an old ball filled with goat's blood. The ball split during the demonstration and he ended up covered in blood in front of the villagers. His quest took an emotional toll, and the woman for whom he undertook this venture deserted him, unable to cope with the humiliation. He said:

> My wife didn't understand me. She left me. My mother left me. This topic is such a taboo, even my mother won't discuss it with her daughter and here I was, a man, trying to do something. The community thought I was a pervert. They wanted an exorcism because they thought I was possessed by demons.

The lack of access to hygiene products was only half the battle. Tackling the misconceptions around menstruation was perhaps more challenging. 'There are regions where it's believed that if an unmarried girl uses a pad and a dog smells it, she will never get married. We worked at a village where they believed that if women went out after sunset during menstruation, they will go blind.'

What message does that send to a young woman about her body—is her body something to be cherished or to be ashamed of? On one hand, why is the fertility of a woman deified, but on the other, her sexuality bound by rules set by a patriarchal agenda? Sita found that even today in India, many double standards existed—such as the social expectation of the young woman being a virgin at the time of marriage (whereas previous sexual experience is acceptable for the male), the be-all and end-all for women in a traditional society.

Sita's spirits soared when she heard the news that a centuries-old humiliating tradition in Maharashtra was being challenged by youngsters, despite facing hurdles from the community and apathy from law enforcers. In the Kanjarbhat community, every girl has to undergo the traditional virginity test on her marriage day. Failure invites punishment, such as the branding of body parts, stripping, making her pick a coin from boiling oil and placing hot iron in her hands. In the case of fifteen-year-old Savita, the caste panchayat members tied her to a pillar and thrashed her till she was nearly unconscious. Her parents pleaded with them and the bridegroom to 'accept' their daughter. It was eventually decided that the girl would be 'forgiven' and the parents would pay money to the bridegroom as compensation. God intervened in the form of some educated youngsters, who joined hands to question this practice, and formed a WhatsApp group to stay connected and keep vigil on instances of girls being subjected to virginity tests. A college student recently recorded a video where community heads were bargaining to 'settle' a case, saying, 'I approached the police, but they dismissed it as a social issue and no action was taken.'[77]

All these instances only prove that girls in India continue to be considered the property of males, and are denied opportunity and resources to experience their sexual selves in a safe and positive environment. Girls who dress in western attire are stigmatized and branded as 'shameless', and those who interact with boys are 'fast' or 'promiscuous'. As the former president of the United States of America said:

> We need to keep changing the attitude that punishes women for their sexuality and rewards men for theirs...We need to keep changing the attitude that raises our girls to be demure and our boys to be assertive, that criticizes our daughters for speaking out and our sons for shedding a tear.[78]

Sita remembered the stories of the passionate love-making between Lord Shiv and his wife for over a 100 divine years (36,000 mortal years). Vishwamitra, relating the legend to Ram, said:

> *On his getting married to Uma, the sublime ascetic and bluish-throated God Shiv, as his throat became blue when he consumed poison during the churning of Milky Ocean, at one time with a predilection towards his consort started lovemaking with her. While that sublime, sagacious and blue-throated God Shiv is in lovemaking, a hundred divine years have elapsed … All the gods headed by Brahma have then started to ponder, 'Is there is anybody who can inevitably sustain that being which emerges from this goddess Uma after this prolonged yogic act of copulation with Shiv?'*[79] [sic]

Unfortunately, in modern India, Sita found a lack of openness and education on sex, due to which young men and women gravitated towards easily accessible, but often-problematic sources of information, such as the internet. Studies showed that children spend hours everyday on the internet, uploading selfies and texting friends. But they are often clueless about evaluating the accuracy and trustworthiness of what they find, making them vulnerable to being easily duped. For the youth, this heightens the risk of problems that could emerge from watching pornography—from interfering with normal sexual development at the lower end of the spectrum, to inciting addictive behaviour and incidences of sexual violence on the other end of the spectrum. For the young girl, it increases her vulnerability to sexual abuse. Sita paid attention to the exponential growth of the internet and unrestricted access to material related to sexuality, sexual crimes, and violence, which was affecting young men's perception and attitude toward sexuality.

Sita felt reassured to know that at least the representatives of the people were raising questions. She read that the Telecommunications Department (DoT) had informed the Parliament that it had directed internet service providers (ISPs) to block 4,694 Uniform Resource Locators (URLs) that contained material related to child sexual abuse. Besides, instructions for blocking 1,791 URLs, including Facebook pages and YouTube videos, have been issued by the DoT to ISPs in 2016 and 2017, said the Telecommunications Minister in a written reply to the Lok Sabha. The government does not directly regulate content appearing on social networking sites, he said, adding that law enforcement and security agencies make searches on the internet on a specific case-to-case basis or as they deemed appropriate.[80] Fast-moving changes were taking place in Indian society, with girls claiming their position in public spaces. However, there was no one to guide them about healthy relations with the opposite sex. No one to encourage conversations about feelings, friendship and relationships; how to accept break ups in relationships; how to say no if someone's pushing you to do something you're not comfortable doing; how to deal with unwanted sexual advances and peer pressure. Young people needed to be supported and directed. Furthermore, in a country where child marriage is widely prevalent and where adolescent girls are not trained in parenting skills, child pregnancy and adolescent fatherhood become a serious challenge.

Sita was amazed that in spite of the high level of gender-based sexual violence, formal sex education in schools in India still did not exist. Where it did, it was mostly inadequate. A topic rarely touched upon was that of children sexually abusing other younger children. Young boys often indulged in exploration with children younger than them, which often lead to other harmful behaviors. Sita discerned a trend where the older boy, being an authority figure, won the trust of the young boy by cultivating a friendship, having heart-to-heart conversations, or giving gifts, gradually grooming the younger child to engage in sexual behaviour. She laid her eyes on an unpublished study by SAFMA,[81] according to which almost half of the cases of sexual offences by juveniles related to sexual assault by minor boys on younger boys. The predatory tactics used by the older boys were as banal as tempting the young boy with colourful marbles, or giving him an extra chance to bat in cricket. Substance abuse and viewing of pornography were also contributing factors, with children being more inclined to use violence under the influence of drugs, when they lost control of their emotions and reason.

Sita identified the existing socio-economic conditions in India as the key problem which rendered children vulnerable to exploitation and neglect. She lay her hands on a study[82] by the government which revealed the extent and pervasiveness of this problem. A major finding that clearly emerged was that it is young children, in the 5–12 year group, who are most at risk of abuse and exploitation. In fact, more than half of the child population have reported facing one or more forms of sexual abuse. New Delhi and the states of Andhra Pradesh, Assam, and Bihar reported the highest percentage of sexual abuse among both boys and girls. The study also stated that 'most children did not report the matter to anyone', which is a matter of grave concern since it conceals the extent of the problem, leading to a lack of an in-depth understanding of the issue or any effective legislative enforcement. Sita was inspired to note a bold move by the Delhi government, which was aware of the urgency of the situation, and was considering a proposal to control instances of sexual offences against children by educating them.[83] The Ministry of Women and Child Development was also planning to use film as a media to assist girls in schools to identify and learn the difference between a 'good touch and bad touch'.[84]

What was more disturbing was the growing tendency of crimes by children.[85] Sita found it unimaginable that young children could commit rape, and even more heinous—gang rape.[86] Shuddering at what was happening in the *Kalyug*, she thanked her stars that Kush and Luv had been born in another era, and not in 2017 when at least one juvenile was arrested on charges of rape every four hours on an average in India.[87] It was not unexpected when people in Uttar Pradesh put their faith in the new Chief Minister, Yogi Adityanath, who earnestly intended to fulfill the pre-poll pledge to check 'eve-teasing' (a term which is commonly used, but in context seem misplaced and tends to minimize the nature of the problem). She was curious if there were any special laws to protect children from offences of sexual assault, sexual harassment and pornography[88], or which penalised[89] them when they came in conflict with the law. Sita felt that children should undoubtedly be punished for their wrongdoings so that they could learn the difference between wrong and right. But she was revolted at the thought of these vulnerable, tender minds being sent to prison, where they might be prone to sexual exploitation, suicide, recidivism, and physical assault. Her compassionate nature recommended correction and rehabilitation of children, and not condemnation to a life in jail. She felt the problem was not only sociological, but also psychological, and laid bare the flaws in society that encouraged people to view women in a violent and destructive manner. The sexual abuse of children by other children is an issue of national concern, and Sita felt that the state had the responsibility of giving priority to children's interests, so that they grow up in a safe and caring environment, and become responsible citizens.

Freedom of Choice

On seeing Ram, Sita instantly selected him as her life partner. If it was a normal *swayamvara*, Sita would have garlanded Ram, the man of her choice, without any hesitation. But her situation was different, and she found herself in a difficult predicament, unable to do what she wanted. Her father, King Janak, had tied her marriage to the outcome of the bow contest.

The proclamation of the heralds stunned many when they said:

> *Harken all ye princes; with our long arms uplifted we announce to you Janaka's pledge … Shiva's bow … is massive and unyielding, as is well known to all. Even those great and mighty champions, Ravana and Banasura slipped quietly away as soon as they saw the bow. Whoever in this royal assembly breaks today the yonder unbending bow of Shiva, him shall Videha's daughter wed forthwith without any hesitation, and he shall triumph over all the three worlds.*

On hearing the story of the might of Shiv's bow, some lost heart, and some, on beholding it simply gave up wanting to try stringing it. Others quietly slipped away. Those princes who prided themselves on their valour were highly offended. They rose impatiently and, bowing to their respective deities, forged their way towards the bow. Casting an angry look at Shiv's bow, they grappled with it with steady aim and exerted all their strength. But the bow refused to budge, forget being lifted or being strung. Foolish kings indignantly strained at the bow and retired in confusion when it refused to dislodge from its position. With each attempt it appeared to grow more and more bulky, absorbing the might of each successive warrior. In the gathering, there were some princes who were sensible enough to not even try to approach the bow. Then 10,000 kings proceeded to try to raise it all at once, but it stopped all attempts at moving it. Shambhu's bow did not stir in the same way as the mind of a virtuous lady who refuses to yield to the words of a gallant. All the princes made themselves butts of ridicule, like a recluse without dispassion. Helplessly forfeiting their fame, glory and great valour to the bow, they retired. Confused and disheartened, the kings went and sat in the midst of their own company.[90]

Sita, given a chance, would have most willingly garlanded Ram, but being dependent on her father, she did not have the authority to take any decisions on her own. She needed her father's seal of approval. She could not go against her father's wishes, especially in a patriarchal society which treated a woman as property—first of her father, then her husband, and then her sons. Even in the twentieth century, a patriarchal and intolerant approach towards women deprives them of their right to choose. If the woman is bold enough to dare going against society, then she may have to face the wrath of zealous, bigoted moral-keepers of society, who will justify their savagery in the name of religious fervour. Matters often reach the court, with the parents of the girl manipulating her age in order to prove she is a minor. Sita perused a case[91] of a letter written by a young girl to the Chief Justice of India. Treating it as a writ petition, the Supreme Court directed the parents of the girl to produce her in front of the court. On being asked by the court, she expressed her desire to live with her husband. The apex court proceeded by taking into consideration a woman's right to personal liberty, particularly in the matter of the custody of a married woman. Referred to was the decision in the case of Lata Singh,[92] where the Supreme Court considered the question of the right to life and freedom, particularly a woman's right in the the matter of marriage. It opined that such acts of violence, threats or harassment are wholly illegal, and those who commit them must be severely punished. The apex court held that:

> This is a free and democratic country, and once a person becomes a major he or she can marry whosoever he/she likes. If the parents of the boy or girl do not approve of such inter-caste or inter-religious marriage, the maximum they can do is that they can cut off social relations with the son or the

> daughter, but they cannot give threats or commit or instigate acts of violence and cannot harass the person who undergoes such inter-caste or inter-religious marriage. We, therefore, direct that the administration/police authorities throughout the country will see to it that if any boy or girl who is a major undergoes inter-caste or inter-religious marriage with a woman or man who is a major, the couple is not harassed by anyone nor subjected to threats or acts of violence, and anyone who gives such threats or harasses or commits acts of violence either himself or at his instigation, is taken to task by instituting criminal proceedings by the police against such persons and further stern action is taken against such persons as provided by law. We sometimes hear of 'honour' killings of such persons who undergo inter-caste or inter-religious marriage of their own free will. There is nothing honourable in such killings, and in fact they are nothing but barbaric and shameful acts of murder committed by brutal, feudal-minded persons who deserve harsh punishment. Only in this way can we stamp out such acts of barbarism.[93]

The sexuality of a woman is the most potent threat to the patriarchal system and the authority of those who uphold it. For them, silence, immobility and obedience are the most desirable female attributes, which are under threat in the modern setup of the free intermingling of the sexes in public spaces, especially in educational institutes and the workplace. The central government was giving a financial incentive to every inter-caste marriage involving a Dalit. Earlier, the scheme was meant only for such couples whose income does not exceed Rs five lakh per annum. However, in a push to encourage inter-caste marriages involving Dalits, the Union Ministry of Social Justice and Empowerment decided to remove the income cap.

The scheme, started in 2013 and known as the 'Dr Ambedkar Scheme for Social Integration through Inter-Caste Marriages,' is meant to enable such couples who have taken a 'socially bold step' to settle down in the initial phase of their married life.[94]

The Delhi High Court[95] in a matter, boldly held

> A father has no right to forcibly marry off his daughter, who is below 18 years against her wishes. Neither has he the right to kill her, because she intends to marry out of her religion. If a girl around 17 years of age runs away from her parents house to save herself from the onslaught of her father or relatives and joins her lover or runs away with him, it is no offence either on the part of girl or on the part of the boy with whom she ran away and married.

Sita was horrified at the barbarity of the lynching of a young couple in Pune, carried out by the girl's family in full public view,[96] simply because the girl had married a person of her choice against the wishes of her family members. Another couple was beaten to death and their dismembered bodies were burnt after a local panchayat ordered their killing. This was, again, only because they had married against the wishes of their parents.[97] A different couple in a village in Jharkhand were tonsured and paraded naked for tying the knot against the wishes of their parents, as they belonged to different castes.[98] People were so incensed that they even beat up an old woman who tried to cover up the girl. Sita could not fathom such brutality and savagery in a society. Back in her time, even the rakshasis did not persecute her in the brutal and inhuman manner that this so-called civilized society did.

The High Court,[99] referring to this brutal incident, observed that the scenario in some regions or families, with respect to out-of-caste/religion marriages, was sufficient to create fear in the mind of a young girl whose parents rebuked her and told her that she would be killed if she insisted on marrying her love. If such a girl left her parents' house, the boy she loved could not be held criminally liable for enticing and kidnapping her. The tragedy is that the perpetrators of this kind of violence on a girl are her own natal family, sometimes alone, but often in association with other relatives and friends, or on the orders of the caste or '*khap*' panchayats—community-based kangaroo courts. Who can believe that a stone's throw away from Delhi, the law takes a medieval turn, and kangaroo councils—the unelected guardians of morality, decide that 'People kill their daughters out of fear that one day, they might elope with men of the same *gotra*. The minds of the younger generation have been corrupted by an obscene and vulgar culture. Our youngsters have forgotten the rich values and customs of our society.'[100] Topping it all was a study[101] launched by the *khap* panchayat which 'proved' that junk food, jeans, mobile phones, the Hindu Marriage Act, and the victim were all responsible for a woman getting raped. In short, they would give any plausible excuse to stop their daughters from exercising their choice, resulting in the curtailment of their freedom of movement and expression.

Khap panchayats or kangaroo courts are a union of villages found mainly in North India, although similar forms exist throughout the country. Taking the law in their hands, *khaps* have emerged as quasi-judicial bodies, pronouncing harsh punishments and using regressive measures for modern problems, especially relating to the youth. When a Dalit girl in Haryana committed suicide after she was allegedly gang raped by four men, instead of condemning the incident and recommending measures to discipline perpetrators of gender-based violence, it went on another tangent, declaring that girls should be married off early so that rapes can be avoided.[102] 'Any adult girl or adult man has the right to marry anyone of their choice. No panchayat, no society, no parent can question this', said the Supreme Court bench headed by the Chief Justice of India, Dipak Misra.[103] 'Whenever there is any kind of collective attack on a boy or girl who are adults, it is absolutely illegal,' it said. The Supreme Court had invited *khap* panchayats to give their views, but reprimanded them saying, 'Changes do not take place in a regressive manner.' Appeasement and vote bank politics have taken over, with even retired government servants jumping into the fray. A retired lieutenant general and a former chairman of the Haryana Public Service Commission, sought to intervene on behalf of *khap* panchayats, contending that *khaps* were often misunderstood.[104]

Sita's knees gave away on reading[105] about the dastardly and barbaric acts of a father, brother and two uncles of a twenty-one-year-old, who allegedly gang-raped her for eloping with a man. The woman and her lover had already eloped twice, and the woman's family had filed an abduction complaint with the police both times. The first time, the man was let off by a court after the woman said she left with him by choice. After a second case was registered, she approached the Allahabad High Court, alleging she was gang-raped by her family members at a nursing home and forced to miscarry. This terror of honour killing has continued unabated. In Rajasthan, a woman who had an inter-caste marriage was allegedly burnt to death by her own family after eight years of her marriage. She had returned to her in-law's house in her village after eight years, following which her family came to know about her whereabouts. On locating her, they dragged her out of her house, beat her up and set her on fire, after which her charred remains were quietly cremated. The police registered a case against 35 people, out of which only seven were arrested.[106]

Lost in thought, Sita was walking sluggishly, when she almost stepped on a semi-nude body of a girl. Gang-raped and murdered, her body had been badly brutalized, evoking memories of the 2012 Nirbhaya case. It turned out to be the body was of a fifteen-year-old Dalit girl who had gone missing after leaving home for her coaching class. The case took a new turn after police recovered the body of a man from the bank of a water channel. He was the person whom the girl's parents had named in the police complaint as the prime suspect. Although both the girl and man were Dalits, the girl belonged to a community that considered itself higher in the social order than the man's family. Sita was nauseated at the thought that parents could get their own daughter gang-raped.[107]

For Sita, love was intertwined with freedom, so she was alarmed at the hate campaign on inter-faith marriages, with courts also jumping into the fray. The Kerala High Court had sent ripples of unrest across the nation by annulling the marriage of a twenty-four-year-old woman, against her wishes. The marriage of the woman from Kerala, who had converted to Islam and married a Muslim man, took a controversial turn when the Kerala High Court annulled her marriage and placed her in the custody of her father against her will. The Court was acting on a petition filed by her father, who had expressed apprehension that Muslim organisations planned to take her abroad to get her to join the terrorist group, the Islamic State. The Kerala High Court reiterated the patriarchal attitude of having no faith in the capacity of women to take informed decisions regarding their lives, and held,

> A girl aged twenty-four years is weak and vulnerable, capable of being exploited in many ways. This Court exercising parens patriae jurisdiction is concerned with the welfare of a girl of her age. The duty cast on this Court to ensure the safety of at least the girls who are brought before it can be discharged only by ensuring that Ms Akhila is in safe hands ...[108]

When her husband, Jahan, appealed against this decision before the Supreme Court, another controversial order was passed. The top court directed the National Investigation Agency to determine if this was a case of alleged organised radicalisation—a conspiracy theory termed 'love jihad' by the Hindu right-wing, in which Muslim men marry Hindu women to convert them to Islam. The investigation was to be monitored by a retired Supreme Court judge[109] who was to be paid handsomely but, having more sense, turned down the job. A second petition was filed in the court questioning the investigation. In the meantime, a change of guard took place in the Supreme Court and the division bench warned against being carried away by the paranoia being fanned by bigoted elements in society. After due deliberation, the Supreme Court thought it appropriate to interact with Akhila, and posed a range of questions pertaining to her qualifications, her interest in studies, perception of life, and what she intended to do in the future. She stated that she intended to continue her internship/housemanship, and that her ambition was to become a full-fledged homoeopathic doctor. She expressed her desire to stay in the hostel and complete the course in the said college, if a seat was made available. In deference to her desire, the Supreme Court directed she be taken to Salem so as to enable her to pursue her internship/housemanship. It opined, needless to say, that when she stays in the hostel, she would be treated like any other student and would be guided by the hostel rules. If necessary, the expenses for pursuing the course and for the hostel would be borne by the State of Kerala.[110]

In another case of inter-religious marriage, a young couple who were in a relationship for several years got married without informing their parents. Fearing an attack from her family, the bride informed the police station at Yellandu. The Circle Inspector claimed to have telephoned the father of the bride and counseled him that since the girl was an adult, the family members should not harass them. 'I spoke to him and other relatives for nearly an hour. They agreed to let the couple live peacefully following which I informed the couple that they are free to go,' he said. The couple spent the night in a hotel in Yellendu and booked a taxi to go to Hyderabad the next day. However, after the couple left the hotel they experienced an action movie-style car chase by the bride's family in which the driver of the car ended up losing his life. He lost control, crashed into a tree and was killed instantly. The couple escaped with minor injuries.[111]

Branding people with tags, not providing them with a non-judgmental space to express themselves, dictating whom to love and when to love, interfering in the personal space of people, and bullying in the name of humanity seemed to have become the norm of the day. But the malevolent behaviour of people never ceased to horrify Sita, especially when she read the report about a twenty-four-year-old woman, who hailed from a village in Muzaffarnagar, Uttar Pradesh and had eloped with a boy she was in love with. The girl's family members, seeking revenge, not only abducted the boy's family members, but also gang-raped his mother. Involved in this vicious act was a former village *gram pradhan*, and his son.[112]

Women who exercised their freedom of choice were not only ostracized by the community but also prohibited from attending the last rites of their dear ones. Sita was impressed with reports of two Parsi sisters, who fought an eight-year battle in courts against religious authorities who declared that the sisters, who had married Hindus (considered to be 'outsiders'), were not welcome in the sacred precincts of the community and should, in fact, be deprived of all rights, including being denied entry into the 'tower of silence'[113] by the the Valsad Parsi Panchayat, a committee of five persons who govern their affairs. Persons of religion, instead of raising awareness of the diversity of their faiths and cultures, and stressing on the need to engage with each other as human beings, were encouraging divisive forces. The Parsi woman was seeking permission to enter the tower of silence to perform her parents' last rites in the event of their death, since she was worried her parents—both eighty-four years of age—were nearing their last days. Sita was astonished that even the High Court, instead of grasping the plurality of India and, it's faiths and cultures, judged (by a 2:1 majority) that a Parsi woman, by virtue of contracting a civil marriage with a non-Parsi man under the Special Marriage Act, ceases to be a Parsi, and hence is prohibited from entry into the tower of silence. According to dissenting opinion, a woman who is born Parsi/Zoroastrian does not cease to be a Parsi merely by virtue of solemnizing marriage with a man belonging to another religion.

An appeal had been filed before the Supreme Court, challenging the final judgment and order passed by the High Court of Gujarat. Prompted by the Supreme Court urging the Parsi community to take a more 'progressive' stand on the issue, a radical decision was taken by the community.[114] It was agreed, on compassionate grounds, to permit the woman to attend the funeral prayers (Paidust ceremony) of her parents performed inside the prayer hall of the towers of silence complex. It was also agreed that she would be entitled to attend the ceremonies of her parents that were to be performed four days after their deaths. The petitioner's children would also be allowed to attend the funeral ceremonies of their grandparents along with members of the community, both Zoroastrian and otherwise.

Even teachers, who play an important role in our life by guiding us, are not spared. A good teacher helps us to become a good human being in society and a good citizen of our country; but what if teachers themselves become the targets of these so-called honour crimes? Sita was bewildered on being informed that two teachers (who were a couple), while attending to guests at their wedding reception, had received a call from the principal of the school where they both worked, terminating their services. The principal told them that their affair had given the school a 'bad reputation' and that was the reason for their termination. 'I was the sole breadwinner in my family and we depend on the salary of Rs 9,000 that we each draw. We have just got married and now we have been rendered jobless,' Bhat said.[115]

Young girls were challenging the repressive system which denied them the right to make their own choices. A young girl, Kausalya, fell in love with a boy in college. He belonged to a Scheduled Caste community, and his father was a daily wager. When the girl's family opposed the match, she left home and the two got married in a temple. 'For the eight months I lived with him, he was more motherly than my mother to me. He would cook for me, wash my clothes, take care of me like a child. He did things that society considers women's chores,' she says. 'For others, love means many things. For me, love gives women self-respect.' The couple's bliss came to a shuddering end when the husband was hacked to death with sickles, and the girl, who had received hundreds of threatening calls from her family during her marriage, was grievously injured. The injuries healed but the wounds didn't, and the victim-turned-crusader helped bring her husband's killers to justice. She was the prime eyewitness in the case, and testified against her parents. She told the court of the harassment meted out to her and her husband and, despite enormous pressure, stood her ground.

Her efforts paid off when the court sentenced her father and five hirelings to death. Her mother, uncle and his friend were acquitted for want of evidence. The incident has motivated Kausalya to prevent other couples from meeting the same fate. 'It was caste that killed Shankar, snuffing out the ambitions of a first-generation engineer graduate. I resolved to fight against it.' An NGO, Evidence, working for Dalit rights, says her transformation has been 'phenomenal'. 'No one else has taken such a strong stand and fought a case against her father and mother', they stated, citing honour killings where the women returned to their parents. According to a study by Evidence, Tamil Nadu has seen 89 honour killings in three years till June 2016. In most cases, the girl's parents would invariably be the accused and go scot free for want of witnesses. Today, sporting denims and cropped hair, Kausalya proudly said, 'I have learnt to drive a Bullet too... The way I look and travel is my choice.'[116]

Sita was heartened on one hand to see young love challenging ideas of religion and honor; but on the other hand was incensed by the increasing powers of vigilante groups.

Freedom of Movement

Sita was not surprised to discover that the rules for a woman had remained the same from ancient to contemporary times. Wherever a women went, she had to return on time. Sita recollected the conflicting emotions she had experienced when she first saw Ram in the garden. She rushed back home with her friends, fearing that her mother may rebuke them for returning late. She was nervous that the slightest infraction of rules of family life, especially in a royal household, may bring admonishment. Men never had any such restrictions—a disparity which is being questioned by the modern Indian girl. On one hand, women have the freedom to move about freely and participate in a variety of activities, and be acknowledged as significant members in society. On the other hand, primitive thinking still prevails that a woman's place is in the home, and that emotional fulfillment for women should be confined to domesticity and motherhood.

Women continue to be defined physically and intellectually as the 'weaker' sex. A number of rules are imposed on them, with which they are expected to comply in order to uphold the 'honor' of the family in society. There is no mention of a *laxman rekha* in Valmiki's *Ramayana* nor in Tulsidas'. How then, over the years, did the concept of *laxman rekha* develop as the ethical limits for a woman? The idea emerged that overstepping the *laxman rekha* would lead to undesirable consequences. The story of Laxman drawing a magic circle around the cottage with the tip of his arrow, and asking Sita not to cross the line, has fired popular imagination seeking to secure a woman's celibacy. A premium is placed on virginity, and is one of the reasons why the chances of a woman remarrying after divorce or the death of her spouse, are difficult. In stark contrast, something rarely invoked is the *vibhandaka rekha*,[117] seeking to secure 'rishyasringa', or simply put, a man's celibacy. The eminent Rishyashringa was a sage who performed a vedic ritual, at the end of which a divine being arose from the sacrificial fire, holding a vessel of divine sweets in his hands. The vessel was handed over to King Dashrath to be distributed among his wives, who would be able to conceive children after consuming them. Dashrath gave half of it to Kausalya, one fourth to Sumitra and one eighth to Kaikeyi. However, there still was some sweet left so he gave it again to Sumitra. This is the story of the birth of Ram, the husband of Sita and hero of the epic *Ramayana.*

Men and women, even in this century, are confined to separate spheres—*zanana* and *mardana*—for women are stereotypically viewed as temptresses and distractions. Diktats issued by colleges curtailing girl's freedom, which according to the authorities are 'in students' best interests',[118] reminded Sita about how scared she was of getting late and disobeying her mother's orders to return home early. In fact, crimes against women in public spaces often provoke comments that the victims should not have been there in the first place, not realising there can be many reasons for a woman to be out late at night. Women in the medical field or hospitality industry,[119] often have to work late or overnight and travel at odd hours. Sita was disturbed on finding the still-entrenched belief that women who violate conservative social norms and stray away from home are 'loose women' and 'fair game' for any aspiring Ravan. In the horrific rape and murder case of Nirbhaya, which shook the conscience of the nation, one cannot use the tired excuse that she was out cavorting during the 'bewitching hours'. It was only 8:30 pm when Nirbhaya boarded the fatal bus.[120]

Sita believed that India would be able to unlock its full economic potential only when it moved beyond the *lakshman rekha* view, and forged progressive ways to address the problem of women's security. The emanciption of women, and not their confinement, was the answer. Her spirits were raised when she saw modern Indian women fighting to reclaim public spaces. The students of Delhi University had organised a campaign under the banner of 'Pinjra Tod' meaning 'break the cage', challenging regressive hostel rules and policies against women in residential accommodations. The hostels, rather than being a home away from home for the girls, end up imprisoning the girls because of their discriminatory restrictions. Authorities, rather than focusing on providing access to safer public transport and more lighting in and around campuses, instead single out women, thus uncovering their bias while formulating hostel rules—the most significant being the 'curfew timing' in girls hostels, which disallow female students from staying out late. The young girls are compelled to protest, only after which do authorities accede to their demands, which are quite reasonable, such as 24-hour hostel entry, ambulance facilities, permission to be a part of all events of the university, abolishing of late-entry fine in the hostels, inspection of hygiene condition, etc.[121] What they do not realize is that rather than restricting women's movement, it is more sensible to assist, advise and caution them. A good example is that of the Chandigarh police, who assist women at night to reach their destination safely.[122]

What responsibility do men have, given that most of the perpetrators of sexual abuse and violence are males? It was noticeable that men and women jointly marched in protest following the Nirbhaya case, but is that enough? Does society not have a duty to teach men that women are to be valued, respected and accorded dignity? The Prime Minister of India, in his Independence day speech, said something no public figure had dared vocalize. He said, 'Control your sons, not just your daughters.'

Today, girls in India are caught between the dilemma of two modes of existence—conservative patriarchy, and what is considered modern 'western' influence. With advances in education, science and technology, Indian society has evolved to adopt different norms, cultures and trends, leading to the formation of a new modern society. Undoubtedly, the joys of both societies do not come without their woes and setbacks, and the question of preferring the modern over the traditional, or vice-versa is highly debatable. According to the Global Gender Gap Index (2017), released by the World Economic Forum (WEF), India had slipped 21 places in gender-gap ranking, leaving it trailing behind even Bangladesh.[123] The country's abysmal ranking was mainly due to two indicators—the first being 'Health and Survival', where India is in the bottom four; and the second being 'Economic Participation and Opportunities for Women'. In addition, the Index also took into account 'Educational Attainment' and 'Political Empowerment'. Sita was sure these figures would soon change, for the gender gaps were fast closing, and decades of economic progress would soon showcase commensurate strides in women's lives. All Indians were proud of their tradition and cherished culture, and a modern society based on gender equality was becoming something to be aspired to, not feared.

Endnotes

1. K.R. Srinivas Iyengar, *Sitayana: Epic of the Earth-born* (Madras: Samata Books, 1987), p.74.
2. Rudyard Kipling, in his speech to the Royal College of Surgeons, 1923.
3. Amartya Sen, *The Argumentative India: Writings on India Culture, History and Identity* (New Delhi: Penguin Books, 2005).
4. Achieving universal primary education is the second Millenium Development Goal (MDG 2) for the United Nations.
5. Sage Satananda was the son of Ahalya, who was turned into stone by her husband Gautama. Satananda was the preceptor of King Janak. When Vishwamitra, accompanied by Ram and Laxman, proceeded to Mithila, then Sage Satananda led King Janak in receiving them ceremoniously.
6. *Navaratnas* or the nine gems was a term applied to a group of nine extraordinary people in a king's court. In India some well-known groups were in the courts of King Janak, Emperor Vikramaditya and the Mughal Emperor Akbar. Notable among the *navratna* in King Janak's court are (i) Sage Yajnavalkya, credited with the authorship of the *Shatapatha Brahmana*, including the *Brihadaranyaka Upanishad*,

Yogayajnavalkya Samhita and the *Yajnavalkya Smriti*; (ii) Maitreyi, the second wife of Yajnavalkya, a Vedic philosopher in her own right. Maitreyi was well-versed in the Vedas due to which she was called *brahmavadini* or 'an expounder of the Vedas'. About ten hymns in the *Rig Veda* are accredited to Maitreyi. According to legend, Maitreyi did not want to marry Yajnavalkya, but she wanted to live with him as his disciple and a spiritual companion to do sadhana or spiritual development; (iii) and Gargi, daughter of Sage Vachaknu, a philosopher, who is mentioned in the sixth and the eighth Brahmana of the *Brihadaranyaka Upanishad.* Gargi is said to have composed several hymns questioning the origin of all existence. The *Yogayajnavalkya Samhita*, a classical text on yoga is a dialogue between the two sages, Yajnavalkya and Gargi.

7. The Vedas, believed to have been composed between 1500 and 700 BC, form the earliest body of Indian scripture. The word 'veda' in Sanskrit literally means knowledge or vision, and in ancient Indian society the laws, as enunciated in the Vedas, regulated social, legal, domestic and religious customs. It is believed that no human composed these revered compositions, but that they were handed down through generations by word of mouth from time immemorial. It is believed that the Vedic hymns are *sruti* (what is heard), which were either taught or revealed by God to the sages, after intense meditation. The Vedas were mainly compiled by Vyasa Krishna Dwaipayana around the time of Lord Krishna (c. 1500 BC).
8. Anurag Dwary, ' "Nirbhaya Could Have Stayed Home": Chhatisgarh Teacher's Shocking Lesson', *NDTV*, January 31, 2018, https://www.ndtv.com/india-news/nirbhaya-could-have-stayed-home-raipur-schoolteachers-shocking-lesson-1806529
9. Sidharth Bhardwaj, 'Cleric Arrested for Raping 9-Year-Old-Girl in Madrassa', *The Times of India*, March 1, 2018, https://timesofindia.indiatimes.com/city/delhi/cleric-arrested-for-raping-9-year-old-girl/articleshow/63118921.cms
10. 'Saluting the Flame for Inculcating "Equality" That Ignited Millions; Nation Recalls Great Visionary Jyotirao Phule', *newsbharati.com,* November 28, 2017, http://www.newsbharati.com/Encyc/2017/11/28/Jyotirao-Phule.html
11. 'Auto Driver's Daughter PCS-Judicial Topper', *The Tribune,* March 1, 2018, http://www.tribuneindia.com/news/uttarakhand/auto-driver-s-daughter-pcs-judicial-topper/551391.html
12. Desiraju Hanumanta Rao and K.M.K. Murthy, trans., *Valmiki Ramayana,* 5:65:26, https://valmikiramayan.net/utf8/sundara/sarga65/sundara_65_frame.htm
13. *Siith bhava* = be cool. Desiraju Hanumanta Rao and K.M.K. Murthy, trans., *Valmiki Ramayana,* 5:53:30, https://valmikiramayan.net/utf8/sundara/sarga53/sundara_53_frame.htm
14. Ibid. This incident is elaborated on in Sarga 53 of the Sundara Kanda of the *Valmiki Ramayana*
15. Gargi Vachaknavi, daughter of Rishi Vachaknu was a *brahmavadini* like Maitreyi. The basic difference between Maitreyi and Gargi is that while Maitreyi's questions

had elements of both jnan and bhakti, Gargi was intellectually interested in ideas about the cosmos and Brahman.

16. Foreign scholars have set the date at around 800 BC for the *Brihadaranyaka Upanishad*, where Gargi appears for the first time. Her conversations with Yajnavalkya are recorded in the sixth and eighth brahmana of the *Brihadranayaka Upanishad,* where the *brahmayajna*, a philosophic congress organized by King Janak, is described. It is said that she challenged Sage Yajnavalkya with questions on the atman or soul.
17. Sandhya Ramesh, 'Have You Heard of Joshee, Medhavi, Jhirad Craters?', *Hindustan Times,* January 27, 2018, https://www.hindustantimes.com/opinion/have-you-heard-of-joshee-medhavi-jhirad-craters/story-bv6Hasz1yLRHIXQRQIkVGK.html
18. Ahalya was the wife of the sage Gautama Maharishi, who was much older than her in age. She was seduced by Indra, the king of gods, who was disguised as her husband. Ahalya saw through his disguise but nevertheless accepted his advances due to which her husband cursed her to assume the form of a stone for her infidelity. She was only liberated from the curse and regained her human form after contact with Ram's foot.
19. K.R. Srinivas Iyengar, *Sitayana: Epic of the Earth-born* (Madras: Samata Books, 1987), pp.70–71.
20. 'Low Literacy Rate Among Tribals', written reply in the Rajya Sabha by Union Minister for Tribal Affairs, press release published by the Press Information Bureau and the Minstry of Tribal Affairs, 23 November, 2016, http://pib.nic.in/newsite/PrintRelease.aspx?relid=154145
21. Malala Yousafzai (born 12 July 1997), the 2014 Nobel Prize awardee, is a Pakistani teenager who spoke out publicly against the Taliban's prohibition on the education of girls. Her father, who established and administered the school she attended—Khushal Girls High School and College in the city of Mingora—encouraged her education. In 2007, the Swat Valley was invaded by the Taliban and, led by Maulana Fazlullah, began imposing strict Islamic law, destroying or shutting down girls' schools, banning women from any active role in society, and carrying out suicide bombings. Yousafzai and her family fled the region for their safety, but they returned when tensions and violence eased.

    When Yousafzai was eleven years old, her father took her to a local press club in Peshawar to protest the school closings, and she gave her first speech—'How Dare the Taliban Take Away My Basic Right to Education?' Toward the end of 2008, the Taliban announced that all girls' schools in Swat would be shut down on 15 January 2009. The British Broadcasting Corporation (BBC) approached Yousafzai's father in search of someone who might blog for them about what it was like to live under Taliban rule. Under the name Gul Makai, Yousafzai began writing regular entries for BBC Urdu.

    In February 2009, Yousafzai made her first television appearance, when she was interviewed by Pakistani journalist and talkshow host Hamid Mir on the

Pakistan current events show 'Capital Talk'. In late February, the Taliban, responding to an increasing backlash throughout Pakistan, agreed to a cease-fire, lifted the restriction against girls, and allowed them to attend school on the condition that they wear burkas. However, violence resurged only a few months later. On 9 October 2012, Yousafzai was shot in the head by a Taliban gunman while she was en route home from school. Fazlullah and the Pakistani Taliban took responsibility for the attempt on her life. She survived the attack and was flown from Peshawar to Birmingham, England, for surgery. The incident elicited protests, and her cause was taken up around the world.

22. 'Malala: Like Father, Like Daughter', *The Telegraph,* http://www.telegraph.co.uk/film/he-named-me-malala/malala-father-daughter-relationship/
23. 'Girls' Education: A Lifeline to Development' (Panel 14), The State of the World's Children (50th Anniversary Edition), Report published by UNICEF, 1996, https://www.unicef.org/sowc96/ngirls.htm
24. '2 Minor Sisters From Jharkhand Rescued in Delhi, 3 Held', *Business Standard,* January 25, 2018, http://www.business-standard.com/article/news-ians/2-minor-sisters-from-jharkhand-rescued-in-delhi-3-held-118012501702_1.html
25. Shradha Chettri and Uma Vishnu, 'ASER Report 2017: More Rural Teen Staying Back in School But Struggling With Reading, Math; Girls Worse Off', *The Indian Express,* January 17, 2018, http://indianexpress.com/article/education/aser-report-2017-more-rural-teens-staying-back-in-school-but-struggle-with-reading-math-girls-worse-off-5027876/
26. 'Rewari Girl Students End Strike After Govt Announces School Upgrade', *Business Standard,* May 17, 2017, http://www.business-standard.com/article/pti-stories/rewari-girl-students-end-strike-after-govt-announces-school-upgrade-117051700935_1.html
27. Kanwardeep Singh, '17-Year-Old UP Girl's Classroom Notes Turned Into a Book', *The Times of India,* January 15, 2018, https://timesofindia.indiatimes.com/city/bareilly/17-year-old-up-girls-classroom-notes-turned-into-book/articleshow/62491080.cms
28. National Family Health Survey 3. The 2005–06 National Family Health Survey (NFHS-3), the third in the NFHS series of surveys, provides information on population, health and nutrition in India and each of its 29 states. The survey is based on a sample of households which is representative at the national and state levels.
29. 'Children in India: A Statistical Approach', Study published by the Ministry of Statistics and Programme Implementation, 2012, http://mospi.nic.in/mospi_new/upload/children_in_india_2012.pdf
30. Teacher Held For Molesting 6-Yr-Old Student', *The Times of India,* December 23, 2017, https://timesofindia.indiatimes.com/city/chandigarh/teacher-held-for-molesting-6-yr-old-student/articleshow/62212448.cms
31. Vibha Sharma and Shiv Sunny, 'Unsafe Public Toilets in Delhi Force Locals to Relieve Themselves in the Open', *Hindustan Times,* December 22, 2017, http://www.

hindustantimes.com/delhi-news/unsafe-public-toilets-of-delhi-force-residents-to-relieve-themselves-in-the-open/story-HWR4ewYJC26LLEvk6Z2htM.html

32. Moushumi Das Gupta, 'In Struggle for Education, Girls of Odisha Tribal Community Break Barriers', *Hindustan Times,* December 8, 2017, http://www.hindustantimes.com/india-news/in-struggle-for-education-girls-of-odisha-tribal-community-break-barriers/story-NbnYaeqYTVqavdziAOjUdJ.html
33. Article 21-A of the Constitution inserted vide The Constitution (Eighty-sixth Amendment) Act, 2002.
    21A. The State shall provide free and compulsory education to all children of the age of six to fourteen years in such manner as the State may, by law, determine.
34. 'Children in India: A Statistical Approach', Study published by the Ministry of Statistics and Programme Implementation, 2012, http://mospi.nic.in/mospi_new/upload/children_in_india_2012.pdf
    According to the report, the percentage of girls in the total enrolment at the primary and upper primary levels was 19 per cent and 46.5 per cent respectively in the year 2005–06.This increased to 48.5 per cent and 48.1 per cent at primary and upper primary levels respectively in 2009–10. The report states that in general, the number of girls enrolled in all levels, i.e. primary, secondary and higher education, is less than their counterparts; however, the female-male ratio in education has been steadily improving over the years.
35. 'Malala: Like Father, Like Daughter', *The Telegraph,* https://www.telegraph.co.uk/film/he-named-me-malala/malala-father-daughter-relationship/
36. Article 15(3)Nothing in this article shall prevent the State from making any special provision for women and children.
37. Article 39. Certain principles of policy to be followed by the State: The State shall, in particular, direct its policy towards securing:
    (f) that children are given opportunities and facilities to develop in a healthy manner and in conditions of freedom and dignity and that childhood and youth are protected against exploitation and against moral and material abandonment.
38. 'Undernutrition Contributes to nearly Half of All Deaths in Children Under 5 and is Widespread in Asia and Africa', Data compiled by UNICEF Data: Monitoring the Situation of Children and Women, December 2017, http://data.unicef.org/topic/nutrition/malnutrition/
39. In July 2015, the Government of India released malnutrition figures from the Rapid Survey on Children (RSoC) data collected in 2013–14, conducted by the Ministry of Women and Child Development with technical support from UNICEF. This data assumes significance as the world adopts the UN Sustainable Development Goals. Goal 2.2 seeks to end all forms of malnutrition by 2030, including achieving, by 2025, the internationally-agreed targets on stunting and wasting in children under five years of age. It found 29.4 per cent of chlldren (aged less than three years) to be underweight (low in weight for their age), while 15 per cent were wasted (low weight for their height) and 38.7 per cent were stunted (low in height for age). On the face of it, this compares well

with the NFHS-3 data, in which the corresponding figures were 40.4 per cent (underweight), 22.9 per cent (wasted) and 44.9 per cent (stunted).

40. Rajib Dasgupta, 'India's Malnutrition Shame', *The Indian Express,* September 17, 2015, http://indianexpress.com/article/opinion/columns/indias-malnutrition-shame/
41. Karen Hulshoff, 'Child Undernutrition in India: A Gender Issue' (speech given at a panel on Undernutrition and Gender in India by the Ministry of Women and Child Development), http://unicef.in/Story/108/Child-Undernutrition-in-India-A-Gender-Issue
42. Sushmi Dey, '51% of Indian Women Aged 15-49 Anaemic, Most in World: Study', *The Times of India,* November 7, 2017, https://timesofindia.indiatimes.com/india/51-of-indian-women-aged-15-49-anaemic-most-in-world-study/articleshow/61538152.cms
43. 'Govt Approves launch of National Nutrition Mission', *Business Standard,* December 1, 2017, http://www.business-standard.com/article/pti-stories/govt-approves-launch-of-national-nutrition-mission-117120101216_1.html
44. *Anganwadi* centres in India are a form of mother and child care centres under the Integrated Child Development Scheme (ICDS), where basic health care is provided, including contraceptive counseling and supply, nutrition education and supplementation, as well as pre-school activities. The main objective of the programme is to cater to the needs of the development of children in the age group of 3–6 years. Pre-school education aims at ensuring holistic development of the children and to provide a learning environment which is conducive to the promotion of the social, emotional, cognitive and aesthetic development of the child.
45. According to legend, Rishi Vishwakarma, the celestial craftsman, forged three bows for the three gods: the *Vijaya Dhanush* for Vishnu, the *Shiv Dhanush* for Shiv, and *Gaandeeva* for Brahma. After their use, they passed them on to other lower gods or very famous humans. Thus the *Vijaya Dhanush* was inherited by Parasurama and passed on to Karna. The *Shiv Dhanush* was inherited by King Janak's forefathers and lay for generations in Mithila's eight-wheeled box. *Gandeeva* was inherited by Agni and then given to Arjuna. King Janak was worried about finding a match for his daughter, Sita, for whom he wanted a strong and educated groom. He declared that whoever lifted and strung the Heavenly Bow—the *Shiv Dhanush* (lying in a corner of his stores for centuries, unused but worshipped daily with *Dhoopa* and *Deepa*), would win her hand.
46. Arjun Chaudhuri (trans.), translator's note to *The Adbhuta Ramayana* by Saudamini Devi, http://poetry.sangamhouse.org/2014/10/the-adbhuta-ramayana-by-saudamini-devi-translated-by-arjun-chaudhuri/
47. Kali comes from the Sanskrit root word *Kal* which means time. Mother Kali is the Goddess of death; symbolically she causes the death of the ego as the illusory self-centered view of reality. Kali wears a garland of skulls and a skirt of dismembered arms because the ego arises out of identification with the body. She is considered the counterpart of Lord Shiv, the destroyer.

48. Desiraju Hanumanta Rao and K.M.K. Murthy, trans., *Valmiki Ramayana,* 5:56:5, https://valmikiramayan.net/utf8/sundara/sarga56/sundara_56_frame.htm
49. K.R. Srinivas Iyengar, *Sitayana, Epic of the Earth-born* (Madras: Samata Books, 1987), p.43.
50. *Dangal.* Directed by Nitish Tiwari. Aamir Khan Productions, UTV Motion Pictures, and Walt Disney Pictures India, 2016.
51. Geeta Phogat (as told to Ritu Sejwal), 'I Had to Wrestle Before a Crowd of Men. I was Shy', *The Times of India,* January 1, 2017.
52. 'Geeta Phogat's Mom Wanted a Boy: Book', *The Times of India,* December 21, 2016, http://timesofindia.indiatimes.com/sports/more-sports/wrestling/geeta-phogats-mom-wanted-a-baby-boy-book/articleshow/56098540.cms
53. Shari L. Dworkin, ' "Holding Back": Negotiating a Glass Ceiling on Women's Muscular Strength', *Sociological Perspectives,* vol. 44, no. 3 (2001): 333–350.
54. Snigdhendhu Bhattacharya, 'Razia's Power Punch Threw Naysayers Out of the Ring', *Hindustan Times,* August 11, 2017, p.11.
55. Anuja Upadhyay, 'Are Sports an Unfair Game for Women in India?', *FutureChallenges.org,* August 30, 2012, https://futurechallenges.org/local/is-sports-an-unfair-game-for-women-in-india/
56. Manas Tiwari, 'Less Than a Year After Playing World Cup Final, No Live Telecast For Indian Women's Cricket Team', *Financial Express,* February 6, 2018, http://www.financialexpress.com/sports/less-than-a-year-after-playing-world-cup-final-no-live-telecast-for-indian-womens-cricket-team-not-even-a-tweet-from-bcci/1053938/
57. Vishwas Manohar Deshpande, 'Gender Discrimination in Sports', *International Journal of Physical Education, Sports, and Health,* vol. 3, issue 3 (2016): 545–47, http://www.kheljournal.com/archives/2016/vol3issue3/PartF/3-3-15-713.pdf
58. Siddharth Saxena, 'Discrimination For Indian Sportswomen at All Levels', *The Times of India,* July 31, 2010, https://timesofindia.indiatimes.com/sports/hockey/top-stories/Discrimination-for-Indian-sportswomen-at-all-levels/articleshow/6239724.cms
59. 'It is Difficult to be a Sania Mirza in This Country', *The Indian Express,* November 26, 2014, http://indianexpress.com/article/india/india-others/it-is-difficult-to-be-a-sania-mirza-in-this-country/
60. According to Google, based on trillions of searches made by Indians over the year.
61. The exception being China.
62. 'Meet Four Female Sports Talents that India Lost', http://www.jaagore.com/power-of-49/meet-four-female-sports-talent-that-india-lost
63. Nitin Sharma, Daksh Panwar and Samudra Gupta Kashyap, 'Out of the Box: Stories Behind India's Five Gold Medals at the Women's Youth World Boxing Championship', *The Indian Express,* December 3, 2017, http://indianexpress.com/article/sports/sport-others/out-of-the-box-stories-behind-indias-five-gold-medals-at-the-womens-youth-world-boxing-championships-4965318/

64. Many years ago while examining the palm of her hand, Narada had forecast that she would meet Ram, the son of King Dashrath, who would later be her husband.
65. R.C. Prasad, ed and trans., *Shri Ramcharitamanasa or The Holy Lake of the Acts of Rama,* (New Delhi: Motilal Banarsidass Publishers Pvt. Ltd), 1:228–229, 231.
66. The King James Bible, The New Testament, Romans 1:20, https://www.bible.com/bible/1/ROM.1.kjv
    For the invisible things of him from the creation of the world are clearly seen, being understood by the things that are made, even his external power and Godhead; so that they are without excuse.
67. R.C. Prasad, ed and tran., *Shri Ramcharitamanasa or The Holy Lake of the Acts of Rama,* (New Delhi: Motilal Banarsidass Publishers Pvt. Ltd), 1:229, 230.
68. Ibid, 1:231-233.
69. Ibid, 1: 234.
70. The Hindu God of love and desire, the Indian equivalent of Cupid.
71. R.C. Prasad, ed and trans., *Shri Ramcharitamanasa or The Holy Lake of the Acts of Rama,* (New Delhi: Motilal Banarsidass Publishers Pvt. Ltd), 1: 234.
72. Loyola University Health System, 'What Falling in Love Does to Your Heart and Brain', *ScienceDaily*, February 6, 2014, https://www.sciencedaily.com/releases/2014/02/140206155244.htm
73. Sharmila Ganesan Rami, 'Sex Sells Everything, Except Safe Sex', *The Times of India,* December 17, 2017, https://timesofindia.indiatimes.com/home/self-goals-a-bigger-threat-to-bjp-than-opponent-rahul/sex-sells-everything-except-safe-sex/articleshow/62099308.cms
74. National Family Health Survey – 4, study conducted by the International Institution for Population Sciences for the Ministry of Health and Family Welfare, 2015–16, http://rchiips.org/NFHS/pdf/NFHS4/India.pdf
75. Vishakha George, 'Myths, Poverty, Inconvenience—Why the Simple Sanitary Pad is a Luxury For Most of India, *The Better India,* September 19, 2017, https://www.thebetterindia.com/115873/myths-poverty-inconvenience-sanitary-pad-rural-india/
76. Alia Waheed, 'India's Sanitary Towel Hero Pad Man Bound For Bollywood Glory', *The Guardian,* February 4, 2018, https://www.theguardian.com/society/2018/feb/04/india-sanitary-towel-hero-padman-bollywood-glory-arunachalam-muruganantham
77. Radheshyam Jadhavi, 'These Siblings are Using WhatsApp to Campaign Against Virginity Tests', *The Times of India,* January 14, 2018, https://timesofindia.indiatimes.com/home/sunday-times/these-siblings-are-using-whatsapp-to-campaign-against-virginity-tests/articleshow/62490705.cms
78. Barack Obama, 'President Barack Obama Says, "This is What a Feminist Looks Like."', *Glamour Magazine,* August 4, 2016, http://www.glamour.com/story/glamour-exclusive-president-barack-obama-says-this-is-what-a-feminist-looks-like

President Barack Obama celebrated his fifty-fifth birthday by publishing a lengthy and deeply personal article in Glamour Magazine about feminism. He is the first sitting President of the USA to publicly proclaim that he's a feminist.

79. Desiraju Hanumanta Rao and K.M.K. Murthy, trans., *Valmiki Ramayana,* 1:36:5-8a, https://valmikiramayan.net/utf8/baala/sarga36/bala_36_frame.htm
80. Prior to 2012, when the Protection of Children from Sexual Offences Act, (POCSO) had not yet been enacted, children committing sodomy were charged under Section 377 of the Indian Penal Code (the subject of study by SAFMA) which deals with unnatural offences or carnal intercourse against the order of nature.
81. Loveleen Kacker, Srinivas Varadan, and Pravesh Kumar, 'Study on Child Abuse: India 2007', report prepared under the Ministry of Women and Child Development, 2007, https://www.childlineindia.org.in/pdf/MWCD-Child-Abuse-Report.pdf
82. Aneesha Mathur, '"Educate Children About Good Touch and Bad Touch", says HC', *The Indian Express,* August 23, 2014, http://indianexpress.com/article/cities/delhi/educate-children-about-good-touch-and-bad-touch-says-hc/
83. 'WCD Minister, Smt. Maneka Sanjay Gandhi Interacts with Women Journalists on International Women's Day', press release by the Ministry of Women and Child Development, March 8, 2015, http://pib.nic.in/newsite/PrintRelease.aspx?relid=116541
84. The Ministry of Statistics and Programme Implementation report, 'Children in India 2012—A Statistical Appraisal', discloses that crimes under the Indian Penal Code by children have increased.
85. NCRB 'Crimes in India 2014' reveals that Madhya Pradesh has reported the highest number of rape cases by juveniles. Gang rape by juveniles is highest in Uttar Pradesh, and attempt to commit rape is highest in Bihar.
86. Chethan Kumar, 'One Minor Held for Rape Every 4 Hours in India', *The Times of India,* October 25, 2017,https://timesofindia.indiatimes.com/india/one-minor-held-for-rape-every-4-hours-in-india/articleshow/61212482.cms
    The Union Home Ministry's latest data reveals that between January 1 and December 31, 2016, some 2,054 juveniles were arrested for rape (one every 4.2 hours to be exact) and 1,627 were apprehended for assaulting women.
87. The Protection of Children from Sexual Offences Act, 2012 (POCSO), No.32 of 2012. An Act to protect children from sexual assault, sexual harassment and pornography and provide for establishment of Special Courts for trial of such offences.
88. The Juvenile Justice (Care and Protection of Children) Act, 2015 (JJ Act) No.2 of 2016. An Act to consolidate and amend the law relating to children alleged to be found in conflict with law, and children in need of care and protection.
89. R.C. Prasad, ed and trans., *Shri Ramcharitamanasa* or *The Holy Lake of the Acts of Rama,* (New Delhi: Motilal Banarsidass Publishers Pvt. Ltd), 1:249, 250.
90. Dr Sudesh Jale (II) vs the State of Haryana and Others, Writ Petiton (Crl) No.233 (2004).

91. Lata Singh vs State of U.P. and Another, Writ Petition (Crl) No. 208 of 2004.
93. Ibid.
94. 'Govt to Give Rs 2.5 Lakh Incentive to Every Inter-Caste Marriage Involving a Dalit, Removes Income Cap', *Outlook India,* December 6, 2017, https://www.outlookindia.com/website/story/govt-to-give-rs-25-lakh-incentive-to-every-inter-caste-marriage-involving-a-dali/305229
95. Vivek Kumar and Another vs The State Govt. of NCT of Delhi and Another 2007, https://indiankanoon.org/doc/390627/
96. 'Couple Lynched for Marrying!', *Hindustan Times,* Febraury 4, 2018, https://www.hindustantimes.com/india/couple-lynched-for-marrying/story-eu5CNbOKilJwCi2oibgWHO.html
97. Vivek Kumar and Others vs The State, Govt. Of NCT of Delhi And Another (2007), https://indiankanoon.org/doc/390627/
98. 'Couple Paraded Naked as Caste Rears its Ugly Head', Dalit Rights (blog), blogspot.com, December 11, 2004, http://ambedkar.blogspot.in/2004_12_01_archive.html
99. Vivek Kumar and Others vs The State, Govt. of NCT of Delhi And Another (2007), https://indiankanoon.org/doc/390627/
100. Suruchi Sharma, 'Rapes, Chowmein and Hormonal Imbalance', *The Times of India,* June 18, 2013, https://timesofindia.indiatimes.com/life-style/relationships/love-sex/Rapes-chowmein-and-hormonal-imbalance/articleshow/17533253.cms
101. Ibid.
102. 'What is Khap Panchayat', *India Today,* October 11, 2012, https://www.indiatoday.in/india/north/story/what-is-khap-panchayat-118365-2012-10-11
103. Shakti Vahini vs Union of India and Others, Writ petition (Civil) No. 231 of 2010.
104. 'Adults Have the Right to Marry Anyone, Khaps Can't Question Them', *The Indian Express,* January 17, 2018, http://indianexpress.com/article/india/adults-have-right-to-marry-anyone-khaps-cant-question-them-supreme-court-5027871/
105. Ishita Bhatiyal, 'Dad, Brother Rape Girl for Eloping with Lover, Held', *The Times of India,* November 29, 2017, https://timesofindia.indiatimes.com/india/dad-brother-rape-girl-for-eloping-with-lover-held/articleshow/61842139.cms
106. 'Honour Killing Horror: Rajput Girl Burnt to Death by Parents in Rajasthan', *Deccan Chronicle,* March 6, 2016, http://www.deccanchronicle.com/nation/current-affairs/060316/honour-killing-horror-rajput-girl-burnt-to-death-by-parents-in-rajasthan.html
107. Manveer Saini and Pankaj Arora, 'Haryana's Nirbhaya Case: Youth She Had Eloped With Found Dead', *The Times of India,* January 18, 2018, https://timesofindia.indiatimes.com/city/chandigarh/haryanas-nirbhaya-case-youth-she-had-eloped-with-found-dead/articleshow/62548297.cms
108. Asokan K.M. vs The Superintendant of Police, Writ Petition (Crl) No.297 of 2016, https://barandbench.com/wp-content/uploads/2017/05/kerala-muslim-high-court-judgment.pdf

109. Shafin Jahan vs Asokan K.M. and Others, Petition(s) for Special Leave to Appeal (Crl) No.(s) 5777 of 2017 (16 August 2017), http://supremecourtofindia.nic.in/supremecourt/2017/19702/19702_2017_Order_16-Aug-2017.pdf
110. Shafin Jahan vs Asokan K.M, Petition(s) for Special Leave to Appeal (Crl) No.(s) 5777/2017 (27 November 2017), http://supremecourtofindia.nic.in/supremecourt/2017/19702/19702_2017_Order_27-Nov-2017.pdf
111. 'Inter-Religious Marriage: Driver Killed in Mishap During Chase by Bride's Kin, *The Indian Express,* January 15, 2018, http://indianexpress.com/article/india/inter-religious-marriage-driver-killed-in-mishap-during-chase-by-brides-kin-5024802/
112. 'Woman Abducted, Gang-Raped After her Son Elopes with His Lover', *Hindustan Times,* December 30, 2017, http://www.hindustantimes.com/india-news/woman-gang-raped-in-up-family-members-abducted-after-her-son-elopes-with-lover/story-zbE6SnMvmwnGswAxyFqjzM.html
113. The tower of silence is where the Parsi community leaves their dead to decompose naturally.
114. Goolrokh M. Gupta vs Mr Burjor Padiwala and Others, Special leave petition (Civil) No.18889/2012, http://supremecourtofindia.nic.in/supremecourt/2012/20212/20212_2012_Order_14-Dec-2017.pdf
115. Naveed Iqbal, 'Day After Wedding, J&K Teachers Couple Sacked for "Giving School Bad Name"', *The Indian Express,* December 15, 2017, http://indianexpress.com/article/india/day-after-wedding-jk-teacher-couple-sacked-for-giving-school-bad-name-4983397/
116. Mayilvaganani, 'How a Young Widow Brought Her Father to Book', *The Times of India,* December 26, 2017, https://timesofindia.indiatimes.com/india/how-a-young-widow-brought-her-father-to-book/articleshow/62246351.cms
117. Rishi Vibhandaka was the son of the great Sage Kashyap, and undertook severe penance to the highest level. Lord Indra became jealous and, feeling threatened, sent Urvashi, an apsara or celestial nymph, to disrupt his penance. Such was her beauty that Vibhandaka lost control of his senses and his semen spilled onto the grass below. A doe, another celestial nymph who had been cursed to be born as a deer, ate the grass and got impregnated. She gave birth to a son Rishyasringa, who was born with the horns of deer on his forehead. Feeling cheated, Rishi Vibhandaka decided to bring up his son in the forest without exposing him to any woman. Vibhandaka drew a line or boundary for Rishyasringa known as the *vibhandaka rekha* or line of celibacy. Nothing feminine could cross the line and approach his son. Neither a cow nor a mare, neither goose, ewe, doe nor sow. Any form of female who dared cross the line would instantly would burst into flames. Hence, Rishyasringa grew up being totally unaware of sexual or gender differences.
118. Mayank Jain, 'Jamia's "No Late Nights" Diktat for Women is Yet Another Reminder of Sexist Hostel Rules, *Scroll.in,* August 15, 2015, http://scroll.in/a/748528

'Residents of the Hall of Girls are informed that no late night is allowed any more. You are, therefore, required to follow the norms, in your own best interests,' stated a notice issued by the university.

119. To meet a longstanding demand for gender parity in the workforce, an amendment in The Factories Act, 1948, to allow women employees to work in nightshifts, was approved. The amendment suggests that nightshift for women should be allowed only if the employer ensures safety, adequate safeguards in the factory as regards occupational safety and health, equal opportunity for women workers, adequate protection of their dignity and honour, and transportation from the factory premises to the nearest point of their residence are met. The Factories (Amendment) Bill, 2003 was introduced on 29 July 2003 and was referred to the Standing Committee on Labour and Welfare, which submitted its report in December 2003. However, the Bill lapsed due to the dissolution of the 13th Lok Sabha. The Factories (Amendment) Bill, 2005, which seeks to allow employment of women in factories during night shift with certain safeguards, has still not been passed.
120. The inhuman sexual assault of a young twenty-three-year-old female physiotherapy intern who was beaten, sexually assaulted and gang-raped in a bus generated widespread national outrage, subsequent to which nation-wide public protests took place against the government for failing to provide adequate security for women. Since the law in India prohibits disclosure of a rape victim's name, she became known as 'Nirbhaya', meaning fearless.
121. Shishir Tripathi, 'Aligarh Muslim University's Female Students Stand Against Discriminatory Hostel Rules', *Firstpost,* October 18, 2016, http://www.firstpost.com/india/aligarh-muslim-universitys-female-students-stand-against-discriminatory-hostels-rules-mismanagement-3058128.html
122. In case any lady is out of her place of stay late at night and is unable to avail a taxi, auto, cab, etc. to reach her place of stay safety, then she may call the PCR at No. 100 or 0172-2749194 or 0172-2744100. The PCR shall send its vehicle to safely drop the lady to her place of stay within Chandigarh, http://chandigarhpolice.nic.in/lndl.html
123. Shalini Nair, 'India Slips 21 Places in Gender Gap Ranking, Bangladesh Ahead', *The Indian Express,* November 3, 2017,http://indianexpress.com/article/india/india-slips-21-places-in-gender-gap-ranking-bangladesh-ahead-4920129/

MARRIAGE

... Soon the great day dawned, and on their coming
To Janak's palace grounds,
Vishwamitra suggested that the Bow
Might be shown to the Princes.

Janak recalled the Bow's history,
The manner of Sita's birth
And the decision to make its stringing
The bride-price of the Princess.

Then he ordered that the marvelous Bow
Be brought to the pavilion,
And offered Sita's hand to Prince Ram
Should he string the Bow indeed.

The formidable Bow was now conveyed
In it's eight-wheeled container,
And on the King's suggestion, the Rishi
Assenting, Ram drew nearer.

A silence vast and profound, and a tense
And taut uncertainty, reigned
In the spacious grounds, and the priests, princes
And princesses held their breaths.

With a light glancing movement, Ram raised
The lid, and sighting the Bow,
He seized and lifted it as if it were
Little more than a feather.

Ten thousand pairs of eyes were riveted
On him when he bent the Bow
And tried to string it—but the massive arc
Cracked and broke in the middle.

And the noise was like deafening thunder,
A mountain breaking apart,
And the earth seemed to tremble for the nonce
And wonderment filled the air.[1]

Marriage, believed to continue beyond one's lifetime upto seven births, is an important stage in the life-cycle of a woman, and generally coincides with her entry into 'womanhood'. An important Hindu *sanskara*, marriage, as an institution, is at the foundation of our society. The purpose of marriage is the satisfaction of 'kama'[2] or desire, and the creation and upbringing of children; after which one would gradually advance towards 'moksha' or renunciation. Like all Hindu fathers, King Janak considered it his sacred duty to find a suitable match to whom he could hand over his daughter.[3] The King was not only anxious to fulfill his duty as a father, but was equally worried for his daughter. She was not like others, for Sita was the divine earth-born. After witnessing her strength, King Janak had taken the pious, although extreme, resolve that her bride price would be the stringing of the mighty *dhanush* or Shiv's bow. As a father, he wanted his daughter's groom to be one who was worthy of her, and her equal, if not more, in qualities.

Years later, Sita herself, relating the story of her betrothal to Anusuya, said:

> *Knowing me to be the one not emerged from a mother's womb, the king after a deep reflection, was unable to find a suitable and worthy husband for me. After reflecting thus deeply, the thought came to him, 'I shall inaugurate a Swayamvara, a process of self-choosing marriage, for my daughter.*[4]

In an era when girls selected their own life partner by garlanding their suitor in a *swayamvara*,[5] Sita's choice, however, was restricted to the man who would be able to lift Shiv's mighty bow. Conventionally, Sita's marriage did not fit into any of the prescribed categories.[6] It could not also be considered a *prajapatya vivah,* where something is sought from the bridegroom in the name of lifting the bow; for the word 'seeking' connotes material assets, not valour or bravery. This unique marriage was preordained for the implementation of a higher purpose of righteousness and is celebrated as a *vivah panchami*[7] every year even today. And for the first time, King Janak did not discuss, nor ask his daughter what she wanted. He took it for granted that she would fall in with his plans. Even if he had asked her, how would she have confessed that his daughter had given her heart to a stranger whom she met in the garden, just a day earlier?

As Ram continued to proceed towards the bow, with each breath, Sita's anxiety increased. She prayed to the gods, asking for their divine strength to help Ram in accomplishing this humongous task. She prayed:

> *Alas, my father has made a cruel resolve, with no thought to good or evil consequences. His ministers are afraid and none of them gives him good counsel—the more the pity—in the great conclave of wise men! While on this side stands the bow, harder to break than adamant, on the other side we find a young prince, dark and delicate of frame. How then, O god, can I be calm? Is a diamond ever pierced with the pointed end of a sirisa flower? The judgement of the whole assembly has gone astray; now my only hope lies in you, O Shiva's bow. Impart your own heaviness to the assembly, and look at Raghunatha and be light yourself.*

Despite taking the name of every known god and goddess, Sita's heart was not at peace. Highly agitated, she would sometimes gaze at Ram and sometimes at the ground, with the moment hanging heavy, as if it were a hundred centuries or yugas.[8] *She felt helpless being stricken with uncertainty at the outcome of Ram's efforts. Dumbstruck, her lips, like the unopened petals of a lotus, sealed her voice. Speechless, modesty was holding her tongue captive, and she was unable to openly declare her love for Ram. Being single-minded in purpose and never one to give up, Sita was determined—no matter whether the bow was broken or not—she still would marry Ram. The heaviness of her heart could not even be lightened by tears, for the tear drops remained hidden in the corner of her eyes, like the gold of a niggardly miser which remains buried in a hidden nook of his house.*[9]

It gave comfort to Sita that in 2017, fathers in India still regarded it their sacrosanct duty to find a suitable match for daughters. However, they were unaware that it is within marriage that violence against women and girls was most prevalent—ranging from premature marriage, forced marriage, physical violence and battering, to rape and sexual abuse, dowry or bride price-related violence, and abandonment. She was amazed to see the wedding extravaganzas of 2017, and the sanctity of the ceremony being lost amidst a show of wealth. The cost of this spectacle sometimes leads to financial ruin for the bride's parents, and people over-stretching their means in an effort to gain social status and approval. Misconduct on the part of the groom's party, such as indulging in excessive alcohol consumption, was not unusual, and cases had been reported where someone was accidentally shot dead by celebratory firing.[10]

Child Marriage

When Sita and Ram got married they were minors, for in ancient times girls were married on attaining puberty. In the early nineteenth century, the urgent need for social and religious reform began to manifest itself, and social reformers like Raja Rammohan Roy[11] were no longer willing to accept the repressive traditions, beliefs and practices of Hindu society simply because they had been practised for centuries. It is a known fact that girls who are married as children have higher chances of experiencing physical, psychological, or sexual violence at the hands of their husbands. Married at the tender age of eleven, Phoolan Devi, a marital rape survivor, went on to become a dacoit. She was a saviour for many, but a criminal in the eyes of the law. When asked if she were to be reborn, would she still choose to return as a female, she replied that it didn't matter as long as God didn't make her poor. Her message emphasized the extreme vulnerability of young girls in poverty, and that the double disadvantage of being female and poor meant that the cards were heavily stacked against young girls from birth itself.

Sita scrutinized the magnitude of the problem, especially because 40 per cent[12] of the world's child marriages take place in India, resulting in a vicious cycle of gender discrimination, inter-generational poverty, illiteracy and high infant and maternal mortality rates.[13] Despite the legal age for marriage for girls being eighteen years, the latest Census Report in 2011 discloses that child marriage is rampant, with almost one in every three married women having been wed while she was still under the age of eighteen.[14] What is worse is that a whopping 7.85 million girls (2.3 per cent of all women or girls who were ever married or were married in 2011) were married while they were under ten years of age. The data also shows that 91 per cent of all married women were married by the age of twenty-five years, and that the trend of underage marriages is prevalent among all religious communities, with the percentage of girls being roughly the same among both Hindus and Muslims. Of these child brides, 20 per cent or approximately 3 lakh, are mothers to at least one child. The likelihood of girls under the age of fourteen dying in pregnancy and childbirth is five times more than that of women aged over twenty years.[15] It is estimated that nearly 6000 adolescent mothers die every year in India. Early marriage increases a girl's chances of having more children, and hence weakens her own health, immunity and nutrition. Not only she, but her child too is more likely to be underweight and malnourished.

Sita was stupefied to know that proponents of early marriage saw no conflict between child marriage and the legal age of marriage for girls, and had total disregard for the law. Till 1929, no minimum age of marriage had been legally fixed. It was only after the passing of the Child Marriage Restraint Act in 1929, popularly known as the Sharda Act, that the minimum age for marriage was fixed at fourteen years. In 1940, this age was raised to fifteen years, and simultaneously, an amendment was made to Exception 2 of Section 375 IPC, in which the age of consent for child brides was raised to fifteen years. In 1978, the minimum age for marriage of the girl child was raised to eighteen years but no consequential amendment was made in the IPC. In 2013, after the horrific Nirbhaya case, the Parliament raised the age of consent to eighteen years, but missed out in making a corresponding change in Exception 2 of Section 375 of the IPC. A girl child who was married before the minimum age of marriage, could be subjected to forcible sexual intercourse by her husband and, if she was over fifteen years of age, the husband could not be charged with any offence.

People's traditional mindsets, social pressure, and the deep-rooted beliefs of families that consider girls a liability, were among the many reasons for the rampant occurrence of child marriage. The gravity of this issue was accentuated by the barbarous gang rape, in 1992, of a grassroots worker, employed as part of the Government of Rajasthan's anti-child marriage project, and who had dared to report a child marriage. In retaliation, she was attacked and gang-raped in front of her husband by so-called upper caste men. Her case shaped the women's movement in Rajasthan, but she herself got no relief. However, it led to the Supreme Court framing guidelines[16] for women on the prevention of sexual harassment in the workplace, which subsequently paved the way for legislation 20 years later. Why was it that again and again women were having to pay such a heavy price to protect children and attain the most basic of rights? How could a modern society justify such brutality and inequality? Misguided or so-called well-meaning parents do not realise the negative consequences the child bride is prone to suffer—domestic violence, coerced sex, reproductive health problems as underdeveloped bodies and systems are forced to cope with sexual activity, pregnancy and childbirth, etc. *Akshaya Teej*[17] (Also known as *Akshaya Tritiya* or *Akha Teej*) is considered an auspicious day for weddings, and on this day, even today, thousands of child marriages are solemnized in mass weddings, to save parents' expenses. Sometimes even toddlers are married off in clear violation of the law. In Rajasthan, the state government has, on one hand, directed all its elected representatives to ensure that no child marriage takes place in their constituencies. Whereas on the other, out of 200 members of the State's legislative assembly, 76 were married off when they were minors.[18] Compared to the northern states of Rajasthan and Bihar, where the marriage of minor girls is as high as 70 per cent, the rate of child marriage in South India remains low.[19] Even elected representatives had no qualms about violating the law of the land. Marriage to a child was associated with increasing the man's sexual potency. With great disgust, Sita read about the marriage of a twelve-year-old girl to a fifty-six-year-old village chief in Madhya Pradesh's Morena district.[20] He had been planning an ostentatious marriage ceremony for months, and had booked a helicopter ride for the wedding. His application to build a temporary helipad made the local administration suspicious, who then started to inquire about the marriage. They were told by the villagers that the girl was just twelve years of age, and that he had possibly forged documents to make her nineteen years of age. The girl's family was obviously party to this deception since they refused to comment. According to district officials, the man's first wife was in her forties, and he had taken a no-objection certificate from her. Sita was comforted to know that for the first time a public official had been sacked on allegations of child marriage in a state where such marriages were prevalent.

It was an eye-opener for Sita to discover that many girls were raising their voices and repudiating their child marriages after understanding what its consequences were. She applauded the girl who filed a petition[21] for dissolution of marriage, stating that she was about fourteen years of age at the time of marriage, and that she had repudiated her marriage in a panchayat when she was merely seventeen years of age. Another commendable effort was that of the Muslim girl who filed a suit for dissolution of her marriage on the grounds that she was married by her father before she attained the age of fifteen, and which she had repudiated before attaining the age of eighteen.[22] The Trial Court dismissed the suit. In an appeal, after scrutinizing and evaluating the evidence exhaustively, the High Court upheld the right of repudiation of a minor's marriage on attaining puberty, as, unlike Hindu Law, marriage under Mohammedan Law was in the nature of a contract. In the case of a minor who had not attained the age of puberty i.e. fifteen years, the contract of marriage could be entered into by her guardian, but the minor can always repudiate or ratify the contract made by her father during minority after the attainment of puberty. The minor, on attaining puberty, could apply to the Court for dissolution of marriage on the grounds mentioned under Section 2 of the Dissolution of Muslim Marriages Act, 1939.

What shocked Sita all the more was that forced sexual intercourse by a man with his own wife, who was a minor but above fifteen years of age, was not considered rape in the eyes of the law.[23] Even Ravan had been cursed to have his head splintered into pieces if he possessed a woman against her wishes. While most people are aware of the abduction of Sita, male chauvinists still give credit to Ravan, propagating the myth that he did not force himself upon Sita, and instead, tried every day to convince her into marrying him and win her over by presenting her with luxurious jewels and shimmering silk clothes. Nothing could be further from the truth. According to legend, Nalkuvera—Ravan's brother's son—was in love with Rambha, an apsara or celestial courtesan, whom Ravan had violated.

Quivering like a creeper shaken by a storm, shivering, shrinking with shame and fear, Rambha went to meet Nalkuvera. Seeing him, she fell at his feet. After narrating the horrific incident Rambha said, 'Blinded by lust, Ravan did not hear my pleas and raped me and forcibly had sex with me. Please forgive me.' Begging Nalkuvera for forgiveness, she cried, 'Dear one, unfortunately a woman does not have the physical strength to resist her violator. Being physically weak I could not defend myself.'[24]

On hearing Rambha's account of the rape, Nalkuvera was inflamed with anger. Immediately washing his hands ritually, along with his feet, eyes and lips, he cursed Ravan. Addressing Rambha with respect he said, 'Noble lady, using brute force Ravan ravished you. From now onwards he will never be able to take any woman against her wish. If he ever uses force on a woman to fulfill his desire, his head would break in seven pieces'. After that, Ravan never nursed a desire for union with an unwilling woman. And women were also happy for, becoming aware of the curse, they got the confidence to resist him.[25]

Just as Sita was sitting despondently, her eyes fell on the landmark judgement of the Supreme Court,[26] which criminalized sex with a child bride, removing an exception in India's criminal jurisprudence i.e. Exception 2 to Section 375 IPC, which provided protection to men raping their minor wives. The Supreme Court unequivocally held that sexual intercourse with a girl below eighteen years of age was rape, regardless of whether she was married or not.

> The exception carved out in the Indian Penal Code creates an unnecessary and artificial distinction between a married girl child and an unmarried girl child and has no rational nexus with any unclear objective sought to be achieved. The artificial distinction is arbitrary and discriminatory and is definitely not in the best interest of the girl child. The artificial distinction is contrary to the philosophy and ethos of Article 15(3) of the Constitution as well as contrary to Article 21 of the Constitution and our commitments in international conventions. It is also contrary to the philosophy behind some statutes, the bodily integrity of the girl child and her

> reproductive choice. What is equally dreadful, the artificial distinction turns a blind eye to trafficking of the girl child and surely each one of us must discourage trafficking which is such a horrible social evil.[27]

The Supreme Court touched upon the report, 'A Statistical Analysis of Child Marriage in India Based on Census 2011,' prepared through a collaborative effort between an organization called Young Lives and the National Commission for the Protection of Child Rights. Broadly, it stated:

> Child marriage is not only a violation of human rights, but is also recognized as an obstacle to the development of young people. The practice of child marriage cuts short a critical stage of self-discovery and exploring of one's identity. Child marriage is an imposition of a marriage partner on children or adolescents who are in no way ready and matured, and thus, are at a loss to understand the significance of marriage. Their development gets compromised due to being deprived of freedom, opportunity for personal development, and other rights including health and well-being, education, and participation in civic life, and nullifies their basic rights as envisaged in the United Nation's Convention on the Right of the Child ratified by India in 1989. Marriage at a young age prevents both girls and boys from exercising agency in making important life decisions and securing basic freedoms, including pursuing opportunities for education, earning a sustainable livelihood and accessing sexual health and rights ... Child marriage places a girl under the control of her husband and often in-laws, limiting her ability to voice her opinions and form and pursue her own plans and aspirations.[28]

Sita was overjoyed, but some doubts still plagued her mind. Could the government enact legislation, and could courts issue decrees from an ivory tower without ensuring effective implementation and compliance? Especially in view of the fact that nearly 12 million children were married before the age of ten.[29] Additionally, shouldn't the court have made the government comply with the order and follow up by taking steps or gathering data? If sexual intercourse with a girl below the age of eighteen is rape, then in couples where the girl is under under eighteen, or in cases of cohabitation, would the husband be committing rape? If yes, then what special facilities would the government provide to the police in view of the fact that on a conservative estimate almost 10 million rapes would be occurring? What provisions would the government make to assist the minor bride in filing a complaint? What is the role of the Child Marriage Protection Officer, and to what extent is the officer accountable in ensuring that child marriages do not take place? To address the issue in earnestness, the government needs to be transparent about the steps it has taken or is proposing to take from stopping the occurrence of child marriage. The Supreme Court had opined that marriage poses various risks for the survival, health and development of young girls and to children born to them. In that case, what special steps have been taken by the government after the judgement to address the needs of the adolescent girl in terms of education, and health? Have any awareness programmes been proposed or is there any proposal to include deterrences/showcase the adverse impacts of child marriage in the syllabi of schools? Have the panchayati raj institutions been involved in creating awareness among parents, teachers and community members? If a minor girl gives birth to a child, can she be denied access to institutional labour on the grounds that she is a rape survivor?

As a rape survivor, will she be entitled to compensation? Can the child born from wedlock be denied a birth certificate or the name of the father since he is the perpetrator of a crime?

In this perplexed and confused state of mind, Sita heard the good news of the Supreme Court judgement having emboldened girls to raise their voice against injustice. Less than a month after the judgement, a minor girl from Mathura, Uttar Pradesh lodged a police complaint against her husband, accusing him of raping her. She alleged, 'After our marriage, he tried to force me into prostitution and when I refused, he started harassing me. I informed my in-laws about it but they refused to help me.' The girl added that when she refused to return to her husband's house, he put her picture on Facebook with the alleged rates she charged for sex.[30]

Sita was vexed at the plight of child brides who were being denied protection and social autonomy, and were sexually exploited and trafficked. Poor rural parent were lured into traps by traffickers in the guise of grooms, without any demand for dowry. The minor girls were then sold and trafficked in metropolitan cities like New Delhi, Mumbai, Kolkata, and even Dubai, where virgins were in demand. One such example was of twelve-year-old Ameena, who had been married to a fifty-seven-year-old Arab national.[31] Trafficking for marriage is often disguised, and the money made by the brokers is more than that by the parents of the child bride. In states like Haryana and Punjab, which have a skewed sex ratio, child brides are procured from villages in Orissa, Jharkhand, Bihar, Assam and West Bengal. Often, the girls are shared for conjugal purposes and subjected to gang rape, in addition to torture and abuse, in order to give birth to a male child. India reportedly has the world's largest concentration of child sex workers, accounting for one in every four in the world. Around 60 per cent of the sex workers belong to the Scheduled Castes (SC), Scheduled Tribes (ST) and Other Backward Classes (OBC).[32] The Supreme Court, in the same case, also acknowledged that punishments provided in the Prohibition of Child Marriage Act, 2006 (PCMA) are neither a sufficient punitive measure nor a deterrent. Therefore, the PCMA has been breached with impunity, and the Act needs serious reconsideration, especially in view of the harsh reality that a large section of child trafficking is taking place under the garb of marriage, including child marriage. More stringent punishments, including a minimum punishment, should definitely be provided especially to those mature adults who promote such marriages and who perform, conduct, direct or abet any such marriage. Otherwise, this legislation will never act as a sufficient deterrent to prevent or even reduce the number of child marriages. Special reference must be made to the National Plan of Action for Children, 2016, in which the Government of India itself has recognised the high rate of child marriages prevalent in the country, and the fact that child marriage violates the basic rights of health, development and protection of the child. Sita saw a relevant portion of the report, which reads as follows:

> A large number of children, especially girls, are married before the legal age in India. According to NFHS 3 (2005–06), 47.4 per cent of women in the age group 20–24 were married before 18, the percentage being higher for rural areas. The situation has improved in 2013–14 as the RSOC (Rapid Survey on Children) data shows that 30.3 per cent women in the age 20–24 were married before their legal age. Early marriage poses various risks for the survival, health and development of young girls and to children born to them. It is also used as a means of trafficking.[33]

Sita was firmly of the view that prevention of child marriages is necessary, not merely from a child and human rights perspective, but also in the interest of meeting several national goals and Millennium Development Goals, such as reducing poverty, MMR[34] and IMR.[35] She lauded the steps taken by the government in strengthening the law against child marriage and including provisions for the appointment of officials whose sole jobs were to prevent child marriages.[36] Yet, much remained to be done, and it was imperative to conduct awareness campaigns across the country, highlighting the dangers inherent in child marriage.

Dowry

Sita was still to acquire a clear picture of marriage in modern-day Indian society, when she met women who had been tortured and harassed for providing insufficient dowry. She contemplated the noteworthy gesture of King Dashrath, her father-in-law.

The King of Ayodhya was delighted to see his four sons with their brides, as though he, the jewel of monarchs, had realized the four ends of life, (viz., worldly riches, religious merit, sensuous enjoyment and Liberation) along with the four processes of their realization (viz., sacrificial performances, piety, practice of yoga, and spiritual exercise).

All the other princes were married according to the same rites as Sita and Ram. The richness of Sita's dowry was beyond description. The whole pavilion was packed with gold and jewels. There were a number of shawls, linens and silks of various colours and designs and of immense value; elephants, chariots, horses, men-servants and maid-servants, and cows adorned with ornaments and many other things which were more than one could count, and defied description. Those alone who saw the dowry could have some idea of it; even the guardians of the different realms regarded it with envy. The King of Ayodhya gladly accepted it all and gave to the beggars whatever they liked; only that which was left was taken to the lodgings of the bridegroom's party.[37]

Rather than being avaricious and amassing this unearned wealth, Dashrath magnanimously distributed it among the beggars as largesse. Whereas today, in the arranged marriage system, the girl's parents are expected to provide a 'respectable' dowry, the greed for which is growing exponentially day by day. Even though the giving and taking of dowry has been declared illegal since 1961, the continued prevalence of this social evil has turned marriage into a nightmare for the hapless young bride. Sita came across families spending days first trying to match horoscopes. The bride and groom rarely had any role in their own marriage nor did they have the privilege of taking any decision relating to the most important day of their lives. In case the negotiations over the amount of dowry were successful, allowances were made for discrepancies in the horoscopes as it was presupposed that to get all 36 points in both the horoscopes to match, meaning a 100 per cent compatibility, would be difficult. The dowry amount expected was dependent on a number of factors, including region, religion, caste and sub-caste, the groom's education, the bride's skin tone etc. Politicians, bureaucrats, engineers, doctors, executives and even unemployed men, all came with a price tag. Last and most important was the bargaining clout of both the families involved. In case the negotiations failed, then, in order to ensure the alliance did not materialize, the girl was blamed for having a *dosh* or fault in her horoscope.

Sita mulled over her own wedding. Did not all the good omens occur at once, did not the gods rain down flowers, and was there not rejoicing in heaven? Then how did her marriage end in separation and abandonment?

That very moment, considered most auspicious, had finally arrived. Perceiving propitious omens, the Brahmanas apprised King Videha of its approach. Like any bride's father, Janak was anxious that everything should go off well at the auspicious time. 'I am already ready and awaiting for you remaining at this Altar of Fire. Let everything be done without any deterrents.' [sic] *so said Janak to Vashishta.*[38] *Sage Vashishta conveyed this to Dashrath who, with the baraat or wedding coterie, started the wedding walk—a custom of inching towards the venue, walking leisurely and dancing in a mood of celebration.*

The long-awaited event, close to everyone's heart, was now going to take place. Sita's companions joyously conducted her into the pavilion, forming a circle around her. Each one of them was extremely exquisite and, having practised all the 16 forms of adornment, moved with the grace of an elephant in rut. The sound of their melodious strains charmed the hearts of sages, distracting them into forsaking their meditation. Even the Love God's nightingales hung their head in shame before their sweet symphonious singing. Accompanying their singing was music produced by their ornaments. Toelets, anklets and charming bangles on their wrists produced a delightful sound, in tune with their chants. As usual, Sita, in her native loveliness, shone forth among the bevy of ladies. A charming personification of Beauty in the midst of the Graces.[39]

Then King Janak, giving his daughter's hand to Ram said,

> *This is Sita, my daughter, she's the unique bride whose exemplary worth, beauty and blessedness match your own. She'll share the great burden of your royal destiny. Take her hand, she'll be a partner in your path of righteousness; loving and devoted, she'll follow you. She acquits herself in whatever duty you undertake. Take her wishfully, let safeness betide you, take her palm into your palm …*

Making this formulaic citation, not a king but a father handed over his daughter to her husband. Sita and Ram became one forever. The moment marked the marriage of chit or consciousness to prakriti or nature. An exalted spiritual metamorphosis occurred, when God became manifest and nature became conscious. Both Sita and Ram were unaware of this life-

altering moment, nor did they know that destiny had brought them together for a purpose.[40]

According to Hindu belief, the success of a marriage is determined, among other factors, by astrological configurations. The rites must take place at an auspicious hour, and so must the arrival of the bride and bridegroom. Sita's wedding day was chosen in the delightful month of *Margasirsa,* the beginning of the cold season. Having carefully examined and determined the propitious nature of the planets, the date, the asterisms, the conjunction of the stars, the day of the week and the hour of the wedding, the Creator dispatched a note through Narada, which mentioned the hour of the wedding. It matched exactly with the time determined by Janak's astrologers. Today's astrologers contend that had King Janak decided to match the horoscopes of Sita and Ram, rather than making the stringing of Shiv's bow a pre-condition to her marriage, then he may never have gotten his daughter married to Ram. Since Sita's birth remains an enigma, and the exact time and date of her birth is not known, therefore it would not have been possible for King Janak to get her horoscope made accurately.

Certain communities, where the practice of asking for or giving dowry was relatively less prevalent, seem to have succumbed to this evil today. So much so that it is now commonplace for newspapers to report young brides being tortured, brutally burnt, or poisoned, due to unsatisfied dowry demands, on a daily basis. When a girl gets married, she is told by her natal family to serve and respect her in-laws, and to adjust to her husband's way and obey his every wish, like Sita was instructed by the queen mothers.

When the queens heard that the bridegroom's party was about to start, they all felt miserable, as fish are when faced with shortage of water. Again and again they took Sita in their lap and blessed and exhorted her in the following words: 'May you be ever loved by your lord, and with him live a long and happy life; this is our blessing. Serve your husband's father and mother and the guru, and regarding your lord's will, do as he bids.' Demonstrating their love, Sita's clever companions too, with their overpowering affection, taught her in gentle tones the duties of a housewife. The queens politely advised all the other princesses too.[41]

Just as Sita left her natal home, it is taken for granted even today that a girl will leave her father's house to go to her matrimonial home after she is married. The Supreme Court, reiterating this orthodox view, has held that a wife is expected to be with the family of the husband after marriage. If she makes an attempt to deviate from the normal practice and constrains her husband to be separated from his family, it constitutes an act of 'cruelty', and is sufficient grounds for divorce.[42]

In Indian society, a girl is considered *parayadhan*, or another person's property held in trust by her father, who will one day leave her natal home. Parents are always apprehensive as to how she will adjust in the new environment, or how she will be treated by her husband and in-laws. Will she be able to interact with every member of the family and become a pillar of strength and love? The day of marriage, considered the happiest day in a girl's life, is a paradox, for it is the day she cries the most. This is true, especially during the *bidai* ceremony, when she is separated from her family, friends and relatives. Sita herself had butterflies in her stomach picturing her new life, and what lay ahead for her in the house of her husband and in-laws. Fixed in her mind till date was the heart-rendering scene and emotional trauma her family underwent while bidding farewell to their beloved daughter.

While bidding adieu, the queens lovingly clasped the princesses to their bosom, again and again. As the mothers embraced their daughters time and again, they exclaimed, 'Why has Brahma created women?'[43] *Unable to bear the pangs of separation from Sita and Urmila, many nurses and maids broke down with grief. The mothers held the hands of the sons-in-law and prayed to them to treat their daughters gently and with affection. 'They know no hardship or sorrow, they have grown up soft and tender,' they pleaded in pathetic appeal. They wept as if they were losing their very eyes. At last, they ascended the chariots and moved off. The city was filled with gloom, as much gloom as the ecstasy it was filled with for three days previous*

Mithila became a city wracked with grief, unable to bear the departure of their beloved princesses. Janak, whose daughters were the apple of his eyes, and immeasurable source of joy, experienced a range of emotions. He was relieved and happy that there was a man strong enough to break the bow and be a worthy husband for Sita, but her departure created an emptiness in his life. He constantly thought of her sweet smile and loving antics. Trying to normalize, Janak sent for Sage Satananda and his ministers. In order to free his mind from the upsurge of sorrow, he tried to discuss items of business with them. But in the midst of the discussions, his mind would wander into sadness again. One of his ministers, observing that he was giving replies unrelated to the problems, said,

> *O King! The separation from Sita seems to have caused great grief in your heart. No father can escape this separation and this grief. Once she is gifted to the bridegroom, the father's duty is to reduce the attachment gradually; this is a matter not unknown to your Majesty. And, we know that Sita is no ordinary maiden! She is a Divine Angel. So, separation from her must cause you greater agony. O King! The daughters are Divine; and, note, the sons-in-law too have Divine Splendour! … It is really a wondrous coincidence that such bridegrooms have been wedded to such brides, worthy in every way, in physical, mental, intellectual and spiritual characteristics, in status, wealth, power, family honour, dynastic sanctity and religious faith. This cannot happen to all. Therefore, the daughters will have happiness, without the least diminution. Their lives will be filled with greater and greater joy as the years roll by.*[44]

In the olden days, it was customary for the family of the bride to follow the wedding party up to the outskirts of the village or town. This ceremony, called *bidai*, was of significance for it allowed the girl to enjoy another few minutes with her family before she embarked on another life. The popular adage goes: 'Once a woman leaves her father's house, only her corpse can return.' This makes it difficult for a girl, even today, to seek solace in her father's house if she faces a matrimonial problem. This clichéd line, often used in television serials and film, perpetrates the proposition that an Indian woman must demonstrate total subservience and subjugation to her husband and her in-laws, even at the cost of her own life. A young girl is constantly reminded throughout her life that she is a 'worthless expense', which makes her all the more hesitant to seek the support of her parents who most probably incurred huge debts in amassing the dowry for her marriage. A woman returning to her natal house exposes her poor upbringing, and society blames the parents for not giving their daughter good *sanskar*s on how to adjust. Being financially dependent on their husbands or fathers, most girls choose to live in abusive marriages rather than be a burden on their parents. Sita also did not return to Mithila after her husband abandoned her, but continued to stay in Valmiki's hermitage and give birth to her children there in the forest. Did she not want to dishonor her parents or was she avoiding vicious gossip by the people of Mithila? Even after her second *agnipariksha,* she chose to descend into the womb of Mother Earth, and not go back to Mithila.

Sita's new home and life was filled with bliss and she was treated lovingly by all her mothers-in-law, especially Kaushalya. This made her all the more revolted to see tender young girls, with hope in their eyes, being subjected to cruelty, harassment, and even murder by their matrimonial family. All this was done only to fulfill the never ending desires of the insatiable in-laws. Even the giving of dowry did not guarantee a blissful marriage. In addition to cash and ornaments, consumer goods like refrigerators, air conditioners, and a whole range of other gadgets had become an integral part of dowry, with explicit demands being made about the brand and quality of the products. In a survey conducted by SAFMA, most parents of the girls clearly admitted giving dowry at the time of marriage. About 70 per cent said it was in the form of household items, 35 per cent said it was in the form of cash and about 20 per cent said it was in the form of a vehicle.[45] A woman from an educated background is equally at risk of being harassed for dowry as a woman from an impoverished background. A woman's economic status does not make her any less likely to succumb to such pressure; on the contrary, among the upper classes, the expectations of the in-laws are higher and range from demanding an Audi to demanding cash. The complaints over the inadequacy of dowry begin as early as the honeymoon and continue even after the birth of children. In other words, it becomes extortion under the name of dowry. New Delhi itself witnesses a large number of dowry complaints being registered every day. However, in the last four years there has not been a single conviction in any dowry case registered across the city. There are only 11 persons who have been convicted for dowry harassment, out of over 14,000 prisoners in Tihar Jail.[46] In fact, the moment a woman is married she faces violence in the form of demands for dowry and can even be killed or burnt for bringing insufficient dowry. Extravagant weddings and the parents' incapacity to provide dowry are among the ills prevailing in society.

Media and advertisements made a naked show of wealth by depicting affluent marriages. Advertisement campaigns promote the view that 'money is needed for a daughter's marriage'. Insurance companies, exploiting the unease of the bride's father, propagate the message that a father's success is dependent on the lavishness of the wedding he organises. For example, an insurance company's advertisement depicted a widow being grateful to her deceased husband for his astuteness in taking a life insurance policy, which enabled her to fulfill his responsibility of getting their daughter married. Marriage was no longer a solemn affair, but had deteriorated into a monetary transaction with escalating costs. A daughter's marriage is directly proportionate to the economic strain a family undergoes. The more the daughters, the more impoverished the parents.

Often, girls, wanting an easy life, have encouraged parents to succumb to the demands of the groom's family. Sita watched an episode of a Tamil talk show[47] aired on television which had created quite a bit of hysteria and discussion on social media. The subject of the show was how young women demand dowry from their parents at the time of marriage.

Initially, most of the girls appeared to be selfish, entitled brats, measuring success and happiness only in terms of the goods that they possessed. Some coveted a centrally located house, others a vehicle, or household appliances. One participant desired at least 50 sovereigns of gold as dowry, in addition to a grand wedding. A young women, narrating her childhood, dream said that her childhood dream was to wear a lehenga worn by a famous film star for her wedding reception. But as the show progressed and as the layers unfolded, both parties, although on seemingly opposite sides of the debate, ended up speaking the same language of patriarchy. No one questioned the fundamental assumption that marriage was the biggest event in the young women's lives. Both the mothers and the girls agreed that a woman's worth in her marital home was measured by how much dowry she brought. Young girls immaturely reasoned, 'If the house is in my name, the husband's family can't throw me out, can they', and, 'If I bring a TV to the house, nobody can stop me from watching it. Or even breaking it if I'm angry!'

In this frenzy of a comfortable lifestyle and hullabaloo about flaunting one's status and money, there was a girl from rural Maharashtra whose views seemed like a breath of fresh air. Chaitali, a farmer's daughter, on realizing that her in-laws house did not have a toilet, asked her parents to get a toilet built for her instead of the usual items of dowry like jewellery or kitchen appliances. She is the first Indian bride to have asked for a toilet as a wedding gift for her marriage.[48]

Sita's heart bled for Manjula, a civil engineer and a PhD scholar at the coveted IIT Delhi, who, unable to bear the torture and harassment for dowry by her in-laws, hanged herself from the ceiling fan of her hostel room. Her mother was in tears and, waiting outside the mortuary as doctors carried out an autopsy on her daughter, told Sita, 'It was a mistake to educate my daughter and send her to IIT. I should have saved all the money for her dowry.'[49] Hundreds of women like Manjula are subjected to horrific acts of dowry-related violence, including being burnt, being falsely implicated in cases, or even virtually imprisoned in their matrimonial homes—all to extract more money from the girl's natal family in the form of money, property, clothes, appliances, jewellery and even cars. Despite these acts of gender-based violence, a widespread misleading perception prevails that women misuse the law, with the courts, over a period of time, issuing numerous and divergent guidelines/opinions diluting legislative intent. In one case the complainant alleged that her father had given dowry as per his capacity, but that the husband and in-laws were not happy with the extent of the dowry and had started abusing her. They also made a dowry demand of Rs 3,00,000 (approximately 460 US dollars)and a car, which the family could not arrange. It has been clearly recorded in the order of the court.

> After perusal of the file and the document brought on record. It is clear that the husband Shri Rajesh Sharma demanded car and three lacs rupees and in not meeting the demand. It appears that he has tortured the complainant. So far as torture and retaining of the stri dhan and demanding Rs. 50,000 and a gold chain and in not meeting the demand the torture is attributable against Shri Rajesh Sharma. Rajesh Sharma appears to be main accused … [sic][50]

Yet when the matter reached the apex court, it overgeneralized and stated that most of such complaints are filed in the heat of the moment over trivial issues. It alleged that many such complaints are not bona fide. At the time of the filing of the complaint, implications and consequences are not visualized. At times, such complaints lead to uncalled-for harassment—not only the accused but also to the complainant. If Sita herself refused to compromise when her dignity was doubted, and chose to return to Mother Earth, then why should these women, who suffer abuse and harassment at the hands of their husband and matrimonial family, compromise under pressure? She was curious if the Division Bench had the jurisdiction to brand women in distress as wives who misuse the law. As per the settled provisions of law, while exercising appellate jurisdiction, the Court is required to examine whether the court below committed an error that resulted in a misuse of the process of law. In Rajesh Sharma's case, the Division Bench has not indicated errors committed by the court below. Instead of identifying the errors, it opined that there was a 'tendency to rope in all family members to settle a matrimonial dispute'.

Relying on the Crime Record Bureau data, the apex court Division Bench formed an opinion that a low conviction rate/ high rate of acquittals in these cases meant that the case is false or fake, totally overlooking the fact that the conviction rate in matrimonial matters is low because of pressure from the woman's own natal family, pressure by police to compromise, ineffective investigation, prolonged judicial process, etc. Sita thought that if low conviction decides the truthfulnes and genuineness of the case, then over half the cases registered, whether relating to murder, theft, dacoity or any other crime, would be considered fake since, according to the NCRB Crime in India 2016 statistics[51], IPC crimes reported a chargesheeting rate of 72.9 per cent while the conviction rate was only 46.8 per cent. Sita felt offended, for it was not only misleading but also demeaning to suggest that women in India are untruthful. Since the matter before the Division Bench was dowry-related harassment, the Court should have pondered upon the continuous rise in dowry deaths, rather than simply blaming women.

As per NCRB data, dowry deaths accounted for 1.8 per cent of the violent crimes in India, against murder which was 7.1 per cent. There were 8,455 deaths in 2014, while in 2015 the deaths reduced to 7,634, and by 2016 the number of deaths further dropped to 7,621. Sita wondered whether this data captured the actual figures, or if a large number of cases were reported as natural deaths rather than dowry murders. Little did Sita know that India's crime statistics, as laid bare in the NCRB data, was highly deceptive.[52] Every year, the NCRB presents data for the number of crime incidents in Indian cities. The bureau also provides crime rates, which is the number of crime incidents per lakh of population. The catch, however, is that the NCRB does not change the population of cities between the censuses that take place every 10 years. As a result, the crime rate in cities falls sharply once in 10 years, not because of better policing but because the denominator—population, suddenly sees a jump every 10 years. For example, for all the years between 2001 and 2010, the 2001 population data is used to calculate the crime rate. Similarly, the 2011 census data has been used for all subsequent years and will continue to be used till the 2021 figures are available. This effectively makes crime rates for cities meaningless. International data on crime shows that countries with the best systems of law and order also have high crime rates, while countries with dysfunctional governments mostly show low crime rates. According to data from the United Nations Office on Drugs and Crime, averaged over a few recent years, Sweden reported the highest rate (6,456 per 1 lakh people) of seven serious crimes, followed by Denmark (6,041) and the Netherlands (5,523). In contrast, the lowest rates of these crimes were seen in the most lawless countries: Somalia (1.5 per 1 lakh people), Iraq (2) and Libya (2.9). For India, the number was a mere 87.[53] Sita felt that a poor understanding of the law among data collectors leads to poor data. Also, a high level of cases were disposed of by the police, as compared to those disposed of by courts, which clearly establishes the fact that in most cases the matter is closed in out-of-court settlements, especially in dowry-related cases.

Data collection in India is generally so poor that it fails to unmask issues that even the authorities acknowledge. Sita was puzzled why Bihar, Jharkhand, and West Bengal have reported zero farmer suicides, which was extremely odd for states where the majority of the population is dependent on agriculture. The absence of farmer suicides for years, in these states is attributed to the difference in understanding the idea of 'farmer suicide'. Then, there are the ways in which data is recorded. Usually, the

FIR is lodged by a constable or sub-inspector who visits the suicide spot and talks to members of the dead person's family. The reason he records for the suicide is dependent entirely on what he infers from the situation. 'The immediate cause of a farmer suicide may be a quarrel with his wife over money. So the FIR invariably records the cause as 'family problem' or 'poverty'. However, the real, underlying cause could be distress due to crop failure, which led to indebtedness and financial difficulties.'[54] The inability to arrange finances for marriageable daughters was one of the reasons for farmers committing suicides.[55] However, the category in which the police would register the crime is debatable.

Recurrent reiterations of women misusing the law are made because these victims of gender-based violence are scattered, in addition to having no common identity, whether political, social or cultural. Hence, they are unable to form a group and raise their voice together. Further, it is known that even today, the status of the groom decides the quantum of dowry and the make of car received. Sita thought that considering this social evil is destroying the roots of society, it would have been prudent for the Division Bench to address the culture of violence that has gender inequality at the heart of the problem, and to issue appropriate guidelines to stop the evil of dowry, which not only results in cruelty and the death of women, but also in their fathers committing suicide due to their inability to bear dowry expenses. She was gratified to know that the apex court, in another case,[56] clarified that it was obligated to state that they were not in agreement with the decision rendered in the Rajesh Sharma case, and were disposed to think that it really curtailed the rights of the women.

Many argue that despite changes in the law, women continue to be excluded from a right over their natal property, hence, what is given as dowry essentially amounts to their share of the property or *stridhan*. This argument is mistaken on the premise that the dowry is neither enjoyed by nor in possession of the bride. It is important to clarify the concept of *stridhan,* which has often been confused with dowry. *Stridhan* literally means a woman's property. Different forms of *stridhan* are for the woman alone: the husband cannot lay claim to these except in times of distress.[57] Manu, the ancient Hindu law maker, warned that a husband's heirs will incur a sin if they divide the ornaments worn by a woman during her husband's lifetime. Today, however, Sita saw that it was not uncommon to find a woman's ornaments being misappropriated by her in-laws. The woman was therefore doubly deprived, as gender-based 'ownership inequality'[58] deprived her from inheriting land and property from her family of origin, which typically favoured male heirs.

Sita wondered whether the law in India drew a sufficiently clear distinction between dowry and *stridhan.* Retention of *stridhan* by the in-laws was illegal under section 406[59] of the Indian Penal Code, and giving and taking of dowry was illegal under provisions of the Dowry Prohibition Act, 1961. The Act was implemented with the aim to curb the growing menace of the practice of dowry and the social harm caused by it. The Act makes not only the actual receiving of dowry punishable, but also the very demand of dowry (made before, at the time, or after the marriage, where such demand is referable to the consideration of marriage), illegal. The rules framed under the Act clearly mandate the preparation of a list of gifts received (at the earliest), to be signed by both the parties. This is rarely ever done. In the earlier days, families ensured that proper lists and accounts were prepared, while the dowry itself was put on display at a formal function for all the relatives to take note of, so there were numerous witnesses to the transaction. Today, no lists are signed and most of the giving and receiving is shrouded in secrecy and made known only through whisper networks within the social circle. Despite legislation and a sensitive judiciary, dowry-related crimes are still on the increase. The maximum cases of dowry deaths were reported in the state of Uttar Pradesh, followed by Bihar.

Census data clearly indicated the decline in women's status in India in the last decade, and especially so in states that were considered industrialized. One of the reasons cited for not wanting girls, was the liability they pose in terms of a dowry. Sita felt that unless there was greater awareness, until society itself believed that dowry was an evil, and until parents refused to succumb to pressure to give dowry, the evils of dowry would continue to manifest irrespective of caste, creed or religion. Young men also needed to develop the courage to make a stand against such practices. Sita admired the grit of girls like Mumtaz Ansari,[60] who sent a strong message of deterrence to covetous grooms. She refused to accompany her husband to her marital home when he demanded another bike as dowry and threw tantrums, disrespecting her father. As a parting 'gift', the bride's family tonsured the head of the groom and his brother, and sent them off with a garland of shoes. Also laudable was the courage of a woman dentist in calling off her marriage to a doctor after the family of the groom demanded a last minute dowry of Rupees 10 million or one crore (153,400 US dollars) on the wedding day.[61] At the time of the engagement, the groom was given a car and five gold coins of 10 grams each, but their greed was neverending, and on the day of marriage they sought more gifts, cash, and jewellery worth Rupees 10 million. On discovering that the groom was adamant about the demands, the girl refused to marry into a family of extortionists.

Conveying the decision to call off the wedding to the groom's family, the girl filed a complaint with the police against the groom, his sister, his brother-in-law, and his parents. However, the not-to-be bride's family played the gracious host and broke the news to the guests only after the wedding feast was served. The guests appreciated the woman's decision and said it would inspire other women to fight the menace of dowry.

Marital Life

The outcome of marriage in India depends not just on the attitude of a husband but as much on the kind of relationship a woman has with her marital family and extended kinship group. This is echoed in the words of Uma's mother Mena, who advised her daughter to 'treat her husband like her God' when she was bidding her farewell after her marriage to Lord Shiva.

There is a curious dichotomy for women in Indian families. They represents both ends of the power spectrum; She is the least powerful member of the household when she enters as a young girl and new bride, while the mother of the groom wields considerable power in the household. If a girl is lucky like Sita, she will command respect and affection from her in-laws and can frequently count on them to intervene on her behalf. Sita mused at how the queen mothers were enraptured to behold their four sons along with their brides. As they gazed again and again at the beauty of Sita and Ram, they joyously regarded their life's objective as being fulfilled[62] and extolled their good fortune. Sita was not only welcomed by the queen mothers but also by the whole of Ayodhya, which made her adjustment in the new environs of her matrimonial home easier. She did not feel the sense of alienation often felt by married women. She was wholeheartedly welcomed with love and affection. This was in contrast to another young newly-wed nineteen-year-old bride of modern India from Uttar Pradesh, who ran away from her matrimonial house on the second day of her marriage, after being compelled to defecate in the open. In a swift act of defiance she inspired a widespread movement[63] and returned only when a toilet had been constructed.

Sexual Satisfaction

Sex is a vital part of marriage and the only thing the couple uniquely share with each other that they don't share with anyone else. In spite of the *Kamasutra* or 'The Treatise on Pleasure' being written sometime in the third century by an Indian scholar, Vatsyayana Mallanaga, sex still remains a forbidden word in India. The word 'kama' literally means desire or pleasure, and 'sutra' alludes to a manual or guide. The *Kamasutra,* in addition to being simply a manual of sexual positions, has immense historical importance. It is a book on the art of living and, among others, the chapters demonstrate stimulation of desire, types of embraces, caressing and kissing, superior coition and oral sex, preludes and conclusions to the game of love, as well as to how to acquire a wife, the duties and privileges of the wife, and how to maintain power in a marriage. There can be no two opinions that a good marriage starts with a spark but grows only with careful attention to its needs, and undoubtedly, the most essential ingredient is a healthy sexual life. Simple courtship gestures like holding hands, spending time together, and looking good for each other are critical towards forming a strong bond as lovers, but also towards cementing what is to be a lifelong partnership. Sita was nonplussed on discovering that most women did not have any idea about sex when they got married, and any mention of the word was followed by girly giggles. Sita mused about her meeting with Anasuya in Chitrakut. Despite her advanced age, the pious-minded Anasuya made it clear to

Sita that husband and wife have a responsibility to meet each other's sexual needs, which were the key to a long and happy marriage. Modern-day research findings reveal that Anasuya's advice to Sita was spot on, as falling in love and staying in love is largely due to the chemistry between two people, and that love potions could soon be a reality.[64]

Sita reverently paid homage to the illustrious Anasuya, a devoted and virtuous wife. Her name ranks in the forefront amongst pativratas or devoted wives. She made Sita sit beside her. Sita spent time with Anusuya, eagerly earning the lessons of ideal womanhood and dedicated devotion to a husband. Despite her advanced age, the pious-minded Anasuya made it clear to Sita that the husband and wife have a responsibility to meet each other's sexual needs which was the key to a long and happy marriage. Anusaya said:

> *O, Sita the beautiful lady! Thank heaven! Leaving your relatives, honour and prosperity, you are accompanying* Ram, *who is expelled into a forest. Highly fortunate worlds await those women, to whom their husband is dear no matter whether he lives in a city or in a forest; whether he is sinful or virtuous. To women of noble nature, the husband is the highest deity no matter whether he is ill-behaved or licentious or devoid of riches. O, Sita! On a reflection, I perceive none who is a better friend than a husband, who protects his wife in all circumstances, like the imperishable fruit of one's austerities.*

If both husband and wife stand by each other in times of adversity, no misfortune can separate them. They will draw strength from each other to withstand all their difficulties together. Anasuya instructed Sita to be 'devoted to your lord, loyal to your husband, following established rules, and become an honest wife to your husband and obtain merit and renown.'

Sita, full of reverence for Anasuya, agreed with her saying that even if her husband had ill fortune or a bad character, she would have unhesitatingly obeyed him. She had no words to express how devoted she was to her husband. He was not only absolutely faithful to her, but also renowned for his virtues. He abounded with compassion, was affectionate and religious. His qualities manifested the tenderness of both, a mother and a father, towards her. Praising her husband, Sita said that Ram looked upon all the wives of King Dashrath equally as his own mother. Sita told Anasuya that her words echoed the advice given by her mother-in-law while departing for the lonely and fearful forest, and what her mother had taught her at the time of marriage with Ram. Sita concluded, 'Such excellent women, devoted to their husbands, and by their meritorious deeds, are highly honoured in heaven.'

On hearing Sita's response, Anasuya was very pleased, and kissing Sita's forehead said, 'O, Sita with a bright smile! There is a great merit acquired by me in virtue of my various pious observances. Through that power, I wish to confer a boon on you.' Anasuya had acquired esoteric powers by virtue of her ascetic practice. Being pleased with Sita, she wanted to grant her a boon.

> *O, Sita! Alas! I will create a great joy for you, which will be to your advantage ... Here are divine gifts: a garland, an apparel, jewels, a scented cosmetic and rare body-cream. These are all given by me to adorn your limbs. They will be ever worthy of you and will remain intact even after constant use...Your body, anointed with these heavenly cosmetics, will make you look beautiful to your husband, as Lakshmi (the Goddess of fortune and beauty) does to the imperishable Vishnu (the Lord of Preservation).*

Despite her age, Anasuya realised the need for Sita to remain attractive and desirable to her husband, even in the forest. She gifted her cosmetics and body cream with divine potency, which when rubbed on the body, would arouse her husband's desire. Anasuya recognised the need for a married couple to draw a balance between these two mutually exclusive modes of existence: the householder and the ascetic. Devotion and conjugal activity, both are essential for a balanced harmonious relationship. Anasuya presented Sita with a divine garland, fine clothes, and exquisite jewellery. She also gifted her priceless unguents that would lend her body an eternal lustre, a glow, enhancing her brilliance and making her more attractive to Ram. Anasuya suggested that Sita refrain from being complacent after marriage, and extorted the need to groom oneself, put in some effort to keep herself physically and mentally fit and energetic, and even use fragrance or perfume to make herself more alluring. All this in spite of dwelling in the forest.[65]

In the Hindu scriptures, the mythologies of Lord Shiva allow a free interplay between eroticism and asceticism, without any conflict between the two states. However, in the character of Ram, sexuality does not get full expression. The tension between the ascetic and the householder way of life alludes to the conflict between dharma or righteousness, and the indulgence of individual desire. Questions have been raised as to how the couple drew a balance between these two mutually exclusive modes of existence—the householder and the ascetic, while in exile. Did Sita and Ram refrain from sexual activity for the 14 years of their exile? When Laxman built the straw cottage at Panchvati near the River Godavari, he did not construct it according to his needs, but for the comfort and privacy of Sita and Ram. The narration of the Surpanakha episode generally begins with a two-fold description of idyllic domesticity and the performance of austerities. Surpanakha is punished for her display of unrepressed sexuality, which is harmful to both domesticity and asceticism.[66] Are we to deduce from that event that a woman was not allowed to express her sexuality freely? And in case she did, then she would be the one to suffer the consequences, not the man?

Same-sex Relations

Sexual desire and satisfaction have been liberally discussed by Valmiki in the *Ramayana.* But it has primarily been described between heterosexual couples. Sexual knowledge and skill were considered to be evidence of achievement, refinement, intelligence, and were indulged in by both, the common masses and the princely class. For example, when Hanuman entered the palace of Ravan, he passed by the various wives of Ravan in different stages of desire, and that the 'appearance of those sleeping women, tired from being possessed by lust, was like lotuses sleeping.'[67]

Hindu literature discusses sex, including oral sex and bestiality, but there appears to be no concept of same-sex relations, not even as a prohibited form of sex. In Ravan's house, Hanuman saw thousands of desirable women sleeping naked or in a disheveled state. Their garlands were crushed, their jewellery scattered, and their garments loosened. They had reddened squeeze marks and love scratches on their breasts.

Women sleeping, making pillows out of their arms decorated with bracelets and beautiful clothes. One woman sleeping on another woman's bosom, a woman asleep on a woman's shoulder, another woman asleep on another woman's thigh and breasts. Overcome with heat and friendship, they embraced each other's limbs, their thighs, sides, waist and back clinging to each other. That garland of women tied with the rope of each other's shoulders shone like a garland of flowers with dragonflies on it tied in thread. So closely were they entangled that it was impossible to make out which jewellery or clothes belonged to which body part. The co-wives' smelled each other's faces again and again.[68]

However, the sensual physical proximity of the women was only in context of imagining the other to be Ravan,[69] for women of royal sages, Brahmins and demons and of *gandharvas*, of *rakshasas*—all those unmarried girls surrendered out of lust to Ravan.[70] There was not even one woman who had been obtained forcefully by the strong Ravan, except for Sita.[71] Hence, the only example which can be interpolated out of same-sex relation is in the account of the descent of Ganga. According to legend, King Sagar's 60,000 sons were burnt to ashes by their own sin of insulting Sage Kapila. Dalip, Sagar's progeny, had two wives in Ayodhya, who were determined to bear a child. They both drank a potion created from a *yagna*; one wife drank it in the capacity of a wife, while the other made love to her pretending to be the late husband. It is notable that she made love to another woman, not imagining her to be a woman, but fantasizing that she was her departed spouse. From this union a child was born. Since no male had been involved in the creation of the child, it had no bones or nerves, only flesh and blood. Since he was born only of *bhaga* (vulva), on becoming complete he was known as Bhagiratha—the man instrumental in bringing Ganga down to earth.[72]

This story of two women creating a child is found only in the Bengali *Krittivasa Ramayana* and the Bengali version of the *Padma Purana.* It is believed to have been derived from the ancient Hindu medical text, the *Sushruta Samhita.* In this text, it is stated that since the father contributes the bones and the mother the flesh and blood, a child born from two women's intercourse will be a boneless lump of flesh.[73] The personality of the two queens' has been more developed in another version of the *Krittivasa Ramayana,* and is found in only one manuscript. According to this manuscript,the co-wives, Chandra and Mala, rather than being instructed to make love in order to have a son, spontaneously made love in the romantic monsoon season, while lying in their late husband's bedroom. Kama, the God of love, infused them with his *tej* or energy, due to which the pregnancy occurred. Because Kama inspired the pregnancy, the child was born beautiful and healthy, with bones.[74] Words connoting drenching, pouring, and the flowing of powerful love, have been interpreted both as semen flowing or as energy emitting.

To summarize, if marriage is considered a covenant between a man and a woman which is, by its nature, ordered toward the procreation of children; and if children are considered a gift from God and if whoever welcomes one of these little children welcomes God, then every child is a reward and a blessing, whether born to hetrosexual or homosexual couples. Birth itself is a miracle, and is even more of a miracle in the case of same-sex couples procreating.

Sita boldly supported the basic right of a person to love someone of the same gender, a right which had been criminalized[75] in India. In fact, India was among one of the 13 countries to vote against the passing of a United Nations Human Rights Council (UNHCR) resolution to denounce the death penalty for homosexuality.[76] In other parts of the world that permit same-sex marriages, it has been held that:

> No union is more profound than marriage, for it embodies the highest ideals of love, fidelity, devotion, sacrifice and family. In forming a marital union, two people become something greater than once they were ... Marriage embodies a love that may endure even past death. It would misunderstand these men and women to say that they disrespect the idea of marriage. Their plea is that they do respect it, respect it so deeply that they seek to find it's fulfillment for themselves. Their hope is not to be condemned to live in loneliness, excluded from one of civilisation's oldest institutions. They ask for equal dignity in the eyes of the law. The Constitution grants them that right.[77]

She was intrigued about why homosexuality was considered a taboo or 'deviant behaviour', and was not merely a question of one's sexual orientation or preference.

Equality and Respect

A marital relationship requires mutual respect and parity to be healthy and strong. Sita and Ram had a healthy friendship based on equality, and personal freedom. Both had a unique identity separate from their spouse. They learned to enjoy being in each other's company, and expressed themselves not only through words, but through actions too. They valued each other's presence, which strengthened their union. Even when there was a major disagreement Sita never used harsh words, knowing that it may cause irreparable damage to the relationship. Simultaneously, she had the freedom to question her husband, which she did on numerous occasions, and Ram provided her the space to do so, without taking offense or being insulted. A Tamil author [78] is stated to have said:

> I am not a politician to speak about independence. Independence is nothing but a freedom to do things without affecting the freedom of others. Before we talk about independence and freedom (of the underprivileged, women, dalits, minorities, writers) the question should be whether we have the freedom to discuss these.

Sita always held her own counsel and, being Janak's daughter and Ram's wife, did not shy away from speaking out when she saw injustice being done.

Anasuya's advice to Sita that the husband should be obeyed can interpreted in today's context as appreciating one's spouse and not being too controlling. Often without realizing it, the spouses attempt to control each other by engaging in destructive habits such as complaining, blaming, criticizing, nagging, threatening, punishing, and bribing (or rewarding) to control behaviour. Did not Kaikeyi's tantrums and threats to her husband, King Dashrath, prove to be the reason for the destruction? So, a healthy union is one in which each person can retain their individual identity, whilst still merging into a shared existence—which inevitably entails compromise. Well-known psychologist and marital researcher, John Gottman,[79] identified some key ingredients for a healthy and sound relationship: shared fondness and admiration; attunement to one's partner's needs; managing conflict and accepting one's partner's influence; sexual intimacy; trust and commitment; and creating a shared meaning. In this coexistence, there is bound to be friction and disagreement. An important predictor of the survival of a marriage is not whether couples fight but how couples fight. The most toxic and potent destruction comes from when one or both parties habitually use coercive criticism, contempt and/or stonewalling against their spouse. Undoubtedly, the reason partners complain to each other is because they are not getting their needs met, but how this is addressed and how matters are repaired after arguments is just as crucial as the argument itself. Before pointing a finger at one's spouse, look within yourself. If you have changed, he could change, making the marriage stronger and more joyful. Learn to accept differences rather than try to change the other. Each spouse contributes different qualities to the relationship. Genuine appreciation means that you value each other. Interestingly, Gottman's research showed that the failure of men to accept influence from their female partners was highly correlated with the failure of marriages. Was this the reason Sita did not take Hanuman's offer to help her escape, but wisely said that her husband should get credit for eliminating Ravan and rescuing her?

Men tend to set limits on their wives' ambition and aspirations. Sometimes this limit is clearly articulated, and sometimes it is unspoken, and it is almost as though career aspirations are seen to be the exclusive domain of the man. Even in the courts, a patriarchal mindset prevails and gender subservience is promoted. In a case of divorce where the woman, residing in Mumbai, was not willing to join her husband, who had got a job in Port Blair, the Bombay High Court observed that married women should be like Sita and should give up their all to accompany their husbands.[80] Another leading example is of Rosemary Dzuvichu, whose activism took a toll on her marriage.[81] In a world where men call the shots and a woman is often restricted to weaving, washing clothes and doing household chores, Dzuvichu defied patriarchal Naga society. Her grandmother, Zeliezhu, was one of the first women leaders of the underground Naga National Council, and her mother, Alhouu, broke through and entered the male bastion of traditional apex tribal bodies. She spearheaded a fight to improve Nagaland universities and filed public health litigation on health and education. She said, 'Too many women are seen as liberated, but we struggle with patriarchy, customary laws and social practices. But these have made our women stronger and bolder.' Dzuvichu fought for women's constitutional right[82] of 33 per cent reservation in urban bodies, which was opposed by patriarchs on the grounds that it would alter social equations. Relief came from the Supreme Court in 2016, when it ordered the Nagaland government to hold polls with one-third of the seats reserved for women.

Communication

In a harmonious relationship, feelings and emotions must be candidly communicated. Sita and Ram did not always need words to express themselves, for much of how they felt was conveyed through body language, mood, and expression. Having attained an exceptional level of togetherness, they had the unique ability to 'know' exactly what the other felt and thought. Communicating well is about mastering the craft of what to say, and knowing when and how to say it. Most important is knowing when to say absolutely nothing at all, for words can either draw people toward us or push them away. Sita and Ram, like most ordinary couples, wanted the same things: love, security, and trust. Sita, being self-confident, always knew how to best articulate her feelings to Ram.

Sometimes, despite having a harmonious relationship, egos can get in the way of understanding those whom we love. Ram cared for Sita, which is why he tried to dissuade her from accompanying him into the forest. It is said that the eyes are the windows to the soul, and they reveal what is in our mind. When Ram was trying to dissuade Sita, his eyes frequently darted around nervously, looking down, and he was unable to maintain eye contact with his wife. Sita, however, made of stronger mettle, maintained steady eye contact with Ram and resolutely held his gaze.

Ram faced the grim prospect of having to break the news to Sita. She had been practising for the coronation ceremony, and had no idea of the inner evil machinations transpiring. Taking leave of his mother, Ram entered his own apartments, which were decorated and filled with people rejoicing all around. Sita was sitting in a corner after having performed the daily worship of the deities. Eagerly waiting for her husband, she sprang up from her seat instantly on seeing her beloved enter. She trembled with anxiety on seeing her husband stricken with sorrow. His face was drained of colour and devoid of its usual radiance. Alarmed and concerned to see him in such as state, she exclaimed, 'Oh Rama! It is indeed told by learned brahmanas that today's constellation Pushya (which is presided by Sage

Brihaspati), which is propitious, is suitable (for your coronation). Why are you sadly disposed?

Sita wanted to take him into her arms, so that he could rest his weary head on her bosom. Unburdening all his grief on her and feeling relieved, Sita's selfless love and her loving arms were there for his support. What ailed him? Did he not share his sorrow with her fearing she would be disturbed? Is that why he stood before his gentle tender-hearted beloved, Sita, stiff like a stranger? Ram cringed, remembering the effect the news of his renunciation had on his mother and brother. Inwardly, he was trying to find the best way to communicate to Sita, so that she did not react with feeling of mistrust, anger, fear, or blame. After hesitating for a few seconds, he spoke in a subdued tone. First he mumbled, 'Oh, Sita! My venerable father is sending me to the forest in exile.' Then he slowly elaborated upon how he was caught in the net of dharma and the two boons owed by his father to Kaikeyi. Hesitantly, he advised Sita:

> *Before setting forth to the lonely forest, I came to see you. I should not be praised at any time in the presence of Bharata. Men endowed with power and fortune indeed do not tolerate praise of others. Therefore, my virtues should not be extolled by you in front of Bharata. You need not be attended in a special manner at any time by him. You can stay familiar to him, by behaving with him comformably …*

Emboldened on not seeing Sita react instantaneously, Ram continued to make suggestions on how she should pass her time in his absence, and behave with his mothers and brothers. He was indirectly suggesting that if she stayed on in Ayodhya, and took over the responsibility of caring for his aged parents, it would as though she was fulfilling her duties towards him. Ram said,

> *Oh, Sita the good and faultless lady! You can become interested in religious vows and fasting. You can rise at dawn, perform worship of*

> *the deities as per precept and do salutation to my father, King Dashrath. For me all my mothers are equal in my eyes, in terms of fondness, love and the way they have looked after me (in my childhood). You, in particular, should regard Bharat and Shatrughana, as your brothers or sons. Bharat is indeed king and the master both for the kingdom and for our family. Hence, you should not do what is displeasing to him at any time.* [sic]

The usually soft-spoken and gentle Sita was aghast on hearing Ram's words. Sita was no different. She felt highly offended on her husband pontificating to her in such a formal and emotionless manner. She was filled with righteous indignation that Ram could be so casual, bordering on callous, by talking about the exile and separation. In loving anger, she insisted that since Ram had been ordered to live in the forest, as his wife, her fate had also been decided along with his. Trying to defend herself, Sita asked Ram not to be cross with her for not obeying his advice. Desperate to accompany Ram into the forest, Sita went to the extent of challenging Ram's manhood by saying that if he was capable of protecting others in the forest, then why couldn't he protect her?

Sita then tried to seek support from Kaushalya, her mother-in-law. Kaushalya was aware of the extent of her authority and used it judiciously. Sita and Ram were sitting beside her, waiting for her decision. But she did not give any order, only advice. To agree or not, was the decision of Sita and Ram themselves. Kausalya gave advice as a mother, and as an elder who has seen life. But she did not want to interfere unnecessarily in the marital life of the couple, nor thrust her own views upon them.

To quash Sita's desire to accompany him into the forest, Ram started describing the various afflictions she might have to face. Not inclined to take Sita with him, Ram harboured the mistaken impression that he would be able to frighten Sita with the hardships of forest life. He underestimated her strength of spirit, and ability to withstand difficulty. Ram did not realize that every challenge she faced made her stronger and wiser. Ram, throwing caution to the winds, changed his tactic and tried to gain his wife's confidence.[83]

Ram thought he was being clever by explaining things to Sita, about how a man must do his duty. If she stayed on in Ayodhya, and took over the responsibility of caring for his aged parents, it would be as though she was fulfilling her duty towards him. Ram used a number of endearments to coax her, ranging from calling her a princess to a sensible lady. He thought by calling Sita beautiful, clever and wise, she would be elated and, in an agreeable state of mind, would be prepared to listen to what he thought was 'reason'.

Ram felt like his chest was going to explode, but he had to continue. Pulling himself to his full towering height, Ram again changed his strategy and decided that he must exert his authority and scare her. Highly educated and well-versed in all subjects, Ram had a good idea of human psychology. He understood that when humans sense danger, their brain reacts instantly by sending signals through the nervous system, and that the response to the perceived threat is flight, or, in other words, submission. He hoped Sita would refuse to go on her own. So he commenced his manoeuvre to frighten Sita by exposing her to the reality of the difficulties she may have to face in the forest.

Ram thought that Sita, used to living in luxury and comfort, would be intimidated by physical suffering. Not that Sita was not aware of the hardships of forest life. She was well aware of the difference between life in a forest and a palace. Ram did not intend to give her a lesson in geography or a lecture on jungle life, but was merely trying to convey that living in a forest for 14 long years was not an easy task. It involved intense emotional and physical duress, including the risk of succumbing to either. Human beings find happiness through material items like food, clothing and shelter. Sita had all the comforts available to her in the palace, while life in the forest would be the exactly the opposite. But Ram saw that his words had no effect on Sita.[84]

This private conversation between wife and husband was taking place in the presence of the queen mother, Kaushalya.

Initially they had longed for privacy, but having crossed that threshold, neither Sita nor Ram felt restrained and continued their intense argument in her presence. It was as if two beings were both dreading the instant that would separate them. He was trying to change her heart, but did not want her to know the agitation in his heart. She was trying to change his heart, and wanted him to know the strength of her love. Any other woman would have shunned the thought of living in the forest, even if it was with her husband, however much she loved him. But Sita was no ordinary woman, and Ram had underestimated the strength of his wife, who knew how to treat adversity as an opportunity. She had the ability to endure hardship, and bravely face any trial or tribulation, whether in the palace or the forest. The anger that had momentarily permeated her spirit vanished, for she was by nature soft-spoken and gentle. She wanted, from the depths of her soul, to be with her beloved in times of adversity, and had deep unbridled faith in her beloved. Sita, in her winsome way, argued that riches, houses, land, cities, and kingdoms, were all mere accoutrements of woe to a woman bereft of her husband. She made a compelling argument to advocate her case, and her words seem prophetic, for today the amount of money a man possesses has become the deciding factor for the parents of a girl in choosing a groom.

Remaining adamant, Sita renewed her plea and said it was nothing compared to the utter horror of separation from her beloved husband. With her face filled with tears of agony at the thought of being left behind, Sita, speaking slowly and lovingly, said, 'All the disadvantages you mentioned about dwelling in the forest become advantages to me, if your affection is placed before them.'

Sita then pleaded with Ram to allow her to accompany him. The cold sweat of fear of being left behind for 14 years gripped her. Was she not being able to articulate her agony to her husband? Was her adamancy in trying to convince him making him all the more dismissive of her feelings? Was Ram feeling pushed, and cajoled, which was why he was reacting in the exact opposite manner? How could she convince him? Demurely playing on his vanity, Sita said, 'Oh Ram! Antelopes, lions, elephants, tigers, sarabhas (a legendary animal with eight legs), birds, yaks and all others which roam in the forest, run away after seeing your form, since they have never seen your figure before. When there is cause for fear, who would not have fear?' She knew no harm would come to her when Ram was with her.[85]

In order to best accomplish their objectives, people use a variety of arguments and strategies. The most effective of these are the three rhetorical appeals—ethos, logos, and pathos, which are powerful tools for achieving a persuasive goal. Words not only express what is in our heart and mind, they also form the means with which we influence those around us. Ram had used tactics, ranging from admonition, and gentle and friendly reproof, to warnings and threats, in his effort to influence Sita's decision. Similarly, Sita, having proficiency in the Vedas, was well equipped in the art of advocacy and persuasion. Being able to successfully influence someone is a challenging task. Sita had used up all her powers of persuasion tapping into her natural behaviour to persuade Ram into 'complying' with what she wanted him to do. Making direct eye contact with Ram, she addressed him while tipping her words with fire. Asserting her authority, she tried to convince him that she would not follow but lead, and would pave the path in the forest for him. She would be an asset for him and not a liability. She tried to increase Ram's confidence by displaying her grit and strength of character. She sequenced her arguments and finally appealed to his nobler motives, expressing her love and devotion, and even tried to appeal to his masculinity.

When no logic appeared to have effect, in spite the right mix of the tactics, resorting to astrological predictions, she said, 'When I was an umarried girl, the prediction of my dwelling in the forest was heard by me. In the past, you have been really pleased for many a time to take me along with you, indeed, for the tour of a forest, as longed by me.'

On seeing that neither of her arguments were cutting any ice with Ram, then ramping up the urgency, Sita said that she would take resort to poison or fire or water to kill herself, if Ram was not willing to take her. In her passion to be with Ram, this was the second time she mentioned suicide. The first was when she resolved that if Ram failed to string Shiva's bow, then rather than live without him, she would terminate her life!

Ram, in vain, tried to pacify her, saying that rendering service to elders and staying back at home was advisable. Finally overwhelmed with grief, unmindful of propriety and her mother-in-law's presence, Sita embraced Ram tightly. Sita had reached her 'breaking point', and was on the verge of losing consciousness with fatigue and grief. Finally, Ram uttered the most endearing words that she had ever heard. He said, 'Give up lamentation and accompany me to the forest. Grief is out of season today. Prepare yourself for the journey to the woods at once.'[86]

Unable to bear seeing his beloved in this condition, Ram perceived that Sita could not be deflected from her purpose. He did not misunderstand her but, on the contrary, instinctively inferred it to be a sign of her honesty and trustworthiness. No one had compelled her to go to the forest, she wanted to go on her own volition, because her love and devotion did not allow her to abandon her husband to a solitary life in exile. Not in a position to refute her arguments, he was convinced that if left her behind against her will, she would not survive. There had always been a powerful mutual understanding between Ram and Sita and he realized how much this meant to her. In a marriage love increases through *voodal*[87] which brings happiness, just as salt brings taste to food, but in excess makes it bitter. Similarly, a little friction in a marriage increases compatibility. Seeing how distraught Sita was, Ram tried to lighten her heart by addressing her in a jovial loving manner, saying, *'Oh, lady with charming hip and loins! Now itself, begin with duties appropriate for living in exile. Oh, Sita! Even a heaven is not a liking to me without your presence.'*[sic][88]

Sita had always given primacy to her husband, insisting that a hut of leaves in his company would be as comfortable as the abode of the gods. Today, on the contrary, the amount of money a man possessed was the deciding factor for the parents of a girl in choosing a groom. Often, the girls themselves wanted their parents to select wealthy husbands. Sita saw women who were more determined than ever to bag a partner who would improve their financial prospects. Character, gentleness, and the good old-fashioned qualities of listening to each other and caring for each other seemed a thing of the past. In case the man selected lacked in material resources, then the girls often demanded that their parents provide for their needs, including a car and other comforts, as they were hesitant to start life with struggles. Sita glanced at an article featuring the life of a successful woman who said that 'the seeds of resilience are planted in the way we process the negative events in our lives'.[89]

Sita never shied away from expressing herself. It was the role of a wife to remind her husband of his dharma if she felt he was straying from the path of righteousness, like she did when she cautioned the *maryada purush* Ram. Sita was not only highly educated in the scriptures, but could also argue coherently and cogently. She did not act superior, but simply tried to reason with Ram and, using the art of persuasion, compelled him to dwell upon what was appropriate.

Sita could foresee danger in Ram's decision to eliminate the rakshasas of Dandaka forest, without any provocation. Seizing an appropriate moment to remind Ram of his dharma, she said, 'Gross injustice will accrue to any in an abstruse way, if his indulgence is enkindled merely by his own desire…'

The characteristics that influence the behavior of offenders are mentioned in the Manusmriti, and abusing others and indulging in women have been identified among the ten desires. Sita continued in her endeavour to dissuade Ram, totally unmindful of the fact that it might create conflict in their relationship. Standing by what she considered her dharma, and combining her knowledge, noble reasoning, logic, and wisdom, she addressed Ram in a friendly manner, expanding on self-gratifying acts. She said:

> *Only three self-gratifications, the definite products of desire, are there: one is speaking fallacious utterances, which itself is worse, and worst than the other two malefic self-gratifications, where the other two are the fascination for other's wife, and the cruelness without enmity ...*[90] *The habit of telling specious words is not there with you … You are conscientious, adherent of truth, and obliging father's orders, and in you virtue and truth, nay everything is established in you ... Oh, dextrous one, all this can possibly be shouldered by one with controlled senses ... That third tendency to torture others' lives without enmity has now suddenly chanced on you. Intending to safeguard the sages you have promised the dwellers in Dandaka forest, oh, valiant one, that you would eliminate demons in a fight ...*[91] [sic]

Sita did not believe this was a wise decision and counselled Ram accordingly. Her words were only prompted by her love for him and not any desire to moralize. She said, 'Always tread along the righteousness with a pure mind, oh, gentle one, and especially in these sagely forests ... you know everything in all the three worlds, in all its nuances...'

Ram gracefully accepted that Sita's words have been said in friendship, good-heartedness, and in his best interest, for uninterested ones, indeed, do not forewarn. Her words of caution were appropriate and seemly. 'Oh, graceful Sita, you are the co-pursuer in dharma with me, hence you are loftier to me than my own life ...' so said Ram to Sita.[92] *This reflected the perfect understanding between the couple, where love had erased ego. Both of them were united in heart, mind, and spirit. One automatically understood what lay in the other's heart.*

A woman who knows how to handle her partner is at a distinct advantage. Sita remembered the time when she was fascinated by the golden deer, but she did not insist or nag Ram. Instead she just said, '*Tradition says that this sort of unruly self-seeking is unbefitting to women, yet that deer's beautiful body is inducing curiosity in me.*'[93] Her words contained neither a demand nor a compulsion for Ram to bring the deer. She left the fulfilment of her desire to the discretion of Ram, who himself was allured by the deer and went to fetch it for his wife, not knowing it was a ruse by the diabolical Ravan to kidnap Sita—an event which lead to the historic battle between good and evil. Ram and Laxman were aided in their attempt to rescue Sita by many powerful creatures and deities. Ravan was defeated and Sita was finally finally saved after much trial and tribulation. However, before the royal couple returned triumphantly to Ayodhya, Ram made some morally questionable decisions. Ram was heady with success, but from here commenced Sita's trial as a woman. This is a story history has repeated in every century, when women, despite being victims, are forced to prove their innocence.

The auspicious moment had arrived for the reuniting of the separated lovers. Sita stood before Ram, her eyes raised hopefully towards his face. A little embarrassed, she hid her face with the edge of her sari.

To everyone's shock, Ram behaved contrary to all expectations. Ram rejected Sita, doubting her chastity. Dispelling any false notion that he had fought for her sake, Ram coldly informed Sita that he had done what ought to be done by a man to defend his wife's honour. In killing Ravan, he had wiped away the insult meted out to him and Sita. He had done it to wipe off the scandalous insinuations on his illustrious dynasty. He said,

> *Sita as you stand before me, doubts arise on your character. You are extremely disagreeable to me, as the flicker of a flame is to one suffering from a poor eye-sight. O Sita! That is why, I am permitting you now to go wherever you like. All these ten directions are open to you, my dear lady! Which noble man, born in an illustrious race, will take back a woman who has lived in another's abode?*

Unbelievable! Sita thought that the communication she shared with her husband had always been perfect, which is why she was deeply hurt when Ram publicly denounced her. Shocked, Sita was overcome with emotions. A depressive stillness prevailed while his words sank in. Words are meant to heal, but Ram's words were like sharp weapons. Words can cement relationships, but the words of her beloved were destroying their bond. Bathed in tears, she kept on staring at him with her eyes wide open like a doe. Although Ram's eyes were fixed on Sita, his heart was being torn apart between a king's fear of public scandal, and a man's love for his wife. This was a dilemma he would face once again, and again he would submit his wife to humiliation on the pretext of upholding dharma.[94]

Hearing this unpalatable speech from her beloved husband, Sita trembled like a tender creeper crushed by the trunk of an elephant. It was difficult to make out whether she was shedding tears of sorrow, or if she was crying out bitterly against an unjust fate. Sita, accustomed to hearing only endearments from her beloved husband, was deeply hurt. She was humiliated and embarrassed at being spoken to in such a harsh manner and denounced in public. It was not in Sita's nature to stand silently when it was time to speak. Feeling betrayed, Ram became the target of her fury. Addressing him in a stammering voice, she said:

> *O valiant Ram! Why are you speaking such harsh words, which are even cruel to hear, like a common man speaking to a common woman? I am not the one in the way you understand me. Have a faith in me. I swear to you by my own character. By the conduct of vulgar woman you cannot cast a slur on the entire race of women. Give up this doubt, if I have*

> *been actually tested (and found trustworthy) by you. O lord! It was not my wilfulness when I came into contact with Ravan. I was helpless. My adverse fate was to blame on that score. My heart, which was subservient to me, was abiding in you. As regards my limbs, what could I do, I was completely helpless being in somebody's power, I had no control over myself. I did not desire it. O bestower of honour! If I could not be fully known to you, in spite of our love having simultaneously grown, and despite our living together, then I am ruined permanently by your ignorance [sic].*

How could Sita convince Ram that it was not her fault' It was a crime of opportunity. Ravan, incited by Surpanakha and mad with lust, looking for the right moment, chose to abduct her. Why was she being made to take responsibility for her abduction by Ravan? Did Ram not know of her sufferings? Did Hanuman not disclose her condition, and the torture she had to undergo at the hands of the rakshasis? Hanuman had seen everything with his own eyes; did he not feel the need to inform Ram?

Sita had preserved her precious chastity, with devotion, scrupulousness, and ferocious care. But her efforts seemed to be futile. Sita, taking command of the situation and her life, turned to Laxman, who himself was highly disturbed. Demanding he light a pyre for her, she said:

> *O Laxman! Create a pile of fire, for me, which is a remedy for this disaster. I no longer wish to survive, smitten as I am with false accusations. I will enter the fire, to obtain the only course appropriate for me, who has been abandoned amidst an assembly of men, by my husband who was not satisfied with my virtues.*[95]

Sita remembered how no one had spoken out on her behalf. There was a hushed silence. The crowd, milling around, had collected to get a glimpse of Sita, not her trial by fire. Feeling sheepish, they all were concerned for her safety. Yet not a soul spoke up. No one cried or tried to convince Ram of his folly as they had done when he had been determined to leave Ayodhya and go into exile. If the consensus was that Sita was an innocent victim, then why was there no protest or uproar? Why did no one cry, 'She's not guilty of any crime! She's innocent!'

Sita proceeded towards the blazing fire and reverentially circumambulated her husband, who did not even raise his head to look at her. Offering salutations to the gods and brahmins, she invoked the fire, witness of whatever happened in the world, to protect her.

Sita, the devout wife, was now being doubted by the very man she worshipped. With dignity, she demanded the fire burn her if she had ever erred in thought, deed, or word. Cupping her palms she said, 'As my heart never moves off from Ram, so may the Fire God, the witness of the world, protect me from all sides. As Ram apprehends me, though of unimpeachable conduct, to be spoilt, let the Fire God the witness for all creatures, protect me from all sides.'

Fearlessly, Sita walked around the Fire God. Her mind free from any hesitation, she plunged into the blazing fire. All the women screamed with horror on seeing this horrific sight. Possibly dreading that one day their chance may come, to be tested! The incident was not only about Sita, but the whole of womankind.[96]

This argument has relevance even today, for however good the equation may be between the married couple, yet women are still disbelieved on the slightest suspicions, whether it is in context of their being sexually assaulted, or on facing matrimonial violence. How did Ram go wrong? Why did he need the gods to intervene when they saw him abandon dharma and resort to adharma? The Fire God, unable to bear the heat of Sita's chastity, emerged to testify on behalf of character.

Restoring Sita to Ram, and testifying to her purity, the Fire God said,

> *Here is your Sita. No sin exists in her. This auspicious lady, whose character has been good, has never been unfaithful. This Sita, who was*

> *fixing her mind upon you and looking on you as her final attainment, was detained in the gynaecium and hidden there. She was guarded by rightful female-demons with horrible intellect. Sita, whose mind was directed towards you, ignored that demon even though she was allured and frightened through various means.*[97]

Ram remained silent, making no acknowledgment of all that had just been said by the gods. Nor did Ram give any reason for his accusations against Sita. A man will believe another man but not his own wife. If Ram needed the gods to testify to Sita's purity and innocence, then it's not surprising the courts in India, through their judgements and implications, brand women as liars. In fact, it was Dashrath who made the important statement to Sita that the ordeal was meant only to publicly demonstrate her chaste character, '*as one passes gold through fire to reveal it's purity*'. But this occurred later and only after Ram himself had announced that the trial was only intended to convince the world of Sita's chastity.

Immediately, in a voluble self-justifying outburst, Ram wanted to clarify to all present that his actions were only aimed at establishing Sita's innocence in the eyes of the world. In his defence Ram said:

> *I also know Sita, the daughter of Janak, who ever revolves in my mind, is undivided in her affection to me. The world would chatter against me, saying that Ram, the son of Dashrath, was really foolish and that his mind was dominated by lust, if I accept Sita without examining her with regard to her chastity.*

Concluding with finality he said, 'Sita, the daughter of Janak, is completely pure in her character, in all the three worlds and can no longer be renounced by me, as a good name cannot be cast aside by a prudent man.[98]

When Sita emerged unscathed from the trial by fire, was it not enough proof to clear the doubts and suspicions of her husband and the public at large? Then why did Ram have reservations about being candid with his own wife when vicious rumours were circulating about Sita? Instead of confronting her about the rumours, he surreptitiously ordered Laxman to abandon Sita in the forest. Many believed that he feared she would question him, for when Ram had asked her to stay behind with her mothers-in-law, Sita had insisted on accompanying him into exile. And when he tried to set her free from all obligations of marriage after killing Ravan, she walked through fire to prove her chastity. Did Rama fear that if he told her about the rumours, she would argue or ask questions which he would not be able to answer? Sita underwent only two trials by fire, but the ordinary woman is doubted every other day and is expected to pass an *agnipariksha* at every turn of her life. Introspecting on this matter, Sita inferred that until the time when men do not have the courage to accept their mistakes, they will continue blaming the 'Sitas' of this world, and every woman will be expected to endure the accusations silently, without a chance for rebuttal.

A harmonious marriage is maintained not by perfect spouses, but through integrity and devotion. Companionship or marriage does not solve existential problems, it just takes care of some of your needs. If you accept, respect, love, include, care for, and take responsibility for each other, it can be a beautiful relationship.[99] On one hand, marriage should be a union one feels ready for and freely seek, but on the other, it is an institution that is socially prescribed and layered with gendered politics. How then do we preserve its sanctity and spirit and protect it from being hijacked by social pressures and expectations?

Widowhood

India is perhaps the only country where widowhood, in addition to being a personal status, exists as a social institution. What happens when a loving relationship is turned upside down due to the death of a spouse? It is worse for women, especially in India, who not only have to deal with the loss and the pain, but also with losing their financial anchor. Being widowed in India can be a living death. Indian widows are often financially destitute, marginalized, and socially rejected as *manhoos* by the very network of friends and relatives who should stand by a woman as a support system so that she can restart her life with renewed strength and purpose. In India, widowhood tends to bode a grim fate, in contrast with the developed world where women have more choices. Sita discovered that the world had moved far ahead, and remembered the time when Ravan had ordered Vidyujjihva to use his conjuring trick to fool her into believing that Ram was dead.

After giving a gory description of the massacre, Ravan summoned Vidyujjihva to ring the head of Ram. Sita distraught and shocked, burst into uncontrollable tears. She examined the illusionary head carefully, and recognised Ram's eyes, facial complexion, hair, expanse of his forehead and the beautiful jewel worn on the top of his head. Her soul was consumed with sorrow to the point of death.

Trembling, the miserable girl fell on the ground, like a plantain tree cut at the roots. Regaining consciousness, she mourned the death of her husband. How could Lord Brahma, without thinking of the repercussions, shower a boon on a monster like Ravan. Addressing what she thought was the severed head of Ram, she said,

> *O, the long-armed Ram! The pursuer of a strong will! Alas, you have been killed! I have become a witness to your last fate. I have been made a widow. It is said that the early death of a husband is the misfortune of*

> *a wife. You, having good conduct, have preceded me in death. Even you who were actually intent on protecting me, fallen in great affliction and immersed in an ocean of grief, have been killed by the enemies ... O, Ram! Take me also with you.*

For Sita, life had no meaning without her beloved Ram. She wanted to put an end to her torment and longed for death—a death which would release her from this fire of separation in which she was burning. Sita, turning towards Ravan, pleaded with him, 'O Ravan! Unite the wife with the husband and, without delay, arrange to kill me right at the head of Ram. Thus, you will perform an admirable and auspicious act.'

Unexpectedly, without any warning, an emissary of Ravan appeared on the scene, calling the king for some urgent work. To fulfil his kingly duties, Ravan rushed off with him. Lo and behold! The moment Ravan left the garden of Ashoka, the severed head and bow also vanished.[100]

A widow dying with her husband is not her personal choice, but only illustrative of her succumbing to social pressure. In ancient India, there was no custom of women being burnt on their husband's funeral pyre. Did not the wives of King Dashrath survive his death? However, being a widow often meant loss in stature, and there are many instances in the epic which portray their piteous condition. For example, when Ravan was about to kill Madhu, his wife Kumbhinasi fell at Ravan's feet pleading, *'Do not kill my husband. Widowhood is the worst misfortune that can befall a woman. Widowhood is a woman's greatest fear. Indeed, there is nothing in this world more terrible than being a widow.*[101]

Sita was horrified to see culturally sanctioned practices, even in this day and age, holding the wife accountable for her own widowhood. Sita had questioned traditional wisdom in that she considered herself as being an exemplary wife, so she could not accept the fact that Ram had predeceased her. She had blamed herself for her husband's death, since she thought he had died trying to rescue her from the clutches of Ravan. Sita had said, *'I shall follow',* an allusion to the practice of *anugamana,*[102] or going after, i.e., when a wife followed her husband shortly after his death. This is in variance with the infamous *sahagamana* or sati. It is pertinent to point out that there is no mention of *sahagamana* whatsoever in vedic literature or the *Dharmasutras.* Comprehensive data is lacking on how the custom of sati, in which the wife lies, or is usually forcibly made to lie on the burning pyre of the deceased husband, became popular amongst the so-called higher castes of Indian society, despite the fact that Brahmins originally condemned the practice. Over the centuries this custom died out in the south only to become prevalent in the north, particularly in the states of Rajasthan and Bengal. Thankfully, this dehumanising and barbaric social evil has been outlawed,[103] for it had degraded into a practice where greedy in-laws and relatives of the widow, having an eye on the property of her deceased husband, would build up a fervor and push her into the burning funeral pyre. The last sati in India occurred in 1987, when a woman was burnt to death on her husband's pyre. It is debatable whether she did it voluntarily or was forcibly thrust into the funeral pyre.[104] It may also be possible that the covetous relatives took advantage of her depressed and compromised state of mind, and planted the idea of suicide in her distraught mind.

Sita wondered how the public burning of Roop Kanwar was different from the thousands of married women burnt alive in their matrimonial homes with the tacit consent of society, on the pretext of a gas burst or the excuse that she fell in the well while drawing out water.

In India, a woman is usually identified either through her father or through her husband. On the death of her husband, her life becomes a nightmare, especially for those women living in rural areas. After the death of a spouse, women are often forced to adhere to strict codes of dress. In some communities the widow is forced to be in a constant state of mourning, wearing a white sari for the rest of her life. Her diet is downsized (made vegetarian), and in more extreme cases she is made to shave her head. Social norms restrict women's right to property, and remarriage is not encouraged. In sharp contrast, widowed men in India are not subject to the same restrictions, and are encouraged to remarry. Was not Surpanakha, a widow, punished for her display of sexuality, which was considered harmful to society? If a woman's husband expires, does that mean she has no sexual needs or that she should not be allowed to have a healthy sexual life? Sex is a basic need and it is only natural for a mature woman to crave a sexual touch every night she goes to sleep.

In many parts of India, a widow is still considered inauspicious, and it is believed that even her sight or touch can bring bad luck to a person. She is often expected to be confined to the home, without any interaction with the outside world. In many communities, when the husband dies, his widow is immediately made to discard the symbols of marriage such as *sindoor* (vermillion on the forehead), *mangalsutra* (necklace), toe rings, bangles etc. She is also forbidden from enhancing her appearance with makeup, jewellery, or any ornate apparel. It is the custom in several communities to lock up widows for months in a dark room after their husband's death. In some communities, if she does not have children, she is forcibly married off to the deceased husband's brother to provide an heir. In Punjab, among the predominantly agricultural tribes, there is a custom, called *karewa*, which has legal sanction.[105] The brother marries his brother's widow in a highly informal ceremony by *chaadar andaazi* or plain cohabitation *(karewa).*

Despite laws being enacted, widows are seldom allowed nor are they in a position to exercise their right to maintenance and property. Prevailing regressive customs strip her of all rights and dignity, making it inevitable for a large number of widows from lower middle-class families to find escape in the towns of Vrindavan and Varanasi. These towns are known to be havens for widows, where they coexist in solidarity, confining themselves to a life of prayer and solitude.

Widows in different age groups face specific challenges pertaining to loss of adolescence, access to employment, skill development, property rights, shelter, access to healthcare etc. According to the Census of India 2011,[106] child widows in the age group of 10–19 years comprise 0.45 per cent of the total number of widows, while 9 per cent are in the age group of 20–39 years, 32 per cent are in the age group of 40–59 years, and 58 per cent are above 60 years. It is indeed a matter of concern that India has 1.94 lakh child widows despite the Prohibition of Child Marriage Act, 2006. The plight of widows being beaten, stigmatised, declared a *dain* or witch, and shunned from the village has been well documented,especially in Andhra Pradesh, Assam, Bihar, Chhattisgarh, Gujarat, Jharkhand, Karnataka, Madhya Pradesh, Maharashtra, Orissa, and West Bengal. Women are hacked, hanged, or burnt to death. Their families don't escape either, and the heads of their children are smashed on rocks. Women who escape death are subjected to different forms of inhuman treatment, such as being forced to eat human excrement, or drink urine.

Sita read about the Dalit woman who was burnt and branded as a witch, with her son witnessing the barbaric assault. The fifteen-year-old boy said that the mob forced his mother to eat faeces, and paraded her around after stripping her naked. He said, 'They thrust hot coal in her hands and also hurt her in other places … they refused to listen to her pleas for mercy.'[107] A hurried funeral was followed by the *khap* panchayat deciding that no police action should be taken after a fine of Rs 2,500 was paid by the accused—one of whom was the nephew of the deceased woman's husband. It was left to a distant relative and social worker to struggle to register a case with the unwilling police. It's not surprising that often, out of sheer despondency, the widow may resort to committing suicide.

At the root of many accusations of witchcraft is not superstition, as is the common misconception. Fundamentally, it is socio-economic factors that are the driving force for this form of violence. The only way for a male relative to get his hands on the property, and to prevent it from passing on to the widow, is to label her a witch. Sometimes it is because the woman has rejected a male relative or a neighbour's advances, so he wants to stigmatise her in the name of revenge. Sometimes, it is even for political reasons, as a method to thwart the woman from exercising her rights. There are cases where members of upper castes have wanted to grab the land distributed to Dalit or tribal families. When a widow is denied her property rights, she is browbeaten and brainwashed by her relatives, and in sheer desperation she often resorts to ending her life on her husband's cremation pyre.[108] In India there are thousands of widows struggling each day against economic hardships, violence, and neglect. While little public concern is focused on them, the media tends to highlight aberrant incidents of sati.

Since a woman is conferred social status through a man, in his absence she becomes a non-entity, and suffers a social death. A widow is expected to live by herself, and withdraw from society, being regarded as an 'evil eye', and a 'purveyor of ill fortune'. A large number of women, having been widowed at an early age and living on the brink of starvation, dare not even think of expressing their sexuality. They are expected to spend the remainder of their life in the memory of their late husband and God. Widow remarriage is rare, and they are more likely to be judged than their male counterparts if they embark on a new relationship. A widow, in vernacular language, is often referred to as *rand*, while the word for prostitute is *randi*. This affirms cultural anxieties about the sexuality of women, especially of young widowed women, who are perceived to pose a danger to society. Hence, she has to be 'neutered' and 'un-sexed.' Young widows were considered sexually dangerous and had the potential to disrupt, pollute, and desecrate the dead husband's lineage, and therefore she had to be emasculated of all her sexuality. There was also another objective in treating a widow this way. This was to prevent her from making any demands on her husband's property or from asking for a share in the parental property. In a cloistered life, the property was of no use, and even if she had property, she was not permitted to administer it or draw benefits from it. It cannot be said that that this cruel practice existed universally in all parts of India. Since the Brahmins were the custodians of morality, this was more strictly applied by them than by other communities where property and patriarchal values were not in vogue. Certainly it found no acceptance among the socially lower categories who had to survive on their labour. They could not afford to maintain a non-productive widow in the family for long, and nor was there physical space for such secluded surroundings. Studies among the lower castes found that while in non-manual jobs the number of widows was smaller than non-widows, in agricultural and outdoor field activities the number was equal.[109]

Sita could perceive a change in mindset, but the pace was too sluggish. She applauded the efforts of Ishwar Chandra Vidyasagar,[110] a leading nineteenth century social reformer, who argued for social change and improvement in women's status. He urged the British to pass legislation to allow widows to remarry and, to support his request, collected almost 1000 signatures and sent his petition to the Indian Legislative Council. This resulted in The Hindu Widow Remarriage Act being passed in 1856. Like Vidyasagar, even in modern India there are harbingers of hope in the form of people like Bindeshwar Pathak, the founder of Sulabh International, an organizations which arranges events for widows so that they can participate and enjoy cultural activities like other women. For the past five years Sulabh has been celebrating festivals like Holi, Diwali, and Christmas with the widows from the ashrams of Vrindavan, challenging misogynistic conservative practices, and infusing women with a different level of enthusiasm.

Sita, on reading Sheryl Sandberg's post, felt that there was a stark contrast between the status of widows in India and those in the contemporary western world. In the immediate aftermath of her husband's death, Sheryl Sandberg said she got help from Facebook users, whom she didn't know. She said, 'Strangers posted, "I've lost this person. I've lost a twin. I lost a baby. I lost a husband." Rather than feel so isolated, I felt connected to all of these people who were experiencing loss, and breaking the isolation really helped.'[111] Sheryl said that it actually helped, and although it did not take away the grief, it took away a great deal of the isolation from their lives.[112] Although things are changing, India still has a long way to go to protect the basic human rights of women who have lost their husbands, who have been through a heartbreaking tragedy, and are subjected to alienation for no fault of their own.

Endnotes

1. K.R. Srinivas Iyengar, *Sitayana: Epic of the Earth-born* (Madras: Samata Books, 1987), pp.80-81.
2. Hindu dharma prescribes four basic pursuits of life, called the *Purusharthas:* Dharma or duty, Artha or wealth, Kama or desire, and Moksha or renunciation.
3. Similar to traditional Christian ceremonies where the father of the bride escorts his daughter down the aisle before handing her over to her groom.
4. Desiraju Hanumanta Rao and K.M.K. Murthy, trans., *Valmiki Ramayana,* 2:118:37–38, https://valmikiramayan.net/utf8/ayodhya/sarga118/ayodhya_118_frame.htm
5. *Swayam* in Sanskrit means 'oneself' and '*var*' means groom.
6. The *Manusmriti* describes the following eight types of marriages:

i. *Brahma Vivah* - Considered the best form of marriage in which the boy and girl belong to the same caste, where the boy should have completed his *Brahmacharya* ashram (education).

ii. *Daiva Vivah*– Unable to find a suitable boy, the girl's family marry her to a priest.

iii. *Arsha Vivah*–The groom gives a gift (a cow and a pair of bulls) to the girl's family since they are unable to afford the expenses of the marriage.

iv. *Prajapatya Vivah* - Similar to *Brahma vivah*, except here instead of *Kanyadaan*, the bride's father hands over protection of his daughter to the groom during the *Panigrahan* ritual.

v. *Gandharva Vivah* - The girl and boy marry of their own choice.

vi. *Asura Vivah* - The boy, not being of the same stature as the bride, gives gifts to the bride's family in order to gain their approval.

vii. *Rakshasa Vivah* - Where force is involved in solemnization of the marriage.

viii. *Paishacha Vivah* -Where during solemnization of the marriage, the girl was not in her senses due to unsoundness of mind, intoxication or any other reason.

7. According to the Hindu calendar, a month contains two fortnights called *paksh*, literally meaning 'side'. One fortnight is the bright, waxing half where the moon size grows till becomes a full moon. The other half is the darkening, waning fortnight which ends in the new moon. *Vivah panchami,* also known as *Ram vivah utsav* falls on the fifth day of the *shukla paksh* or waxing phase of the moon in the month of *Margashirsha*, which usually is in November–December.
8. The precession (caused by the gradual rotation of the Earth's axis) of the equinoxes is the period of time that it takes the Earth's axis to pass through one complete cycle of the zodiac. It takes the planet 72 years to pass through one degree of the zodiac and 25,920 years to complete one full circle of 360 degrees. One half of the journey takes 12,960 years and covers the four yugas. The Satya Yuga lasts 5184 years. The Treta Yuga lasts 3888 years. The Dwapara Yuga lasts 2592 years. The Kali Yuga lasts 1296 years. These four yugas taken together come to a total of 12,960 years; http://isha.sadhguru.org/blog/yoga-meditation/science-of-yoga/kali-yuga-end-lies-ahead/

9. R.C. Prasad, ed and trans., *Shri Ramcharitamanasa* or *The Holy Lake of the Acts of Rama* (New Delhi: Motilal Banarsidass Publishers Pvt. Ltd), 1:257, 258.
10. Dean Nelson, 'Groom Shot Dead at Wedding by Uncle's Stray Celebratory Bullet', *The Telegraph,* February 19, 2010,http://www.telegraph.co.uk/news/worldnews/asia/india/7271134/Groom-shot-dead-at-wedding-by-uncles-stray-celebratory-bullet.html
11. Raja Rammohan Roy, born in 1772 into a Bengali Hindu family, is known as the 'Father of the Indian Renaissance'. A great patriot, scholar and humanist, he founded the Brahmo Samaj at Kolkata in 1828. A vociferous social reformer, he organised a movement against the inhuman custom of sati, in which a widow was compelled to sacrifice herself in her husband's funeral pyre. Due to his efforts this practice was banned by an Act passed in 1829 during the time of Lord William Bentinck. Rammohan Roy advocated widow remarriage and giving daughters equal rights to that of sons over parental property. He raised his voice against child marriage and polygamy and promoted women's education.
12. The National Family Health Survey (2005–06) reveals that almost half (46 per cent) of the women get married before the legal minimum age of 18. The median age of women at the time of their first marriage is 17.2 years. Men get married more than six years later, at a median age of 23.4 years.
13. 'The State of the World's Children: Maternal and Newborn Health', Report prepared by the United Nations Children's Fund, 2009.
14. Sagnik Chowdhury, '30% Women Married Under Age 18', *The Indian Express,* May 31, 2016, http://indianexpress.com/article/explained/child-marriage-women-india-census-data-2011-2826398/
15. 'Report on Prevention of Child Marriages in the State of Karnataka', report prepared by the core committee headed by Justice Shivraj Patil, for UNICEF and the Department of Women and Child Development, 2011.
16. Vishaka and Others vs the State of Rajasthan and Others, Writ petition (Crl) Nos.666-670 of 1992.
17. The third day of *shukla paksh* (bright fortnight) in the month of *Vaisakha*, in the Hindu calendar. Every year since then, this day is celebrated as *vivah panchami.* Since the word 'akshaya' means imperishable or non-diminishing, people believe that the purchase of a valuable metal, like gold, will lead to an increase in one's wealth, and any new venture started on this day will grow forever.
18. Prakash Bhandari, 'Std VIII Barmer boy father at 15', *The Times of India,* May 8, 2008.
19. 'A Study on Child Marriage in India: Situational Analysis in Three States', study conducted by the National Institute of Public Cooperation and Child Development and the Centre for Social Research, 2008, http://www.nipccd-earchive.wcd.nic.in/sites/default/files/PDF/A%20Study%20on%20Child%20Marriage%20in%20India%20-%20three%20states.pdf
20. Shruti Tomar, 'Sarpanch Fired for Bid to Marry Minor', *Hindustan Times,* December 28, 2017, http://www.htsyndication.com/htsportal/ht-mumbai/article/sarpanch-fired-for-bid-to-marry-minor/25060981

21. Ramesh vs Rajpati, F.A.O Appeal No.30 of 2001.
22. Shabnam (Mst.) vs Mohd.Shafiq, D.B. Civil Misc Appeal No.539 of 1996.
23. IPC S.376 Exception 2.—Sexual intercourse or sexual acts by a man with his own wife, the wife not being under fifteen years of age, is not rape.
24. Chaturvedi Dwarka Prasad Sharma, trans., *Srimad Valmiki Ramayana,* (Allahabad: Ramnarayana Lal Publisher and Bookseller, 1927), 7:26:51, 52 (This version is originally in Hindi. The English translation is the author's own).
25. Ibid, 7:26:56.
26. Independent Thought vs The Union of India and Another Writ Petiton (Civil) No. 382 of 2013.
27. Ibid.
28. 'A Statistical Analysis of Child Marriage in India Based on Census 2011', report prepared by Young Lives and the National Commission for Protection of Child Rights, 2017.
29. Ranjana Kumari, 'The Shocking Realities of Child Marriage in India', Gender Matters (blog), project from the Centre of Social Research, New Delhi, June 13, 2016, http://gendermatters.in/2016/06/child-marriage-in-india/
30. 'Uttar Pradesh Police Book Mathura Kathavachak after Minor Wife Files Rape Case against Him', *Firstpost,* November 6, 2017, http://www.firstpost.com/india/uttar-pradesh-police-book-mathura-kathavachak-after-minor-wife-files-rape-case-against-him-4194915.html
31. J.S. Ifthekar, 'The Marriage Trap', *The Hindu,* March 7, 2013, http://www.thehindu.com/news/cities/Hyderabad/the-marriage-trap/article4484790.ece
32. It is estimated that there are about 3 million sex workers in the country, of whom 40 per cent are children. Almost 15 per cent of the sex workers enter the profession before the age of fifteen, and 25 per cent between fifteen and eighteen years.
33. 'National Plan of Action for Children, 2016', report prepared by the Ministry of Women and Child Development, 2016.
34. Measles, Mumps, and Rubella Diseases vaccine.
35. Infant Mortality Rate.
36. The Child Marriage Restraint Act, 1929 has been repealed and The Prohibition of Child Marriage Act, 2006 has been enacted.
37. R.C. Prasad, ed and trans., *Shri Ramcharitamanasa or The Holy Lake of the Acts of Rama,* (Motilal Banarsidass Publishers Pvt. Ltd), 1:325; Desiraju Hanumanta Rao and K.M.K. Murthy, trans., *Valmiki Ramayana,* 1:74:5,7a, https://valmikiramayan.net/utf8/baala/sarga74/bala_74_frame.htm
38. Desiraju Hanumanta Rao and K.M.K. Murthy, trans., *Valmiki Ramayana,* 1:73:16, https://valmikiramayan.net/utf8/baala/sarga73/bala_73_frame.htm
39. Summarized in sarga 72 and 73 of Book 1 of *Valmiki Ramayana* (Desiraju Hanumanta Rao and K.M.K. Murthy, trans., *Valmiki Ramayana,* VR 1:72–73) and in verses 312 and 322 of Book 1 of *Shri Ramcharitamanasa* (R.C. Prasad, ed and trans., *Shri Ramcharitamanasa or The Holy Lake of the Acts of Rama,* [Motilal Banarsidass Publishers Pvt. Ltd], 1:312, 322).

40. K.R. Srinivas Iyengar, *Sitayana: Epic of the Earth-born* (Madras: Samata Books, 1987), p.84.
41. R.C. Prasad, ed and trans., *Shri Ramcharitamanasa* or *The Holy Lake of the Acts of Rama*, (New Delhi: Motilal Banarsidass Publishers Pvt. Ltd, 1990), 1:333:3-4.
42. Ashok KM, 'Forcing Husband to Get Separated From His Parents, Amounts to "Cruelty": SC', *LiveLaw.in,* October 6, 2016, http://www.livelaw.in/forcing-husband-get-separated-parents-amounts-cruelty-sc
43. R.C. Prasad, ed and trans., *Shri Ramcharitamanasa or The Holy Lake of the Acts of Rama,* (New Delhi: Motilal Banarsidass Publishers Pvt. Ltd, 1990), 1:333:4.
44. Sri Satya Sai Baba, *Ramkatha Rasvahini,* Chapter 7 (d) Winning Sita, http://vahini.org/ramakatha/chapter7d.html
45. Charu WaliKhanna, *Laws on Violence Against Women*, (New Delhi: Serials Publications, 2009), p. 115.
46. Prawes Lama and Manas Sharma, '715 Dowry Related Deaths in Delhi, but No Convictions in Last Four Years', *Hindustan Times,* August 14, 2017,http://www.hindustantimes.com/delhi-news/715-dowry-related-deaths-in-delhi-but-no-convictions-in-last-four-years/story-Y7Voo4ODJ6kNwSi5fFD2yI.html
47. Sowmya Rajendran, '" I Want a Helicopter at My Wedding": The Latest "Neeya Naana" Show on Dowry Shouldn't Shock You', *The News Minute,* March 20, 2017, http://www.thenewsminute.com/article/i-want-helicopter-my-wedding-latest-neeya-naana-show-dowry-shouldnt-shock-you-58924
48. 'The Unsung Heroes of Swachh Bharat: No Toilet, No Marriage', *Sulabh Swachh Bharat,* November 13-19, 2017.
49. Prawesh Lama and Manas Sharma, 'Dowry Cases Double in 5 Years', *Hindustan Times,* August 14, 2017, http://www.htsyndication.com/htsportal/hindustan-times/article/dowry-cases-double-in-5-years/22376293
50. Rajesh Sharma and ors. vs State of UP and Anr., Criminal Appeal No.1265 [Arising out of Special Leave Petition (Crl.) No. 2013], 2017, https://barandbench.com/wp-content/uploads/2017/07/6593_2017_Judgement_27-Jul-2017-watermark.pdf
51. 'Crime in India, 2016', report published by the National Crime Records Bureau under the Ministry of Home Affairs, 2016, http://ncrb.gov.in/StatPublications/CII/CII2016/pdfs/NEWPDFs/Crime%20in%20India%20-%202016%20Complete%20PDF%20291117.pdf
52. Atul Thakur, 'Three Googlies Make India's Crime Statistics Deceptive', *The Times of India,* December 25, 2017, https://timesofindia.indiatimes.com/india/three-googlies-make-indias-crime-statistics-deceptive/articleshow/62235951.cms
53. Deeptiman Tiwary, 'Why Crime Data Does Not Always Add Up to the Complete Picture', *The Indian Express,* December 6, 2017, http://indianexpress.com/article/explained/ncrb-crime-records-why-crime-data-do-not-always-add-up-to-the-complete-picture-4969741/
54. Ibid.

55. As observed by the High Court of Bombay in the case of The Secretary, All India Biodynamic and Organic Farming Association vs The Principal Secretary to the Government of Maharashtra and Others [2006 (3) Bom CR867].
56. Nyayadhar vs the Union of India Ministry of Home Affairs and Ors., Supreme Court Writ Petition (Criminal) No. 156 of 2017.
57. P.V. Kane, *History of Dharamasastra*, Vol.3 (Poona: Bhandarkar Oriental Research Institute), p. 777.
58. Amartya Sen, 'Many Faces of Gender Inequality', *Frontline,* vol. 18, issue 22 (2001), https://www.sas.upenn.edu/~dludden/MANY%20FACES%20OF%20GENDER%20INEQUALITY.htm
59. 406. Punishment for criminal breach of trust. Whoever commits criminal breach of trust shall be punished with imprisonment of either description for a term which may extend to three years, or with fine, or with both.
60. Richa Taneja, 'Jharkhand Groom Demands Dowry, Bride's Family Teaches Him a Lesson He Will Never Forget', *NDTV Every Life Counts Campaign,* April 28, 2017, http://everylifecounts.ndtv.com/jharkhand-groom-demands-dowry-brides-family-teaches-lesson-will-never-forget-12645
61. 'Kota Bride Calls Off Wedding After Dowry Demand', *The Indian Express,* December 5, 2017, http://indianexpress.com/article/india/kota-bride-calls-off-wedding-after-dowry-demand-4968920/
62. R.C. Prasad, ed and trans., *Shri Ramcharitamanasa or The Holy Lake of the Acts of Rama*, (New Delhi: Motilal Banarsidass Publishers Pvt. Ltd, 1990), 1:348:2.
63. 'Unsung heroes', *Sulabh Swachh Bharat,* November 13-19, 2017, p.25.
64. Rachel Hosie, 'Love Potions Could Exist Within Ten Years, Scientist Claims', *The Independent,* April 14, 2017, http://www.independent.co.uk/life-style/love-sex/love-potions-exist-ten-years-scientist-anders-sandberg-oxford-a7683771.html (quoted in *The Times of India*, 15 April 2017).
65. Desiraju Hanumanta Rao and K.M.K. Murthy, trans., *Valmiki Ramayana*, 2:117-118, https://valmikiramayan.net/
66. Paula Richman, ed.*Many Ramayanas: The Diversity of a Narrative Tradition in South Asia,* (Berkeley: University of California Press, 1991), p.83, http://publishing.cdlib.org/ucpressebooks/view?docId=ft3j49n8h7;chunk.id=0;doc.view=print
67. Desiraju Hanumanta Rao and K.M.K. Murthy, trans., *Valmiki Ramayana,* 5:11:34, https://valmikiramayan.net/utf8/sundara/sarga11/sundara_11_frame.htm
68. Ibid, 5:9:61,62, shttps://valmikiramayan.net/utf8/sundara/sarga9/sundara_9_frame.htm
69. Ibid, 5:9:58, https://valmikiramayan.net/utf8/sundara/sarga9/sundara_9_frame.htm
70. Ibid, 5:9:68, https://valmikiramayan.net/utf8/sundara/sarga9/sundara_9_frame.htm
71. Ibid, 5:9:70, https://valmikiramayan.net/utf8/sundara/sarga9/sundara_9_frame.htm

72. Sagar, a benevolent king started to perform the 'Ashvamedha Yagna' in order to establish his superiority. Lord Indra, jealous of his success, stole the horse. On hearing this, Sagar commanded his 60,000 sons to search for it, They found the horse tied close to Sage Kapila. The horse had been tied there by Indra to mislead them.Under this mistaken impression, the sons of Sagar accused the sage of stealing the horse. The sage, who was in deep meditation, opened his eyes spewing fire, and all 60,000 were burnt to ashes instantly. The sage informed King Sagar that the only way for his sons to attain salvation was purification by the sacred waters of Ganga, by bringing her from the heaven to earth. Sagar gave his throne to his sole surviving grandson, Amshuman, and went to the forest to pray, but died before his prayers could be answered. Then Amshuman, relinquishing the throne in favour of his son Dalip, continued penance from where Sagar had left off. After sometime, Dalip also went to the forests to pray for Ganga, but he too died. He was childless and had left behind his two wives in Ayodhya, who were determined to bear a child. The wives called a sage to conduct a yagna which would yield the magic potion to make women pregnant. One wife drank the magic potion in the capacity of a wife, while the other made love to her pretending to be her husband; and from this union a child was born. Since no male had been involved in the creation of the child, it had flesh and blood, but no bones. The two queens took the mass of flesh to Kapila who, through *siddha* or yogic powers, created bones and nerves for the child. This child, known as Bhagiratha, was instrumental in bringing Ganga down to earth. There is another version that the queens took this mass of flesh and left it on the banks of River Sarayu, where it was spotted by Sage Ashtavakra, whose body was bent in eight places. Accidentally stepping on the mass of flesh, he thought someone was playing a practical joke on him. Cursing the mass, he said that whoever was mocking him would burn to death, but if this was genuinely a deformed child, then they would become normal.
73. Kaviraj Kunja Lal Bhishagratna, *An English Translation of The Sushruta Samhita*, vol.2 (Varanasi: Chowkhamba Sanskrit Series Office, 1963), p. 132.
74. Ruth Vanita, 'Born to Two Mothers, the Hero Bhagiratha', *Manushi,* issue.146, http://www.manushi-india.org/pdfs_issues/PDF%20146/Pg%2022-33.pdf
75. Section 377 of the IPC. Whoever voluntarily has carnal intercourse against the order of nature with any man, woman or animal, shall be punished with imprisonment for life, or with imprisonment of either description for a term which may extend to 10 years, and shall also be liable to fine.

    The Delhi High Court, had in July 2009, had de-criminalised consensual homosexual acts in private by declaring as unconstitutional a part of Section 377 of the IPC that criminalises unnatural sex, saying 'the section denies a gay person a right to full personhood...' The Supreme Court chose to reverse the High Court's order in December 2013, saying it was for the legislature to take a call on the desirability of the controversial provision.
76. Ekta Handa, 'India, US Vote Against UNHRC Resolution to Denounce Death

Penalty for Homosexuality', *India Today,* October 3, 2017, http://indiatoday.intoday.in/story/unhcr-resolution-death-penalty-homosexuality-india-us-vote-against/1/1060790.html

77. Max Ehrenfreund, 'The One Supreme Court Paragraph on Love that Gay Marriage Supporters Will Never Forget', *The Washington Post,* June 26, 2015, https://www.washingtonpost.com/news/wonk/wp/2015/06/26/the-one-supreme-court-paragraph-on-love-that-gay-marriage-supporters-will-never-forget/?utm_term=.88b8fc69ad6b
78. Arun Janardhanan, 'Perumal Murugan: I Didn't Know Who My Enemy Was, Didn't Know Whom to Testify Against', *The Indian Express,* August 22, 2016, http://indianexpress.com/article/india/india-news-india/perumal-murugan-criminal-case-tamil-writer-madras-high-court-2989333/ Tamil author Perumal Murugan declared himself 'dead'.The English translation of his controversial novel *Maadhorubaagan*, translated to *One Part Woman*, won the Sahitya Akademi's Translation Prize in 2016. In January 2015, he announced that he was giving up writing after he came under attack by those who claimed that his novel *Madhurobhaagan*, first published in 2010, was blasphemous. He said on his Facebook page that *'Perumal Murugan the writer is dead. As he is no God, he is not going to resurrect himself. He also has no faith in rebirth. An ordinary teacher, he will live as P. Murugan. Leave him alone.'*
79. 'Debunking Relationship Myths: An Interview With John Gottman and Julie Schwartz Gottman', *Huffington Post,* February 6, 2014, https://www.huffingtonpost.com/omega-institute-for-holistic-studies/debunking-relationship-my_b_5413323.html?utm_hp_ref=gps-for-the-soul&ir=GPS+for+the+Soul
80. 'A Wife Should Be Like Goddess Sita: Bombay HC', *The Times of India,* May 8, 2012, https://timesofindia.indiatimes.com/city/mumbai/A-wife-should-be-like-goddess-Sita-Bombay-HC/articleshow/13054421.cms
81. Rahul Karmakar, 'Fighting For Rights in a Patriarchal Naga Society', *Hindustan Times*, August 11, 2017.
82. The 73rd and 74th constitutional amendments were introduced in the Indian Parliament in September, 1991 in the form of two separate bills: the 72nd Amendment Bill for rural local bodies (also known as panchayats) and the 73rd Amendment Bill for municipalities. The amendments were then officially enacted through the issuance of government notifications—the Constitution (73rd Amendment) Act, 1992 (commonly referred to as the Panchayati Raj Act) which came into effect on April 24, 1993, and the Constitution (74th Amendment) Act, 1992 (the Nagarpalika Act), which came into effect on June 1, 1993.

    This landmark amendment to the Constitution led to women's political empowerment, by providing of one-third of all seats in all panchayats at all levels for women, with the reservation for women applying to the seats reserved for Dalits and Adivasis as well.
83. Desiraju Hanumanta Rao and K.M.K. Murthy, trans., *Valmiki Ramayana*, 2:24, 26, 27, 60; R.C. Prasad, ed and trans., *Shri Ramcharitamanasa* or *The Holy Lake*

of the Acts of Rama, (New Delhi: Motilal Banarsidass Publishers Pvt. Ltd, 1990) 2:60:1–4; and K.R. Srinivas Iyengar, *Sitayana: Epic of the Earth-born* (Madras: Samata Books, 1987), p.138.

84. R.C. Prasad, ed and trans., *Shri Ramcharitamanasa* or *The Holy Lake of the Acts of Rama*, (New Delhi: Motilal Banarsidass Publishers Pvt. Ltd, 1990), 2:62–63.
85. Desiraju Hanumanta Rao and K.M.K. Murthy, trans., *Valmiki Ramayana,* 2:29, https://valmikiramayan.net/utf8/ayodhya/sarga29/ayodhya_29_frame.htm; and R.C. Prasad, ed and trans., *Shri Ramcharitamanasa or The Holy Lake of the Acts of Rama,* (New Delhi: Motilal Banarsidass Publishers Pvt. Ltd, 1990), 2:63.
86. Desiraju Hanumanta Rao and K.M.K. Murthy, trans., *Valmiki Ramayana,* 2:30 https://valmikiramayan.net/utf8/ayodhya/sarga30/ayodhya_30_frame.htm; and R.C. Prasad, ed and trans., *Shri Ramcharitamanasa or The Holy Lake of the Acts of Rama,* (New Delhi: Motilal Banarsidass Publishers Pvt. Ltd, 1990), 2 :68.
87. The Thiruvoodal Festival is enacted by Shiv and Parvati to convey social truths to their devotees, and takes place inside the compound of the Arunachaleswarar Temple. Celebrated on January 16th (the movement of the sun from the southern to the northern hemisphere), the word 'Thiru' signifies deity, sacred, holy, and wealth, and the word 'Voodal' actually means 'tiff' or 'petty quarrel', and represents the friction between the male and female in a love relationship. The distinguishing mark of *voodal* is that it should arise and stay only for a brief period and not be prolonged, as its focus is the bliss when the *voodal* is withdrawn.
88. Desiraju Hanumanta Rao and K.M.K. Murthy, trans., *Valmiki Ramayana,* 2:30:42, https://valmikiramayan.net/utf8/ayodhya/sarga30/ayodhya_30_frame.htm
89. Kif Leswing, 'Sheryl Sandberg just Spoke About Her Husband's Death in Public For the First Time in an Emotional Speech', *Business Insider*, May 15, 2016, http://www.businessinsider.in/Sheryl-Sandberg-just-spoke-about-her-husbands-death-in-public-for-the-first-time-in-an-emotional-speech/articleshow/52274349.cms
90. Hunting, sleeping in the daytime, abusing others, indulgence in women, three artistic impulses music, (dance and drama), and wasteful wandering are among the ten desires, according to the *Manu Smriti.*
91. Desiraju Hanumanta Rao and K.M.K. Murthy, trans., *Valmiki Ramayana,* 3:9, https://valmikiramayan.net/utf8/aranya/sarga9/aranya_9_frame.htm
92. Ibid 3:10:21b, c https://valmikiramayan.net/utf8/aranya/sarga10/aranya_10_frame.htm
93. Ibid, 3:43:21, https://valmikiramayan.net/utf8/aranya/sarga43/aranya_43_frame.htm
94. R.C. Prasad, ed and trans., *Shri Ramcharitamanasa* or *The Holy Lake of the Acts of Rama*, (New Delhi: Motilal Banarsidass Publishers Pvt. Ltd, 1990), 6:60B:6.
95. Desiraju Hanumanta Rao and K.M.K. Murthy, trans., *Valmiki Ramayana,* 6:116:1–19, https://valmikiramayan.net/utf8/yuddha/sarga116/yuddha_116_frame.htm
96. Ibid, 6:116:23–36, https://valmikiramayan.net/utf8/yuddha/sarga116/yuddha_116_frame.htm

97. Ibid, 6:118:1–10, https://valmikiramayan.net/utf8/yuddha/sarga118/yuddha_118_frame.htm
98. Ibid, 6:118:11–19 https://valmikiramayan.net/utf8/yuddha/sarga118/yuddha_118_frame.htm
99. Sadhguru, 'How to Make Marriage Work', Sadhguru Spot (blog), August 10, 2016, http://isha.sadhguru.org/blog/sadhguru/spot/how-to-make-marriage-work/
100. Desiraju Hanumanta Rao and K.M.K. Murthy, trans., *Valmiki Ramayana,* 6:32, https://valmikiramayan.net/utf8/yuddha/sarga32/yuddha_32_frame.htm.
101. Chaturvedi Dwarka Prasad Sharma, trans., *Srimad Valmiki Ramayana*, (Allahabad: Ramnarayana Lal Publisher and Bookseller, 1927), 7:24:42,43
102. Desiraju Hanumanta Rao and K.M.K. Murthy, trans., *Valmiki Ramayana,* 6:32:32, https://valmikiramayan.net/utf8/yuddha/sarga32/yuddha_32_frame.htm
103. The Commission of Sati (Prevention) Act, 1987(No. 3 of 1988).
104. Madu Kishwar and Ruth Vanita, 'The Burning of Roop Kanwar', *Manushi,* issue No.42–43, 1987, http://www.manushi-india.org/pdfs_issues/PDF%20files%2042-43/15.%20The%20Burning%20of%20Roop%20Kanwar.pdf. After a great deal of pressure and agitation by women's organizations and human rights groups all over the country, the government of Rajasthan filed a case in the court of the Additional District Judge, Neem Ka Thana, Rajasthan. On 11 October 1996, the judgement was delivered, acquitting all the accused.
105. The Hindu Marriage Act, 1955. Section 5. Condition for a Hindu Marriage.- A marriage may be solemnized between any two Hindus, if the following conditions are fulfilled, namely: (iv) the parties are not within the degrees of prohibited relationship unless the custom or usage governing each of them permits of a marriage between the two.
106. M.K. Arora, 'A Ray of Hope For Widows', Press Information Bureau, Union Ministry of Women and Child Development, June 7, 2016, http://www.pib.nic.in/newsite/mbErel.aspx?relid=146020
107. Deep Mukherjee, 'Kin Lynch Dalit Woman, Khap Imposes Rs 2,500 Fine', *Hindustan Times*, August 14, 2017.
108. Charu WaliKhanna, *Law on Violence Against Women* (Serials Publication, 2009), p.110.
109. Bindeshwar Pathak and Satyendra Tripathi, *Widows in India: Study of Varanasi and Vrindavan*, (Jaipur: Rawat Publications, 2016), pp.43–44.
110. Ishwar Chandra Vidyasagar (26 September 1820–29 July 1891) was a great social reformer, writer, educator, and entrepreneur who worked tirelessly to transform society. His contribution towards education and change in the status of women in India is immeasureable. He strongly protested against polygamy, child marriage, and favoured widow remarriage and women's education. He ran many schools for girls at his own expense, and was popularly called 'Dayar Sagar' or 'Karunar Sagar' (literally, 'ocean of kindness') because of his charitable nature and generosity. Born in a humble orthodox family, he used to study under street

lights at night, yet he acquired vast knowledge on different subjects, due to which he was given the title, 'Vidyasagar'.

111. Eric Johnson, 'After Sheryl Sandberg's Husband Died, Strangers on the Internet helped Her Cope', *Recode,* May 8, 2017, https://www.recode.net/2017/5/8/15569304/sheryl-sandberg-husband-death-grief-optionb-dave-goldberg-facebook-recode-podcast

112. Kim Hubbard and Sam Gillette, 'Sheryl Sandberg Says people "Judge" Women More Than Men When They Start Dating Again After a Loss', *People Magazine,* April 20, 2017, http://people.com/books/sheryl-sandberg-talks-dating-as-a-widow/Sandberg also discussed one step she's taken in recovering from Goldberg's death—finding companionship again. She is currently in a relationship with Bobby Kotick, the owner of Activision Blizzard, a gaming company. 'I found someone who has brought me joy and laughter,' she says.

Gender-Based Violence

Ravan's mad act of desecration
A crime against the ancient
Sanctities, smashed the cosmic symphony
Into a scream of chaos.

It was as though Nature's sustaining Law
Denied itself and blasphemed:
Salt lost its savour for the nonce, water
Froze, and darkness reigned at Noon.

The terrible spectacle of Sita,
Has hair disheveled, her voice
Hoarse crying 'O Rama, Rama, Rama,
Her sweat melting her tilak

Nature felt ashamed and paralysed by this
Horror of the lecherous
Ravan making off with Maithili
Defying the universe![A]

Sita was gratified to see the principle of gender equality enshrined in the Constitution of India. Accordingly, several measures to preserve gender equality had been undertaken, including the enactment of laws to ensure equal rights and the protection for women from social discrimination and violence. This upheld Sita's belief that life was a gift to be cherished and lived to the fullest by all, and not the exclusive domain of one gender, while the other half suffered in silence.

Sita was learned enough to comprehend that a vital part of understanding a social problem, and a precursor to addressing it, is astuteness as to what causes it. The *Manusmriti* refers to ten desires that influence the behavior of offenders, which include being abusive and disrespectful towards others and indulging in the exploitation of women. Sita had been disturbed about Ram's vow to eliminate the rakshasas of Dandaka and, to convince Ram to change his mind, had said that there are three self-gratifications that are the products of desire, which call for rejection: unqualified falsehood, adultery, and violence without cause.[2] Adultery had been considered a sin for the commoner in every era, but double standards always prevailed, with rules being different for kings, who had multiple wives and lovers. Sita's father-in-law, King Dashrath, himself had over 300 wives. Ravan, considered highly amorous, had many wives and innumerable lovers, including women who had been callously violated by him. It is only after being cursed by Nalkuvera that he could not possess an unwilling woman, and this was the only reason he suppressed his desire to molest Sita. In fact Ravan deridingly told her, *'You claim to be my daughter-in-law. It cannot be true. If you had been a chaste and devoted wife to only one person, I may have regarded you as my daughter-in-law. But apsaras do not have husbands, and gods are never attached to one wife'*[3]

In an age where even gods had multiple wives, Ram proved everyone wrong by marrying only once. Ram returned Sita's trust and confidence in him with a covenant of love and fidelity. He remained monogamous, and was devoted to Sita. In spite of abandoning Sita because of the vicious rumours about her chastity, he continued to keep a golden image of her on his left side, representing his wife.

Having had a husband as devoted as Ram, Sita was astonished to see culturally sanctioned beliefs legitimizing a man's use of violence to control his wife, and 'un-wifely' behaviour being used as an excuse and a justification for the abuse. In the India of today, Sita regarded the statements of the leaders and politicians which were replete with sexism and misogyny. Women were being called prostitutes, designated as 'dented, painted models', and wives of many years were being called 'not as fun as they used to be'.[4] What was odious was that even rape was being justified by saying 'boys will be boys', and political party leaders were exhorting their workers to rape women.

Sita heard horrific stories of acid attack survivors, and of their families being driven to bankruptcy to support medical costs. Sita thought that acid attacks were possibly the worst infliction on another human. She recollected how mutilation had been used as a form of punishment for women. Had not Surpanakha's nose, ears and breasts been cut off?

Obsessed with the idea of having Ram as her husband, and jealous of Sita, Surpanakaha suggested that Sita was unworthy of being his wife. She offered to first devour Sita, and then Laxman. With those two out of the way, she argued, they could wander the Dandaka forest together forever, taking in all the sights.

Ram tried to speak to her clearly and softly, with a smile preceding his words. Averting Surpanakha's advances, he asked her to divert her attention to Laxman. He said, 'Oh, honourable one, I am married and this is my dear wife, thus it will be distressing for your sorts of females to live with a co-wife. Here is my brother Laxman, he is of good conduct, good-looking, a promising and valiant one, and he is without a wife.'

Why did Ram trifle with her emotions, hoodwinking her, rather than telling her to go away, in the first instance itself? Was it because she was single, and single women are vulnerable to being mocked and considered 'easy game'? Or was he just trying to defuse the situation, and in a lighter tone suggested Laxman was 'without wife' since his wife was not with him in the forest?

Succumbing to her overpowering unbridled sexual urge, she promptly discarded Ram. Surpanakha then turned to Laxman, making a similar proposal. Laxman, being totally devoted to Sita, whom he considered a mother, could not tolerate anyone insulting her. Internally he was outraged at Surpanakha for trying to belittle Sita. Without revealing his true feelings, he quipped, 'Why do you wish to become the wife of a slave? Oh, black-colored lotus one, when you know that I am just a vassal of my adorable brother… you better become the wife of my brother Ram who is abounding in means.

Surpanakha took Laksmana's words at face value, unaware that a cruel joke was being played at her expense by the two brothers. Exasperated, Surpanakha, with eyes burning red like charcoal, dashed towards the deer-eyed Sita. Ram immediately became alert to her intentions and tried to stop the rakshasi with a roaring threat. Surpanakha had been prevented in her attempt to devour Sita, but Ram was still seething with anger. Enraged, he instructed Laxman and said, 'She is freakish, knavish and overtly ruttish, O tigerly man it will be apt of you to deface this paunchy demonness.'[5] *On hearing his brother's words, in an instant Laxman drew his sword and chopped off Surpanakha's ears and nose. Her breasts were even not spared.*[6] *Roaring with pain, and with blood spewing like a burst fountain, Surpanakha speedily fled into the forest where she came from.*[7]

Was the 'bad woman' punished in order to protect the 'good woman'? Or perhaps it was as a deterrent for the 'good woman' to remain good and never even dream of following the path of the 'bad' woman. Breasts are considered a symbol of female power, and by cutting them off the victim is not only punished but also humiliatingly deprived of her power. Interestingly, in the performances of the *Ramayana,* this incident is often presented in a humorous manner, evoking ribald jokes and laughter from the male audience—an experience which can be quite humiliating for the woman performer, although in India usually male actors impersonate female characters.

A number of women in the *Ramayana* are killed or mutilated on the grounds of their being demons, which is simply a metaphor used to tarnish women who do not accept male violence or male domination over women. Tadaka, who is trying to avenge her father's death, is transformed by Sage Agastya into a hideous demonic creature with cruel, cannibalistic qualities. Ayomukhi, another rakshasi, who had the gumption to propose to Laxman, has her nose, one ear and one breast cut off by him. Hanuman ruptured Simihika's internal organs with his sharp nails. This show of 'taming' women is lapped up by the male spectators, further reinforcing the belief that violence is an acceptable way to make a woman compliant. Sita found it hideous that primitive practices like female genital mutilation still persisted in modern India. In some communities, warped cultural socialisation teaches society to fear female sexuality, and to adopt barbaric methods in an attempt to stifle this. Due to the inaction of the government, a petition was moved before the Supreme Court to impose a complete ban on the inhuman practice of '*khatna*' or female genital mutilation, also known as 'female circumcision' or '*khafd*'.[8] The Supreme Court intervened and issued notices to four ministries i.e. the Ministries of Law and Justice, Health and Family Welfare, Social Justice and Empowerment, and Women and Child Development.

Sita tried to analyse the statistics on crimes against women given in the National Crimes Records Bureau,[9] which fell under two categories—the Indian Penal Code (IPC) and the Special and Local Laws (SLL). Cases under crimes against women reported an increase of 2.9 per cent in 2016. The majority of cases under crimes against women were reported under 'Cruelty by Husband or His Relatives' (32.6 per cent), followed by 'Assault on Women with Intent to Outrage her Modesty' (25 per cent), 'Kidnapping and Abduction of Women' (19 per cent) and 'Rape' (11.5 per cent). Uttar Pradesh, the most populous state of the country, reported 14.5 per cent of the total cases of crimes against women, followed by West Bengal (9.6 per cent). Ironically, West Bengal and Uttar Pradesh have had women as their Chief Ministers. New Delhi reported the highest crime rate in the country (160.4 crimes reported in a population of one lakh, compared to the national average rate of 55.2 crimes).

Marital Abuse and Victimization

Sita had heard the maxim that once married, a woman should only leave the 'matrimonial home when she is taken for her funeral rites'. For the first time, she saw evidence of this chilling truth in the countless women who lived by these words, suffering abuse and trauma at the hands of their husband and in-laws. She thought that while there was much pontification about the duties of a devoted and virtuous wife, the scriptures were often silent about the duties and treatment by the husband to his wife. Did not Draupadi have five husbands, and yet none protected her when she was being publicly disrobed by the Kauravas? In fact, all those present, including the 'elders', should have been held guilty of abetting the offence. Yudhisthira had no right to wager his wife—common or personal—in a game of dice. Draupadi was forced to be exhibited in the assembly. Greatly afflicted, but not one to be cowed down easily, she prostrated herself on the ground and bravely challenged everyone in the assembly by saying, 'Did my husband even have a right to stake me, considering that he had become a slave already?'

Marriage is the socially ratified union between two individuals, largely with the objective of promoting procreation and family life which, among other economic and psycho-social functions, preserves the human species. Marriage entails the sharing of responsibilities to provide for the household and children. In this partnership, the woman is entitled to be valued, and to reside with dignity and respect. Sita found this sacred institution in tatters in modern India and 'the manner in which sometimes the bride was treated in many a home by the husband, in-laws and the relatives, created a feeling of emotional numbness in society'.[10] In spite of gender equality being enshrined in the Constitution vide Article 15(3), the reality was quite the opposite.

A special section[11] had been introduced in the Indian Penal Code to protect married women from being subjected to cruelty by the husband or his relatives, and was made punishable under the law. The expression 'cruelty' has been defined in wide terms to include physical or mental harm to the body or health of the woman, or indulging in acts of harassment with a view to coerce her or her relatives to meet any unlawful demand for property or valuable security. Creating circumstances that drive a woman to suicide is also included in the criteria and definition of 'cruelty'. The majority of the cases of crimes against women were registered under Section 498A—'Cruelty by Husband or His Relatives', with West Bengal leading the category, followed by Rajasthan and Uttar Pradesh. Despite having a share of 32.6 per cent, however, this crime had the lowest conviction rate at 12.2 per cent[12] when compared against the high conviction rates in cases of immoral trafficking (38.5 per cent) and acid attacks (37 per cent). In 19 metropolitan cities where data was collected, New Delhi, followed by Hyderabad and Jaipur, had the maximum number of cases of cruelty by husband or his relatives. In these metropolitan cities, the conviction rates under Section 498A and the Dowry Prohibition Act dropped further. Data showed that in 2016, the police could achieve conviction in only 9.5 per cent of cases under Section 498A and a meagre 1.6 per cent under the Dowry Prohibition Act.

Sita couldn't help but wonder why a woman's credibility is the first to be doubted and questioned. Why is the finger so easily pointed at her? This seemed to be a trend prevailing in each era, irrespective of whether it was ancient or modern India. Did not the Fire God Agni swear for Sita's purity in her first *agnipariksha*; then why was she abandoned by her husband because of a random rumour? And why was she made to undergo the humiliating experience a second time even when Rishi Valmiki testified to her chastity? Digging into the past, the terrifying ordeal sent shivers down her spine.

The next morning, people came from different lands, far and wide. All those who had come to attend the celebration of the rite of sacrifice, assembled. Some showed up out of interest. Some out of curiosity. Some out of perversity. And some out of the sheer novelty of the occasion. All congregated to witness Sita giving proof of her purity. Once again no one raised their voice in support of Sita. There was no one to champion the cause of humanism and social justice. Even if they wanted to, they had suppressed their souls. A woman who had scorched the fire with the intensity of her purity was once again being challenged to prove her innocence. This was the dharma of King Ram which attracted great crowds of spectators.

First Valmiki entered. Then Sita followed. Her face was the embodiment of sorrow. Uncomfortable, exposed to the public's steady gaze, she stood with her hands folded in reverence. Then the best among sages, Valmiki, spoke and took an oath on behalf of Sita. He said:

> *O Ram, son of Dashrath! Here is the same Sita, virtuous, chaste and wholly devoted to her husband, you, Ram. She was once abandoned near my hermitage. Fear of false rumours regarding her chastity became reason for you to banish her. Ram, you were scared of slanderous gossip. Now ask her to give proof of her fidelity and convince you that she has been chaste. I speak truthfully that these twins are your sons. If Sita is pure, only then let me get the fruits of my austerities. I, who am the tenth son of Praceta (Varuna), who am sinless and always truthful, am vouching that Sita is pure and guiltless and that these boys Kush and Luv are your very own sons! I took her into my hermitage knowing for certain, knowing as much as can be known by my five senses and by my mind too, that Sita is absolutely pure in mind, body and speech. I know that you abandoned your beloved wife even though you knew fully well that she was chaste, only due to fear of public slander and censure which vitiated your mind.*[13]

The truth always stands out by itself and sets us free, just like it did in Sita's case. She found it a little bizarre that her own husband was inclined to trust another man's words, but not his own wife's! Why does a woman's word carry so little weight and is so readily doubted? Why is her word so easily discredited and her reputation sullied? Why should a woman need another man's endorsement? Why should a man's word be so privileged in the world's eyes, and why should he be so quick to silence and dismiss a woman's word, even that of his own wife? Was this the price she had to pay for saving the 'family honour'? Sita was not surprised at this prevailing misogyny when she read a judgement by the Supreme Court.[14] In this case, in spite of the government counsel submitting that Section 498A had been enacted to check unconscionable demands by greedy husbands and their families, it still opined that a majority of such complaints were being filed in the heat of the moment over trivial issues. While passing the judgment, the Court noted its concern that a large number of cases continue to be filed under Section 498A, alleging the harassment of married women. Was the court implying that the cases were not bonafide or the women were not to be believed, even though it is not a secret that even today, the status of groom decides the quantum of dowry? Was a woman always to be silenced and bullied into submission? What right did society have to turn every statement of fact into a question of her motives, just to deny her justice and silence her?

Sita was relieved to know that there was some relief for women and that in New Delhi, a Crime Against Women Cell (CAW)[15] had been established. This cell, after receiving a complaint from a woman, examines the alleged offences and attempts to provide assistance and, where possible, reconciliation. Most of the women in these cases were from economically disadvantaged sections of society, who often entered into arranged marriages as minors. When subjected to violence by their husbands and in-laws, rather than the perpetrators being punished (and the law being upheld), the victims are often placed under pressure to 'compromise and settle', and return to violent and dangerous situations. Many such young women are subjected to horrific acts of violence, and are often falsely implicated in cases or even virtually imprisoned in their matrimonial homes—all to extract more money from the young woman's natal family. The circumstances of these women made Sita all the more disturbed by the recent trend of courts whittling down the provisions of Section 498A of the IPC and claiming that women file false cases to extract money from the husband and in laws.

Conjuring up the past, Sita thought with pain about how, despite her trial by fire, Ram once again needed Valmiki's endorsement of her purity. While Ram may have accepted Valmiki's word, Sita, on her part, rejected Ram and the hypocrisy of society by choosing to return to her own mother, the Earth or *Bhumi Devi.*

Ram, on hearing Valmiki's solemn pronouncement and seeing Janaki standing in the centre of the assembly of people, said,

> *O Lord! What you said is correct. I know she is pure and had taken an oath in front of the devas, only after which I brought her back home to Ayodhya. I am assured by your words. I know that Kush and Luv are my sons. But what can I do? Public opinion is a potent force in public life, due to which I had to abandon her. Despite knowing that Sita is blemish free, I abandoned her. Please forgive me for this crime. I also know that these two boys, Kush and Luv, are my twin sons, but if in the presence of this vast assembly the purity of Sita is established, I will be very happy. I have faith in your words and am convinced of Sita's purity. But when Sita also establishes her purity in front of all these people, then she will establish herself firmly in my affection.*

This sounded like it was a circus, in which Sita was being made to repeat her act. No. Enough was enough! She would foil this humiliating second test of her purity. All of a sudden a divine fragrance filled the air, as it used to in the Satyuga. Everyone was engulfed with a feeling of happiness and rapture as if the Golden Age, the eon of truth, had come once again. The question foremost on everyone's mind was whether the self-respecting Sita would submit herself to yet another test to her innocence. The crowd was restless and anxious to know the result of the test. Unable to bear having to repeatedly prove her innocence, Sita rejected the hypocrisy of society, and with hers palms clasped and head lowered facing the earth, she said,

> *If other than Ram, I have never ever thought of any other man, then let Mother Earth cleave open and let me take refuge in her. If in my mind,*

> *by action or speech, I have only been devoted to my husband, Ram, then let Mother Earth open and make space for me. If what I say is true, that other than Ram I have never considered any man as my husband, then let the Earth Goddess let me take shelter in her womb.*

As Sita was swearing the oath, a miraculous occurrence happened. The earth shook and the rocks split. At her invocation, a divine lotus-shaped throne arose out of the earth. Sita sat on the lotus with a quiet dignity. Divine flowers were showered from the sky, as the throne descended back into the chasm of the earth. Years ago, while King Janak was furrowing the land, Sita had emerged forth, splitting up the earth, as a daughter of a king. Now history repeated itself. Only this time Mother Earth split, and the wife of a king retreated back into her lap.[16]

Sita, was welcomed back by Mother Earth, but unlike her, women today often lack an enabling environment to make informed choices; and since the natal family does not want them back, they succumb to the pressure of compromising with their treacherous and/or violent matrimonial environment. A married woman often finds little support from her natal family, as returning is considered a worse fate than death.

Domestic Violence

It is a common myth that domestic violence only happens to poor women, but the fact is that women across race, socio-economic strata, and religion can be victims. Whether it is a wife who is subjected to violence by her husband and in laws, a mother by her son and daughter-in-law, a sister by her brother and his family, or even violence by a partner. It is not uncommon for women to blame themselves, often feeling a deep sense of shame, or thinking that they somehow deserve the 'punishment'. No one deserves to be abused. Wives are beaten for not preparing food to the husband's or in-laws' satisfaction, for arguing, for not sufficiently attending to the children, for refusing to have sex, or for simply talking to other men. Sisters are also battered, with the reasons ranging from not preparing food properly to ensuring that they do not demand their right over property. In homes where there is domestic violence among the adults, children tend to be more at risk of being abused and neglected. It poses a risk to children being physically abused or psychologically damaged from witnessing violence between the adults. Both circumstances tend to have serious negative consequences for the child's safety and long-term development. Clearly, if the child is subject to direct violence, that compromises his/her physical safety. However, witnessing violence towards one's mother can be just as psychologically damaging—living in a climate of fear may not only compromise the development of self-confidence and esteem, but can also lead to behavioural and psychological disorders. Sometimes children physically try to defend their mother, which places them at further risk of harm or, conversely, they align with the perpetrators in mistreating their own mothers.

Comprehension of why women tolerate violence and remain in abusive relationships requires an analysis of the complex interplay of psychological, economic, and social factors that condition these relationships. More often than not, these women are economically dependent on their husbands, they keep quiet for their children's sake as they do not want to break up their families, they lack the education and training to find an adequate job, or even consider it their fate or *kismat* to remain trapped and powerless in their violent relationship. According to the United Nation Population Fund (UNPF) report, around two-third of married women in India were victims of domestic violence. It was noted that women with tangible economic assets were less likely to remain in situations of domestic violence than those who lacked them. The report cited Kerala as an example, where 49 per cent of women without property reported domestic violence, compared to only 7 per cent who owned property.[17]

Sita was glad to find that women could get protection under the Protection of Women from Domestic Violence Act, 2005. This was a new legislation which, in addition to the existing criminal law, empowered courts to grant protection to victims of domestic violence and provide other relief. It also included new concepts such as 'civil wrong of domestic violence, the right to reside in a shared household, and the right to protection against domestic violence by obtaining protection orders including monetary relief and custody of children orders'. The objective of the Act is to preserve the family and 'regulate and improve matters for the future, rather than pass judgements or punish past behaviour.' Easier said than done! There are certain criminal remedies that address domestic violence against a wife/ married woman, but none of them address violence against sisters, daughters, mothers and mothers-in-law. Nor do they address their need for residence or maintenance, or discuss who gets to avail of these remedies under this Act. For the first time, an Act allows women in domestic relations with the aggressor to seek a whole range of civil remedies under a single-window clearance system. The wide definition of domestic violence—physical, mental, economic, and sexual—brings under its purview the invisible violence suffered by a large section of women, and entitles them to claim protection from the courts.

This new statute has finally provided legal recognition to the problem faced by thousands of women, and will hopefully lead to greater awareness of this issue among the judiciary. The legislation is in place, but it will take time for its effects to be seen. Until then, deep-rooted social mores will continue to prevail. While stark gender inequalities remain in our national psyche, the challenge lies in creating a new framework for the inclusion of women's rights, and also in tackling the root causes of violence.

Rape

Wherever Sita went, she saw people with grim expressions expressing concerns about the safety of their daughters and sisters. Cases of molestation and rape were on the rise, a fact corroborated by the finding of the NCRB which, in its latest report, stated that rape cases have reported an increase of 12.4 per cent in 2016 since the previous year. The highest number of rape cases were reported in the state of Madhya Pradesh (12.5 per cent) followed by Uttar Pradesh (12.4 per cent) and Maharashtra (10.7 per cent). Perhaps the most disgraceful aspect was that New Delhi was being referred to internationally as the 'rape capital of the world,' with it having reported nearly 40 per cent of the rape cases.[18] Even courts in India had begun to show concern for the shameful decline of respect and honour of womanhood. Sita was astonished that India, renowned for its culture and respect for women, was placed, by an international study, in fifth position among 10 renowned countries with the maximum number of rape crimes.[19]

Sita, herself a survivor of attempted rape, was cognizant of the fact that rape is a particularly complex crime to analyze, and frequently goes unreported. Often the survivor, due to a number of reasons, does not report the crime—this can be to protect the family honour, fear of social stigma, fear of retaliation by the offender, or because the police would not do anything to help. Who knew better than Sita about the social stigma cast on the survivor, particularly potent within the Indian context, which often resulted in the rape survivor fearing being disowned by her own family or husband. Sita contemplated how beliefs and myths about sexual assault served as rationalizations for those who committed violent acts. Especially in the case of rape, the rapist often rationalizes that his victim either desired or deserved it. Did not Ravan try to justify his actions before raping Rambha?

As the sun set and the moon rose in the clear sky, Ravan's soldiers fell asleep and Ravan, enjoying the cool breeze of spring, started feeling sexually aroused. Just at that moment an apsara or celestial courtesan appeared, adorned by garlands of freshly bloomed celestial flowers. Wanting to seduce her, Ravan seized her hand and smilingly said, 'Whose desire are you going to fulfill, my dear? On whom will fortune smile tonight?' Rambha was overcome with embarrassment at these sexual innuendoes.

She begged him, saying she was like his daughter-in-law, but Ravan cast aspersions on her chastity and devotion to Nalkuvera. He forcibly laid her on the slab of stone and raped her. When he had finished giving vent to his lust, Rambha lay defiled in a pool of muddy water churned by gambolling elephants. Her garlands were torn, her ornaments were in disarray and were falling off, and her hair was totally dishevelled.[20]

Was not Ahalya, wife of Sage Gautam, penalized for being the 'most beautiful' woman, when Indra, the lord of the gods, disguising himself as her husband, raped her? On knowing what transpired, the sage cursed Indra and then scolded his wife and told her that she would lose her beauty and youth. He cursed her to live for the rest of her life as a stone until Vishnu himself graced her by placing his feet on her. Her husband callously ignored her plea: '*The sin you attribute to me was not committed willfully, I was deceived into believing the man in front of me is my husband. I did not know it was Indra.*'[21] Sita recounted the prophetic words of Ahalya, the meaning of which she did not understand at the time, but whose impact still remained. She said:

> *In the cockpit of the penitential earth, Devas, Asuras and Men wage their interminable battles for mastery or survival ... and we are but pawns in their game. My mystic antecedents didn't guard me, nor my being the righteous Gautama's spouse, nor my long-tested relationship with my Lord. The whole brood of Devas was jealous of Gautama's eminence, and Indra too had old scores to settle—the blow had to fall on me. When the so called 'god of gods' plays the cad and conspires to entangle in his meshes of insatiable lust a woman in slumber's daze, the wily rover scores an easy win—but 'tis the woman who pays. It is not the poisoned past that disturbs me, but the abominations that I see on the screen of the future. I see numberless discriminations and squalid aberrations. I see the delicate Nar-Nari harmony mauled and mangled. I see Man stooping low enough to shame the Asura and Beast. I see women enslaved and female children cast out unwanted. I see widows on funeral pyres ... None is spared, alas, only degraded ... Can a time ever unfold when woman will be able to resist the thousand varieties of violence to her body and psyche?*[22]

Ahalya's penance is considered exemplary, but not many realize that she did not have any choice. Her voice for justice went unheard and she was punished for being raped. Even today, femininity is tied up with being obedient and docile, and girls are punished for showing independence and spirit. In his interview, Mukesh Singh, the driver of the bus and one of the rapists in the Nirbhaya case, said, 'Women who go out at night have only themselves to blame in case they attract attention of male molesters ... Housework and housekeeping is for girls, not roaming in discos and bars at night or wearing wrong clothes.'[23]

Young girls did not appear to be safe in modern India, with very little institutionalized attention being paid to the sexual dangers confronting them, especially with the age of the perpetrators becoming younger and younger. Girls were not safe, either in their homes, in their neighbourhoods, or in schools and public spaces. Sita felt her hackles rising on reading the story of a thirteen-year-old boy and his twelve-year-old friend who gang raped a four-year-old girl in Ludhiana,[24] and about the class-eight students who allegedly gang raped a girl three years their junior.[25] According to the police, the boys caught the girl as she was returning from the field after relieving herself, and took turns raping her before escaping from the spot. The girl was a student of the government primary school while the boys were studying in secondary school, which had a different building but was located on the same campus. Since schools in the Rae Bareli district did not have toilets, the girl had gone outside to relieve herself. Gang rape seemed to have become the new normal, making the NCRB add it as a separate category to the list of rapes. Innocence was being exploited, like that of the fourteen-year-old child who was lured into a trap on the pretext of buying colour pencils from a shop nearby, but instead, was taken to the perpetrator's house and raped instead.[26]

Rape is the violation of the very core of an individual's physical, psychological, and emotional being. It violates a woman's basic human rights and her fundamental right—'right to life'—as guaranteed under Article 21 of the Constitution of India. The consequences of rape, the least of which are unjustified shame and humiliation, can be enduring and long term. The very motivation for male rape against women is often to assert dominance and keep her 'in her place'. The woman is often left to contend with the dreadful sense of being shunned by her family and relatives as well as by society, and being forever tainted or seen as 'damaged goods', intensifying her feeling of personal failure and inadequacy. Survivors are frequently compelled to marry their rapist, due to the misconception stemming from a belief that marriage somehow sanctifies or legitimizes what was, in fact, an act of violence. Sita was disconcerted to hear of a fourteen-year-old rape survivor, who gave birth to a child and was compelled to marry her alleged rapist due to extreme poverty. Her father, struggling to pay a loan of over Rs 20,000, was finding it difficult to meet the expenses of the girl and her child, along with eight other family members.[27] When the administration did not take the initiative for her rehabilitation or offer compensation, the girl and her family lost the courage to pursue the case further.

Sita strongly felt that an assault on a woman is an assault on the person of the woman. She read a report where Sohaila Abdulali, a rape victim, recounted her experience which took place 32 years ago in Mumbai.

> Rape is horrible. But it is not horrible for all the reasons that have been drilled into the heads of Indian women. It is horrible because you are violated, you are scared, someone else takes control of your body and hurts you in the most intimate way. It is not horrible because you lose your 'virtue'. It is not horrible because your father and your brother are dishonored. I reject the notion that my virtue is located in my vagina, just as I reject the notion that men's brains are in their genitals. If we take honor out of the equation, rape will still be horrible, but it will be a personal, and not a societal, horror. We will be able to give women who have been assaulted what they truly need: not a load of rubbish about how they should feel guilty or ashamed, but empathy for going through a terrible trauma.[28]

In India, there is a tendency to suppress incidents of sexual assault, especially in rural areas, where notions of honour and prestige are placed on a high pedestal. There is often a disincentive for victims to report the matter to the police for fear of intrusive medical examinations, being subjected to innuendo and gossip, and lengthy legal proceedings, not to mention hostile cross-examination if the matter ever gets to Court. It is not surprising then that rapes tend to be hugely underreported not only in India but also worldwide, and that the rate of successful convictions tends to be extremely low. Sita identified strongly with this injustice as she had been made to prove her chastity again and again.

Rape is usually an act of aggression, aimed at controlling, degrading, and humiliating women or communicating a message to the entire caste group of the woman, so that they do not raise their voice against injustice and discrimination. If Ravan had his way, he would have sexually assaulted Sita, but due to a curse he was unable to do so, for his head would have splintered into pieces. History reveals that rape and other forms of sexual violence have been used as weapons of war in order to humiliate, punish, control, and inflict fear among the male members of the community. Women are generally not directly involved in warfare. In times of armed struggle, the combatants are predominantly male. Women, however, are the major victims of warfare.[29] Marauding armies have frequently taken advantage of women in the course of their military conquests, giving rise to the practise of *jauhar* among Rajput women to save their honour from the enemy. In Jammu and Kashmir, a generation of women not only found themselves sandwiched between the violence of militants and the atrocities of security personnel, but also had to face fanatical attempts by fundamentalists foisting diktats upon them. For example, girls over fourteen years of age were deprived of education in the name of religion, or had become the victim of an acid attack for not being 'modestly' dressed. Media attention was focused in the North-East of India on Thangjam Manorama Devi, a woman alleged to be 'a suspected insurgent, explosives expert and hardcore member' of the banned People's Liberation Army, who was found dead three hours after her arrest, having been raped and shot in her vagina. There was widespread eruption of rage in Manipur, and a group of elderly women gathered in front of the 17th Assam Rifles headquarters and stripped their clothes off, inciting the army to come rape them as Manorama had been raped.[30]

Sita was surprised that India, the world's largest democracy, had what is regarded as a highly corrupt, lawless, and abusive police force, which participated in making arbitrary arrests and illegal detention, custodial torture, and extrajudicial killings. Instead of policing through public consent and participation, the police use abuse and threats as a primary crime investigation and law enforcement tactic.[31] Police infrastructure is crumbling. Decaying, colonial-era police stations and posts across India are stocked with antiquated equipment and lack sufficient police vehicles, phones, computers, and even stationery. A severe police staffing shortage is compounded by additional demands on an already-stretched force. Police are routinely diverted to protect 'VIPs'—usually politicians, businesspeople, and entertainment figures. Senior police officials frequently use low-ranking staff as orderlies and even as personal family servants. The police structure in India is based on a colonial law that did not provide the lower ranks, usually local recruits, with operational authority or advanced professional training. Inexplicably, that system continues, even after six decades after the end of British rule in India. Constables, the bottom rank, make up as much as 85 per cent of the Indian police, but for the most part they are not trained to investigate crime complaints.

None of these reasons justify the lack of empathy and sensitivity in refusing to register complaints of crimes, or what is known as a First Information Report (FIR). This is especially true of the poor and marginalised who are unable to afford to pay the bribe demanded for FIR registration, or for the costs of investigation that victims are expected to cover on behalf of the police. They are less likely to have local political contacts who would intervene with the police on their behalf, while their perpetrators may have police protection due to political connections.

Sita was horrified when she read a report of three police stations refusing to register a complaint of gang rape and mocking the survivor for 'coming up with a filmy story'. A nineteen-year-old college girl was tied up and raped by four men for three hours, while they took breaks for tea and *gutka* (tobacco) before returning to assault her repeatedly under a bridge in the heart of Bhopal. Thousands of cars drove past just a 100 metres from where she was stripped, tied up, and raped repeatedly. Yet, no one heard a thing.[32] The girl's father is a sub inspector with a security force and her mother is with the Crime Investigation Department (CID). Her mother said, 'It's one of the worst experiences of my life. If I, as a policewoman, have to face such problems in filing my daughter's gang rape complaint, I can't imagine what a common man goes through.' Two of the accused were caught, not by the police but the girl herself, who chased them and nabbed them in a scuffle. The girl is reported to have threatened her attackers that she would lodge a complaint against them, and asked them whether they were scared of police, to which they laughingly told her that they had looted several people in the and that and the police had taken no action.[33] The girl rubbished questions that are generally raised about the clothes of a woman after a crime against her is reported. 'I was wearing a full-sleeve shirt and jeans, not a short dress. And yet it happened. Even sari-clad women are raped in villages,' she said. Sita was impressed with the boldness of the girl who proclaimed that it was her attackers who 'should feel guilty for what they did to me. I don't want to spend the rest of my life hearing comments like '*bechari* (poor girl) rape victim.'[34]

What astounded Sita was the reaction of the state government which, duty bound to ensure that public spaces are safe for women, put the burden on civil society by decreeing that coaching centres that didn't close by 8:00 pm would be responsible for the safety of their female students.[35]

Sita felt that women had the same instinct for self preservation, whether they were in ancient or modern India. Today this young girl, having presence of mind, concealed the identity of her parents and said, 'I did not tell them that I was the daughter of a policeman, otherwise they would have murdered me.' Sita remembered the time when she was alone in the hermitage and Ravan appeared before her, in the guise of a Brahmin *sanyaasi* or friar. She had proudly proclaimed that she was the wife of Ram the invincible, thus sending a silent warning that he had better think twice before making any attempt to do anything untoward.

Ravan ogled at the glorious and youthful princess, as a sinister planet looks at the star Rohini *when she is devoid of her husband, the moon. The friar, instead of giving his blessings, leeringly praised Sita's beauty, extolling her physical characteristics. He said,*

> *Your hips are beamy, thighs burly akin to an elephant's trunks, and these two breasts of yours that are ornamented with best jewellery are rotund, rubbing and bumping each other, and they are swinging up and up, their nipples are brawny and jutting out, and they are smooth like palm-fruits, thus they are covetable for they are beautiful. Oh, allurer, your smile is alluring, teeth are alluring, and your eyes allure, oh, beauty, your waist is*

> *a palmful; your hair velvety, your breasts are jostling, and you rob my soul as a river in spate robs the riverbank ...[sic]*

Repeating Surpanakha's words, he said 'I have not hitherto seen any earthly female with this kind of features on the face of earth; or, a goddess—no; a gandharva female—no; yaksha female—no; kinnaraa female—no, none whosoever!'[36]

Sita, confused and disturbed by the disappearance of Ram, was not concentrating on the wanton words of the friar. In spite of being uncomfortable with his sexually graphic utterances, she continued to give due respect to the man in pious garb, and unsmilingly invited him inside, thinking he was a Brahmin. Sita naively believed that the man in front of her was a friar, and thought that he would curse her if not replied to properly. Listlessly, in a half-hearted manner, she provided information about herself. In spite of being in a highly perturbed frame of mind, she somehow managed to maintain her composure and relate her life story to Ravan. She said, 'I am the daughter of noble-souled Janak, the king of Mithila, by name I am Sita, and the dear wife and queen of Ram, let safety betide you.' Revealing her lineage, she indirectly wanted to send the message that she was not alone, but had the support of powerful people. She also informed Ravan of the presence of another male with her, by saying, 'One known as Laxman is Ram's brother from another mother, and he is a valorous one, tigerly-man, and an eliminator of enemies in war.'[37]

According to the NCRB Crime in India 2016 statistics, the conviction rate in cases of rape is appalling—just 23.9 per cent—as against murder, which stands at 30 per cent. This is in spite of numerous court decisions that the sole testimony of the victim, if reliable, can be grounds for conviction of the accused. When the victim supports the case of the prosecution and remains unshaken during cross-examination, then her evidence is material, reliable, and trustworthy. Sita then racked her brains as to why the rate of conviction was so poor. The answer lay largely with shoddy investigation and collection of evidence. In a country like India, witnesses can be purchased for a price, and the persons manning the law enforcement agencies become mediums of corruption. It was beyond Sita's comprehension how, in the famous Priyadarshini Mutto murder and rape case, the father of the perpetrator of the crime could have been made the boss of an agency which was investigating his own son's crime. This was not an ordinary crime of theft or burglary, but a crime against humanity, which shook the conscience of the nation even years later.[38] While the father of the spoiled child-turned-criminal was doing what he could to influence the legal process, the father of the victim was waging a lonely battle while shuttling between Jammu, Kashmir, and New Delhi. The accused exerted so much power that conducting a fair investigation was becoming impossible. The Commissioner of Delhi Police, well aware of the vices and fraility of his own force, made a request to the Lieutenant Governor of Delhi to transfer the case, who in turn submitted the request to the Special Secretary to the Government of India.[39] The Police Commissioner put it in writing that he felt the parents of the victim would not have the required confidence if the investigation of the case was conducted by the Delhi Police. In the light of the same it was decided that the CBI would undertake the investigation of the case immediately.

Barring custodial rapes, the onus of proving rape rests with the victim, and therefore, with the prosecutor. Here, the role of those who examine the rape victim, and collect evidence sent for testing to forensic laboratories, is crucial. Yet doctors in public hospitals are not given the appropriate training and resources for examining rape victims. Even the best forensic laboratory can do nothing if the basic evidentiary raw material is either missing or not collected in a proper manner. Besides, in public hospitals, the victim is made to go from one department to another for different examinations. Surely, given what the woman has been through, the system can ensure that such harassment is minimised. Despite Sita having been the innocent victim and suffering a traumatic abduction by Ravan, she was made to prove her innocence, not once but twice. Sita was resentful that even in this day and age a woman had to struggle to establish her credibility at each stage of the hostile investigation and justice-delivery process. This deterred women from registering complaints with the police, and in cases where they did somehow manage to gather the courage to complain, the hostile legal sytem would wear them out. A female Indian Administrative Service (IAS) officer wrote, 'Such is the state of affairs for women in this country ... Idiots are lined up at every step and people are highly insensitive towards our sufferings. If you are born in this country, better prepare yourself for struggle at every step.'[40] This woman's experience, unfortunately, is not a one-off incident; there are many others like her who have faced traumatic humiliation at the hands of lawyers and judges through the trial of their case in court. For example, the girl who was gang-raped in Kolkata's Park Street; her friend and activist, describing some of her ordeals, said:

> One incident that affected her very badly was when her undergarments that she was wearing when she was raped were openly exhibited. The defence lawyer held it with a stick and asked her if it was hers, and whether she wearing it on that day when she was 'allegedly' raped. She told me that she broke down in court and pleaded to the judge, asking her to intervene. The judge, one of her own gender, did not.[41]

Again, Ahalya's ordeal came to her mind when Sita got caught in a fresh debate on 'consent' sparked by a High Court judgement.[42] The question arising before the High Court was whether or not there was consent—whether the perpetrator mistakenly accepted the moves of the woman as consent, whether the feelings of the woman could be effectively communicated to the accused, and whether he genuinely mistook it as consent or if it was only a ruse for his defence. It had been argued in his defence that the history of intimacy and the unabashed liking/attraction of the woman towards the perpetrator may have given an impression of consent. The orgasm which was feigned by the woman, avowedly for the purposes of preventing further damage to her, may have been taken as willingness and been misunderstood as a non-verbal communication of consent. Absence of any real resistance of any kind re-affirmed willingness, for an expression of disinclination alone, that also a feeble one, may not be sufficient to constitute rape. In the present case, the unwillingness was only in the mind and heart of the woman, but she communicated something different. If that were not so, she would not have told the perpetrator that he had gone too far on that night.

Sita shuddered at how the High Court had diluted the interpretation of consent, and stacked the deck against women who seek justice by stating that:

> Instances of woman behaviour are not unknown, that a feeble 'no' may mean a 'yes'. If the parties are strangers, the same theory may not be applied … But same would not be the situation when parties are known to each other, are persons of letters and are intellectually/academically proficient, and if, in the past, there have been physical contacts. In such cases, it would be really difficult to decipher whether little or no resistance and a feeble 'no', was actually a denial of consent.[43][sic]

The court finally concluded that it remained in doubt as to whether such an incident, as had been narrated by the woman, had taken place and whether it was without her consent/will, and if it was without her consent, whether the perpetrator could discern/understand the same.

Marital Rape

Sita found it strange to hear the word 'marital rape' being discussed by people, and tried to enquire more about it in order to form her own opinion. She was told that a case had been filed in the Supreme Court of India,[44] challenging Exception 2 of Section 375 of the IPC, which states that sexual intercourse by a man with his own wife, the wife not being under fifteen years of age, is not rape. The prima facie plea to the judiciary appeared simple and justifiable, for it urged that all minors under the age of eighteen be protected from forcible sex, irrespective of marital status. There appeared to be no rational nexus in classifying girls under the age of eighteen into two groups—those who are married, and those who are not. Moreover, the Protection of Children from Sexual Offences Act, 2012 (POSCO) states that a girl under the age of eighteen is a child, and hence does not have the capacity, whether physical, emotional or mental, to take an informed decision about engaging in sexual intercourse. The petition stated:

> If this is the object for increasing the age of consent to 18 years in 2013, then marriage of girl at the age of 15/16/17 years does not make the girl mature enough [mentally or physically] for the purpose of consent. Thus, the law is ex-facie discriminatory as the classification has no rational nexus with the object.

The government defended the law on the ground that protecting the institution of marriage was a priority. Sita found such a defence disturbing. She was told that the Law Commission of India, while making its 172nd Report on 'Review of Rape Laws' in March, 2000, did not recommend the criminalization of marital rape; however, the Justice J.S. Verma Committee (set up post the Nirbhaya gang rape) Report on 'Amendments to Criminal Law' in January 2013, recommended that the law ought to be amended to delete the marital rape exception. The Department Related Parliamentary Standing Committee on Home Affairs, deliberating on the issue, observed that if marital rape was brought under the law, the entire family system would be under great stress and the Committee may perhaps be doing more injustice.[45] Sita read the reply given by Minister of Women and Child Development to the Upper House of the Parliament, which stated, 'It is considered that the concept of marital rape, as understood internationally, cannot be suitably applied in the Indian context due to various factors, including level of education, illiteracy, poverty, myriad social customs and values, religious beliefs, mindset of the society to treat the marriage as a sacrament.'[46] Sita was also told that the Supreme Court bench refused to look at marital rape as an issue that could be debated and considered a criminal act under the IPC since 'Parliament has extensively debated the issue of marital rape and considered that it was not an offence of rape.'[47] Sita felt that the two issues of child marriage and marital rape were being confusticated. Child marriage was undeniably an offence; moreover since a child does not have the capacity to 'consent', no marriage could be legally entered into without the full and free consent of both parties.[48] However, she felt that criminalising marital rape in case of adult partners would not solve the problem of spousal violence. Not because of the inference that criminalising marital rape can 'destabilise the institution of marriage', but because Sita felt that:

> I don't believe in placing rape on a pedestal within the hierarchy of crimes within a marriage. For a woman who is facing domestic violence, it is equally violating if her skull is fractured, her spine is broken, her cornea is damaged, liver is injured, or her vagina is penetrated forcefully. What women object to is the violence involved.[49]

Sexual violence in a marriage should be seen within the framework of domestic violence, for which relief has been provided in The Protection of Women from Domestic Violence Act, 2005.[50] This clearly illustrates that sexual abuse includes forced sexual intercourse, being forced to watch pornography or other obscene material, forcibly using a wife to entertain others, and any other act of sexual nature—abusing, humiliating, degrading or otherwise, which is violative of a woman's dignity. Considering that India has a track record of gaps in effective implementation of gender laws, which is exacerbated by low conviction rates, against that background, any new law, especially relating to marital rape, will only create more distrust against women. While on one hand there has been a legal expansion of women's rights in India, on the other hand, society still continues to believe that a woman exists only as an appendage to some man in her life, and societal trends still maintain a violent order against women.

Incest

Sita was astonished to find that the failure to implement laws effectively, as well as gaps in the justice system, encouraged violence against women to persist, despite sweeping changes and the expansion of the definition of rape. Simultaneously, the attitudes of law enforcement officers and the tendency of the police to commit serious mistakes while investigating the case discouraged women from reporting cases. There was a lack of adequate and consistent gender sensitivity, and insufficient training for officials responsible for implementing legislation and policies. But what perplexed Sita most was incidents of sexual abuse and rape by blood relatives like fathers, uncles, brothers etc.

Sita was repulsed to read the report[51] of a ten-year-old girl who was allegedly raped by her stepfather several times, and another by her uncle,[52] both of whom were in a precarious condition where abortion and delivery were equally dangerous. In the first case the court granted the small child the right to have an abortion.[53] A request was moved to the local district court because the girl was more than 20 weeks pregnant, and the law only permits termination upto 20 weeks when the 'pregnancy would involve a risk to the life of the pregnant woman or of grave injury to her physical or mental health'. The other girl had a known case of congenital heart defect (Ventricular Septal Defect) which had been corrected earlier, and the Supreme Court of India refused to order medical termination of the pregnancy of the approximately thirty-two-week foetus, on the basis of the report of the Medical Board which stated 'Continuation of pregnancy is less hazardous for the girl child and foetus than termination of pregnancy at this stage'. She was told that she had a stone in her stomach that had to be removed and the ten-year-old gave birth to a premature baby via caesarean section, being too young for a normal delivery. 'Her pelvic bones are not strong enough to push the baby, and she doesn't have the stamina to bear labour pain', a doctor said.[54] Sita's heart went out to the eleven-year-old girl who was compelled to call a child helpline, saying that her mother had died and that she was not safe with her father.

> The girl was brought to the child care institute of the CWC and she told officials there that after her mother's death, she was sent to her uncle's house while her two younger sisters were given in adoption to two other relatives. While in her uncle's house, her cousin, a major, started sexually abusing her. When she brought this to the notice of her father, who once came to see her, he took her with him. However, her father too started raping her.[55]

Sita felt emotionally drained on hearing that children, the most vulnerable of all human beings, were being abused and sold for sex by their own families. She presumed that since children are not a vote bank, their safety is not a priority for politicians, and as a result no preventive plans are in place. Child abuse, and especially sexual exploitation, were unheard of in her time. It was only centuries later, in a 2,500-year-old Buddhist story called 'Sopaka', that one finds a description of a jealous father leaving Sopaka tied to a corpse in a cemetery to be eaten by wolves, until Buddha comes and rescues the boy. Apart from this, sexual exploitation and incest were unimaginable. Sita felt her sanity being threatened with the cacophony of headlines of fathers raping minor daughters, in Mumbai,[56] New Delhi,[57] Kolkata,[58] and even the remote Jhalawar, Rajasthan.[59] The list seemed endless. Instead of sympathy and compassion for the small child, she was being blamed and even thrown out of school.[60] Sita wanted to lambast society for how depraved it had become. Had Indian forgotten their culture and *sanskaras* that *Bharatvarsh*—land of seekers of truth and liberation—was so proud of?

Children are helpless and vulnerable, and a dysfunctional childhood experience can leave enduring scars that persist into adulthood, making it all the more imperative for grown ups to be responsible and protective of children. A child should be encouraged to report abuse and and parents should follow the 'STEPS' approach with children—Stay calm, Tell the child it's not her fault, Encourage disclosure, Provide support, and Seek help. Parents and teachers should maintain close involvement in the child's daily routine, be alert to any suspicious change in appearance or behaviour, teach them to respect their bodies, make them be conscious of the difference between a 'good' touch and 'bad' touch, and encourage children to confide in them about any inappropriate overtures. Incestuous abuse is an area that is still shrouded in secrecy and remains taboo. Fear, as well as social pressure to 'turn a blind eye', tends to cover up this problem, despite its prevalence. The sad irony is that the majority of sexual abuse occurs within the home environment and by perpetrators known to the child. The collective silence within families gives the perpetrators the freedom to repeat their heinous acts.

We can no longer claim the higher moral ground and pretend that incestuous abuse does not occur in India. Sita felt inspired by recent television programmes—like Aamir Khan's show 'Satyamev Jayate'—which have done a valuable service in bringing this issue into the mainstream discussion, and have helped to break the silence by giving the victims a voice.

Kidnapping and Abduction of Women

Sita was petrified on hearing about the kidnapping case of a young woman by a man who wished to marry her. He confessed to having stalked her 150 times in a year, before abducting her. Like Ravan, he was no novice or first timer, but a habitual criminal and had around 30 cases against him.[61] Having undergone the trauma of being abducted herself, Sita could identify with the girls' plight. No doubt sexual needs and desire are a natural part of being human. However, each individual has a responsibility, particularly men in this case, as they are the main perpetrators of sexual violence, to uphold the woman's right to consent and to respect her personhood. Not to mention they also need to be responsible and in control of their impulses and actions. It flashed through Sita's mind that men like Ravan, who abducted woman in order to satisfy their lust, irrespective of the fact whether the woman reciprocated his feeling or not, were on the increase. Examining the Crime in India Report 2016,[62] it was revealed that the 'Kidnapping & Abduction of Women' accounted for 19 per cent of the cases under crimes against women, showing an increasing trend of 6 per cent in 2016. The state of Uttar Pradesh accounted for the maximum number of cases with 17.1 per cent of the total cases of kidnapping and abduction, followed by Maharashtra with with 10.6 per cent and Bihar with 8.3 per cent. In the case of cities, Delhi reported the highest number of cases accounting for 48.3 per cent, followed by Mumbai with 16.6 per cent, and Bengaluru with 7.8 per cent. More than half the kidnappings of women were for the purpose of marriage, and these were increasing every year. Sita's hair stood on end thinking of the time Ravan used his desire to marry her as a ruse to kidnap her.

Ravan, the great-mighty king of demons, revealing his true identity, brusquely said, 'I am that sovereign of hosts of demons, known as Ravan. On seeing you, oh, impeccable one, glittering with golden complexion and attired in ochry-silks, I derive no pleasure in my wives.' He proposed to Sita to become his prime queen.

Furious on being deceived, Sita replied that she was committed to Ram. She said, 'I have avowed to adhere to such a husband, Ram, who is inflexible like a sturdy mountain, comparable to lordly Indra, unshakable like a vast ocean.' Taunting him, she said, 'Ram is a valiant person and confronts, if need be, his enemies straightforwardly, about which you have heard when your Khara, Dushana, and others are eliminated by him … but you are sneaky and slithery ... You are ever a thief, never a valiant one.'[64] *All the while she was berating Ravan with disdain, her fragile body trembled. Yet she continued pouring forth all of her feelings. Unbothered by the consequences, she caught her breath, and felt uneasy.*

On seeing Sita quivering, Ravan, in an attempt to scare her even more, frowned and rudely started talking of his fame, competency, and might. He tried to tempt her by promising her a luxurious life in Lanka, and insisted that the opulence and grandeur of Ayodhya would pale in comparison to what Ravan could offer in Lanka. Sita, on hearing Ravan's monologue was infuriated. Her anger had reached its peak becoming uncontrollable. She even forgot that she was in a vulnerable position, alone with this rakshas in a lonely uninhabited forest. With bloodshot red eyes and her voice rising steadily, she said,

> *All the demons will perforce get completely destroyed, oh, Ravan, for whom you the cruel and culpable one with uncontrolled senses is the king, and you will be blamed for the elimination of righteous demons like Vibhishana. It may be possible to live after abducting the Sachi Devi, the wife of Indra … there will be no liveability after abducting me, the wife of Ram.*

Sita repelled all his temptations and cursed him, saying that there would be no moksha or release from the cycle of rebirth for a man who abuses her or women like her.[64]

On hearing Sita's insolent reply, Ravan became infuriated and roared, wringing his hands loudly with anger. Not willing to tolerate any more imprudence, he discarded the gentle form of a mendicant. Ravan assumed his own titanic ferocious form. Discarding his guise, the evil king stood before Sita in his enormous transformed state, with ten heads and twenty arms. Ravan expected Sita to yield on seeing such a magnificent manly physique, unlike the girlish physique of her husband.

Then evil-minded Ravan, maddened by lust, grabbed lotus-eyed Sita; with his left hand he gripped the plait of hair hanging from the nape of her neck, and with his right hand lifted her by her thighs. It all happened so suddenly that Sita's resistance broke down. On seeing Ravan grab Sita, the forest deities fled, terrorised by his savagery. Sita screamed, 'Leave me! Leave me!' But there was no one to hear her.[65]

Sita had valiantly tried to resist Ravan, but no one came to her help. Such callous disregard seemed to still prevail in modern India. Sita saw CCTV footage going viral on social media in which a distraught woman was being dragged away by two men, followed by a couple of others on motorbikes, yet none of the passers-by stopped to offer any help.[66] It evoked memories of the time when the aged Jatayu was the only one who had the courage to confront Ravan and caution him to change his mind, lest misfortune befall. Alas, Jatayu's discourse had no effect on the lechery of Ravan and, in a fit of fury, he severed the eagle's wings, feet, and sides, leaving him on the ground, almost dead. Known for her tenderness and compassion, Sita ran towards Jatayu and wept while hugging him, as if he was her own relative. Ravan seized her by her hair loosened from her bun and, with death looming large, rose up in the air, taking flight in the sky. Sita recalled how she continued to struggle to be free from Ravan's clutches.

Her anxious eyes were scanning the earth to find a saviour to whom she could turn for help. Unfortunately, she did not see anyone. Her body was wracked with pain, but she continued to grapple with Ravan from under his arm. Just when the terrifying ordeal seemed never-ending, she spotted five prominent oddish monkeys on a mountaintop. On seeing them, Sita quickly dropped her ornaments in the upper-fringe of her sari[67] *in the hope that they would inform Ram of her abduction. She left a trail on the forest floor with her ornaments. Ravan, bent upon fleeing as fast as he could, as though haunted by Ram, did not notice Sita dropping her ornaments.*

The tawny-eyed monkeys gazed at the weeping princess with unblinking eyes. They were Sugriva and four others monkeys, who heard her writhing, resisting, calling for someone called 'Ram', and chanting his name.[68]

None of the so-called valiant and strong monkeys came forward to help the weeping, defenseless woman. Even in this day and age, people continued to be callous and indifferent, and not many persons were ready to give a helping hand to a woman facing a crisis. Real compassion is one which compels you to help even a stranger! Was it possible that male sexual violence against women was somehow seen as acceptable?

The disappearance of loved ones as a result of kidnapping can be deeply traumatizing for those remaining. Often, there is the initial shock and terror, and a deep fear for the safety of the victim and the suffering that might be inflicted on her. This can be accompanied by impaired cognitive functioning (i.e., memory, concentration, and the inability to process information), intrusive and distressing thoughts, or sometimes even a complete denial of the events in an effort to cope. Brothers may become distrustful of each other, and families may break up, blaming each other for not doing enough to get the victim back or protect them from being abducted in the first place. Thus, the trauma dismantles the very supports and structures that need to work together to obtain the victim's safe return. Ram exhibited all the signs of emotional turmoil, ranging from shock and numbness, fear and anxiety, helplessness and hopelessness, to anger, depression, and guilt. On finding Sita missing, Ram became totally desolate.

After killing the deer who turned out to be Maricha, Ram instantly, rushed towards the hermitage. His mind filled with anxiety, he walked back briskly. On the way he saw Laxman, looking equally sad and anxious, coming towards him. Taking Laxman's hand in his own, Ram rebuked him for being thoughtless in leaving Sita behind, alone and unprotected in the forest. Apprehending that something had happened to Sita, Ram said:

> *Oh, Laxman, no doubt Sita is not there in the hermitage, maybe she is whisked away, or wiped out, or wandering around on a wrong path.' She who has come in tow with me to Dandaka forest when I started for peregrination, whom you have now deserted and come here, oh, Laxman, she that Vaidehi, where is she? Without whom I am disinclined to live even for a moment. Oh, valiant one, Sita who is like the daughter of deities and who is my life-force, where is she? I am unambitious for the rulership either on heavens, or on the earth.*[69]

The brothers were astounded on entering their own hermitage. Its calm has been disturbed and ravaged. Scattered around were deerskins and blades of grass. Utterly battered were the tender grass seats and other mats in the compound of the cottage. Articles were strewn around and were in a shattered condition. All evidence pointed towards Sita's involvement in a scuffle, and her attempt to fight back.

Ignoring the evidence, Ram deceived himself into falsely believing that Sita may have gone out to pick flowers or fruits, or gone to the river for water. He rushed out, calling for her. Searching her favourites haunts. Ram rushed from wood to wood, over rivers, hills, mountain-rapids and thicketed forests, speedily and restlessly, pursuing his search for Sita. Like an ordinary mortal, he was distraught by the loss of his soulmate, companion, and partner. The two brothers wandered through the forest in search of her, with Ram becoming despondent and lamenting for Sita. On the advice of Laxman, both of them embarked on a thorough search, looking in every conceivable place in the forest, its mountains, and lakeside. But Sita remained unseen.[70]

The Gendered Concept of 'Modesty'

Women were held in high esteem in ancient India, and their harassment in public places was unheard of, so Sita could not conceive what this modern phenomenon of 'eve-teasing' in India was all about and asked someone for an explanation. She was informed that 'eve-teasing' is a widely-used term for sexual aggression ranging in severity from sexual remarks and catcalls to groping, which added to her bewilderment. She thought, 'Is there any place on earth where women can walk fearlessly?' How is it that such a benign, playful term could be used in reference to what in reality was serious assault and unwanted sexual contact. There was no sympathy for sexually violated women, only curiosity, with society offering little opportunity to both girls and boys to gain experience in dealing with their sexuality. This incongruity has been further magnified by the supposed sexual revolution in the media, where young people are bombarded with sexual imagery, further intensifying the confusing and highly charged messages young men in particular are receiving. In turn, this aggravated the problem regarding the physical and sexual safety of women in India.

The IPC[71] penalizes any person who intends to insult the modesty of any woman, utters any word, makes any sound or gesture, or exhibits any object which intrudes upon the privacy of a woman. The definition of what is 'modesty' is not given in the Code; however it appears to have its origins in the Latin word '*modestia*', meaning 'moderation, sense of honour, or correctness of conduct'. Feminists have argued that the word has a patriarchal view in relation to women's clothing, conduct, and interactions. Throughout history, and even today, women are judged on how 'modest' they are in dress and speech, with femininity comprising modesty, chastity, and innocence; and the degree of respect a woman receives being linked to how 'modest' she is, rather than associating respect to her accomplishments, intellect and abilities.[72] Courts have interpreted modesty as being a virtue which a female has due to her sex, rather than the violation of a woman's right to bodily integrity. The culpable intention of the accused is the crux of the matter. In a case where the woman is not in a position to deny consent, the offender is still liable to be punished under the section. For example, if a woman was unable to appreciate the significance of the act and deny consent because she was mentally challenged, unwell, or under influence of intoxication or anesthesia.

Sita shuddered at the thought of how Ravan, eager to fornicate with her, would stand in front of her and ogle at her, violating her without even touching her.

Sita, on seeing Ravan approach, shook like a plantain tree in a storm. Feeling undressed by Ravan's lecherous gaze, she sat down on the ground, drawing up her knees to cover her stomach, and hiding her breasts with her hands. Ravan stared at her. To him, the frail weeping woman protected by rakshasis appeared divinely beautiful.

Hanuman, witness to Ravan's licentious behaviour, saw Sita flump down on the bare ground like a branch of a tree fallen on the earth. Grieving for her husband and tormented with grief, Sita had turned pasty-faced and had wasted away due to fasting, sorrow, rumination, and fear. Now she had only one desire—the defeat of Ravan at the hands of Ram.

Ravan continued to allure Sita, and at the same time he threatened her with death. Coming closer, he tried to entice Sita in a raunchy tone, dripping with honey. He said, 'O wide eyed one! You are endowed with beautiful limbs, capable of stealing the hearts of many. I desire you. O lovable one! Respect me.' In self-aggrandizement, boasting about himself, Ravan endeavoured to impress Sita with show of his wealth and impressive façade of power and glory. He said, 'In this world I do not see another one who is equally matched to me. Suras and Asuras defeated … by me in war many times are powerless to stand in an army against me.'

Spurning all his offers of gifts, clothes, and jewels, Sita remained silent. In her mind she thought, 'Then how come he was unable to string Shiv's bow?'[73]

The usual defense of the accused is that he did not harbour bad intentions, or loves the woman in question and wants to marry her, like Ravan did. The perpetrator of the crime, often supported by society, resorts to victim blaming and deflects the fault back on to the woman. The crime is justified and the accused, in an attempt to absolve himself of any guilt, blames the girl for dressing provocatively. Sometimes the offender uses criminal force or assaults the woman with the intention to 'outrage her modesty', which makes the offence more severe in the eyes of the law. In India, the state of Maharashtra has reported the highest number of cases of assault on a woman to 'outrage her modesty', followed by Madhya Pradesh and Uttar Pradesh. There is no woman in India who has not suffered the act of her dupatta or sari being pulled, been whistled at or brushed against by strange men, coupled with a request for sexual intercourse, all amounting to 'outraging the modesty' of a woman. The Supreme Court has held that the knowledge that an action is likely to outrage a woman's modesty is sufficient to constitute the offence. The court's definition shows the growing sensitivity to a changing society in which relatively subtle acts of harassment of women have come to be viewed as a crime. In the infamous case of the Director General of Police slapping the posterior of his female colleague, a senior IAS officer, at a party, the court held that the behaviour of the accused was not consistent with the high standard expected of a top-ranking police officer. The findings of the various courts was to the effect that the accused gently slapped the posterior of the woman in the presence of some guests even though he knew fully well that gently slapping the woman's posterior in the presence of other guests would embarrass her.[74]

Centuries ago, Ravan, while regretting his actions, revealed that he had another curse on him from a girl named Vedavati, whose modesty he had outraged by forcibly pulling her hair and humiliating her. The same Vedavati was reborn as Sita to take revenge on him and be the cause of his destruction.

The mighty Ram rushed upon Ravan, shattering his chariot along with its wheels, horses, banner, canopy, great standard, charioteer, darts, spears, and swords. With great force he struck Ravan, and the valiant King of Demons, whom neither thunder nor lightning could cause disturbance or trembling, stumbled, letting fall his bow. Sustaining an ignominious defeat, Ravan escaped with his life and withdrew to Lanka. Ravan, crestfallen and in an introspective mood opened the Pandora's box of his misdemeanours. Downcast he said, 'I was formerly cursed by Vedavati when she was humiliated by me. The same Vedavati is born as the highly fortunate Sita, the daughter of Janak.'[75]

Narrating the story, he said that one day while roaming in the forests of the Himalayas, he saw a young woman wearing the hide of a black antelope, lost in a deep reverie. Attracted to this inexpressibly beautiful woman, he enquired, 'Who are you and why are you doing penance at such a young age? Penance is suitable for older women. You have been made for pleasure'. The meditating girl replied:

> *I am the daughter of the great sage, Kushdhwaja, son of Brihaspati.*[76] *Many gods, gandharvas and rakhshasas wanted my hand in marriage, but my father refused to oblige because he wanted Vishnu, the lord of the three worlds, to be his son-in-law. Sambhu, king of the demons, got so angry at my father's refusal that he killed him one night while he was asleep. My distraught mother chose to die on the funeral pyre of my father.*

> *Now I am performing penance so that I can fulfil my father's desire and become the consort of Vishnu.*

Ravan insisted that she was not suited for such severe penance and requested her to marry him instead, but Vedavati firmly stood her ground. Ravan, taking this as an insult, forcefully pulled her by her tresses. Outraged, she cut off her own hair with her hand, which had turned into a sword, and then lighting a fire said, 'You have defiled me by casting your evil eye on me. Now there is no reason for me to live.' Immolating herself, she entered the blazing fire, to be later reborn as Sita.[77]

Disrobing

Sita brooded over how defiled she felt when Ravan had lifted her by her braid while abducting her. The common feature in both, Sita and Draupadi, is that the perpetrator had 'touched their braids', amounting to molestation and disrobing. Among the first documented cases of disrobing is Draupadi's humiliation and public stripping in the court of the Kauravas, while the elders looked on silently. In the case of Sita, according to Tulsidas, the Sita abducted by Ravan was not the real Sita but 'maya', a surrogate, her illusory image.[78] During Sita's *agnipariksha*, it is the illusory maya that enters the flames and disappears, to reappear as the real Sita. Whereas in Kambana's Tamil version, Ravan does not seize or carry Sita as Valmiki describes it, but simply lifts her with the earth on which she stands, for Sita is 'untouchable'.

Sita was stumped when a woman came to her and, touching her braid said, 'Pretty woman, you have such beautiful long hair, but be careful for there lurks a man on the prowl who chops off women's braids.' Totally flabbergasted, she asked the woman to explain. The woman told her that a mysterious predator had reached New Delhi after spreading panic in Rajasthan, Uttar Pradesh, Haryana, and the Chambal region of Madhya

Pradesh. Villagers were blaming bugs, ghosts, and 'alien-like' creatures. In fact, a picture of the so-called 'hair-eating bug' was doing the rounds of social media in Chambal.[79] In order to fathom the motive, a team of doctors from the Institute of Human Behaviour and Allied Sciences (IBHAS) and a forensic team visited the women, all of whom complained of a severe headache after their braids were chopped off.[80] While the mystery remained unsolved, villagers in the grip of a fear psychosis were taking the law into their own hands and beating suspects. In Agra, a Dalit woman was lynched to death and branded as a witch.[81] Psychologists believe that the women were cutting their hair, either consciously or 'in an altered sensorium'. 'How else does one explain these cases that are happening behind closed doors, in the presence of family members?' an investigator asked. Perhaps this braid chopping is symbolic of the rising gender-based violence by the Ravanas in society; and the internalization of inequalities, humiliations and hierarchies which may be expressed as self-recrimination for a woman's suffering, mistreatment and exclusion. Violence often becomes so normalized that it is rendered invisible. Women often do not perceive it as victimization, with the acts being rooted in profound gendered inequalities that permeate everyday lives, institutions, and state agencies. This omnipresence normalizes the violence.

Foreseeing such crime, and deeply concerned about the rising violence and newer forms of atrocities against women as well as the inadequacy of legal provisions to provide punishment, the issue of disrobing had been taken up in the National Human Rights Commission.[82] They discussed acts of violence and harassment against women including, among others, touching a woman in full public view, forcible chopping off of the hair of a woman, parading a woman naked (in rural areas even the removal of the saree from a woman's head is considered equivalent to nudity/disrobing a woman), being called names etc. It was also mentioned that most of these women belonged to the marginalized sections of society, namely scheduled castes/scheduled tribes..

Prior to the 2013 amendment, there was no specific mention of these crimes in the IPC, and in rural areas such crimes resulted in serious law and order problems, and led to communal/caste violence and tension. Disrobing has been added to the IPC specifically as an offence, and is deemed to occur when a man assaults or uses criminal force on a woman with the intention of disrobing or compelling her to be naked. It is a cognizant and non-bailable offence with a punishment of three to seven years imprisonment.

To be covered under the provisions of this section the perpetrator has to be a man, and the victim a woman. Data on assault or use of criminal force on women with the intent to disrobe was collected separately for the first time in 2014 by the NCRB.[83] The seriousness of the offence can be gauged by the statistics, according to which the total number of cases has risen to almost 10,000 in the year 2016. 18,829 cases are pending trial and 12,859 males having been arrested, with the maximum number of cases registered in New Delhi. In the section Crime/Atrocities against SC/ST (Prevention of Atrocities) Act, the state of Uttar Pradesh occupies the number one position in the country with the maximum number of cases, followed by Odisha. Sita interacted with a survivor from Odisha who said, 'I cannot talk about it because I want to forget it. I have been humiliated enough,' and gestured to her family members to not talk about the incident. Her molesters had even uploaded a video of her being forcibly stripped in public in Bhubaneswar the previous month. With similar videos of molestation and stripping going viral in the state this year, Odisha police are confronted with disturbing statistics that have taken them by surprise. However, the underlying (district) data does not specify if intent to disrobe results in actual disrobement. It is quite possible that in a fight a woman's sari could be pulled off and a case then registered under 354B of IPC. The Police Commissioner of Bhubaneswar-Cuttack said the statistics reflect better reporting standards by police, which has dedicated women units. However, he admited that the high figures for such crimes 'needs research by sociologists'.

According to the police, in many cases, the women targeted were in the company of men not related to them. 'Odisha has been a feudal society, and of late the state has become very unsafe for women,' said Dr Hiranmayee Mishra, a scholar on women's issues in Odisha. 'Prices of gadgets, such as smartphones, have spiralled down and are within reach of people who are not aware of the ethics of using mobile phones and the Internet. These crimes are a reaction of exposure to technology meeting a feudal, patriarchal mindset'. 'A woman in Odisha is considered "loose" or "available", if she is in public in the company of a male friend or boyfriend or colleague,' says Parinita Tripathy, a former teacher at a government engineering college in the state. 'I have personal knowledge of an incident, when a female student, seen with her boyfriend in public, was stripped by a group of men,' she informed Sita.[84]

Often it has been observed that women are victimized by men from their own community, who are clearly establishing disrobing as a manifestation of the patriarchal need to control and subjugate women or grab land and property. Some reported incidents include:

- As per a video[85] taken at Vidisha, a school teacher allegedly tried to disrobe girls of a primary school on the pretext of taking measurements for their school uniforms. This incident also falls in the category of sexual harassment in the workplace since the respondents, being employees, committed the offence in the workplace i.e. the school.
- As per a news reports,[86] about 115 kms from Mumbai, a forty-five-year-old woman was allegedly assaulted and disrobed by six men over a land dispute. The men allegedly pulled her hair, dragged her out of her house and stripped her. The villagers looked on without intervening.

Voyeurism

Voyeurism[87] is a crime where any man who watches or captures the image of a woman, whether he is engaging in a private act or disseminating such images. The term comes from the French 'voyeur' which means 'one who looks'. However, that term is usually applied to a male who observes a woman secretly and, generally, not in a public place. The voyeur does not interact directly with the woman, who is unaware of being observed, with the essence of voyeurism being in the observing. Voyeurism is generally practiced when the woman is doing some activity in private like taking a bath, relieving herself, or having sex etc, but also occurs in public places like public toilets, or trial rooms of shops. The section has two explanations which help understand the term 'private act' and to what extent consent can be used as a defence. The first explanation to the section establishes the meaning of 'private act' to include an act of watching carried out in a place which, in the circumstances, would reasonably be expected to provide privacy, and where the victim's genitals, posterior or breasts are exposed or covered only in underwear—

where, for example, the victim is using a lavatory, or the victim is doing a sexual act that is not ordinarily done in public. When Hanuman went from house to house searching for Sita in Lanka, he saw thousands of women in their most intimate moments, sleeping naked or in a disheveled state. Any other man in his position may have undertaken a voyeuristic journey, but Hanuman remained dispassionate and focused on his task of searching for Sita.

The second explanation to the section clarifies that where the victim consents to the capture of the images or any act but not to their dissemination to third persons, and where such an image or act is disseminated, such dissemination is considered an offence. In the committing of the offence of voyeurism, different techniques are used, like spy cameras, mobile phones etc., and certain image-capturing devices are capable of producing images through materials that are opaque to visible light, including clothing. These devices form images by using electromagnetic radiation outside the visible range.

Sometimes, women in relationships allow intimate photographs to be taken by their partners, who may disseminate the images to a third party without her knowledge, or without the consent of the woman, or may even attempt to subsequently blackmail the woman by implying that if she does not do his bidding, he would put the images/video in the public domain. One of the recently highlighted cases in India is that of a senior Union Minister who spotted a hidden camera in the changing room of a leading clothing chain in Goa. The company denied the allegations and stated that there were no hidden cameras anywhere in the store, including the trial rooms, and that the surveillance cameras installed are prominently displayed. Yet at the same time they conveyed their apologies to the Minister for the inconvenience that had inadvertently been caused to her.[88]

Stalking

Sita, with increasing disquiet read that the capital of India was becoming infamous as the rape and stalking capital. She was unable to comprehend how young men considered stalking to be 'cool', when in reality it was a highly invasive and frightening experience for women. Victims were not only physically followed, but also received texts messages and obsessive telephone calls. Regrettably, this form of violence has been romanticized by Hindi films, and the on-screen stalkers become role models for young boys, who harbour the mistaken belief that the girl will fall in love with them, so much so that there is a total impingement on the girl's right to movement. Stalkers keep tabs on the woman's schedule, showing up at the places she goes to, sending gifts, sending e-mails and messages, repeatedly calling, contacting her or posting about her on social networking sites (Facebook, Twitter, etc.), writing letters (often in blood), damaging her property, throwing semen-filled balloons,[89] and any other action to contact, harass, track, or frighten her. A woman can be stalked by someone she may know casually, a stranger, a past or current friend, or boyfriend. Sita was repulsed to hear about the two teenage sisters who had been set ablaze in their sleep by a local youth who had stalked the younger sister for months. 'He used to follow me on my way to and from school...I had complained about it to my relatives but he kept harassing me,' she cried.[90] Or about the young Dalit girl who was cycling to the vegetable market when some unidentified persons stalked her. The perverts then surrounded her and poured petrol over her, and before she could react, they had set her ablaze. The girl ran for some distance to save herself but finally collapsed and died on the spot.[91]

After an amendment, the offence of stalking[92] has been specifically included in the Indian Penal Code. According to this, any man who follows a woman or attempts to contact a woman to foster personal interaction repeatedly despite a clear indication of disinterest by such woman, commits the offence of stalking and shall be punished with imprisonment. In view of the fact that technology is misused for stalking, the definition also includes monitoring a woman through use of the internet, email, or any other form of electronic communication. This takes into consideration the fact that stalkers use the internet to contact or post things about the woman on message boards or discussion forums. They may also verbally attack or threaten her in chat rooms. Some stalkers post threatening or personal information about the victim online, including her full name and address. Often, stalkers email the victim, fill their inboxes with spam, and send viruses or other harmful programs to the victim's computers. All too often it is seen that the police fail to take stalking seriously, which is why Sita was intrigued when she read a report[93] that the Mumbai police had issued an 'LOC' against a person in a case of stalking. Unable to contain her curiosity she enquired what a LOC was, and was informed that it is a Look Out Circular, commonly issued against terrorists, gangsters, white-collar criminals and murderers. Issued at the local airport by the police, it is shared with all airports in the country. If the suspect tries to leave the country by flight, the immigration department's system alerts the authorities about the person. When the suspect is detained at the airport, the police station concerned is informed about the detention.

It brought some hope to Sita to know that stalking was finally being taken seriously in terms of the law, for not only does it destroy lives, but it also destroys a women's confidence in herself. Stalking can turn life into a living hell, and becomes the victim's first thought in the morning, her last thought at night, and even terrifes her in her dreams. For example, a fourteen-year-old girl who was tired of being stalked and harassed by four youths for a number of months, set herself on fire, sustaining 90 per cent burns.[94] Recognising stalking as a crime sends a powerful message that such behaviour will not be tolerated.

Trafficking

Sita picked up a new term—'trafficking', which she was told was a coercive and violent form of movement, where there was use of force, abuse, violence, deception and exploitation. She found it incredible that in India, human trafficking was an organized criminal process carried out for domestic servitude, commercial sex work, and even organ donation. A frequently used method of deception by traffickers was to lure vulnerable girls by selling them the idea of a 'lucrative job', and thus simultaneously creating the 'urge' to move. After she moved, the woman was trafficked and vulnerable to several harms, including abuse at work, poor living conditions, and health risks. Very often, with rising aspirations and an increase in education, girls who want to make their dream come true fall victim to traffickers who promise them the moon—whether it's the assurance of a job, the rosy picture of marriage, the temptation of money, or the lure of an attractive lifestyle. In the state of Bihar, it has been reported that girls are trafficked for commercial sexual exploitation under the pretext of being offered well-paid domestic help jobs in metropolitan cities. Even in the states of Andhra Pradesh, Kerala, and Tamil Nadu, a large number of women migrate for work but end up being trafficked. There can be no prohibition on women migrating, since they migrate for a multiplicity of reasons, including displacement and dispossession, to search for sustainable livelihoods, Naxal activity, to search for more fulfilling opportunities, or an aspiration for more in life. In the process of migration, the lack of access for women and girls to safe channels for mobility, as well as the absence of legal and social protection, aggravates their vulnerability to trafficking and harm. Sita was plagued with angst and felt that unsafe migration and human trafficking were not recognized as serious community issues and hence were not prioritized.

Sita was appalled to know that extreme poverty, combined with the the low social status of women, often resulted in parents handing over their children to strangers for what they believed was education, employment, or marriage with 'about 200 girls and women entering prostitution daily of which 20 per cent are below fifteen years of age.'[95] According to a study called 'ROSHINI' (Research Study on Human Right Violation on Victims of Trafficking),[96] since in many cases blood relatives and other community members close to the trafficked person benefitted financially from the process, the victim was generally reluctant to make a complaint because the trafficker may be a person known to her. It was not uncommon for families to sell their daughters in times of economic distress to avoid starvation. In the continuum of anti-trafficking initiatives, law formulation and enforcement is more or less restricted to the areas of raid, rescue, repatriation and, to a limited extent, rehabilitation. During the survey, many sex workers denied entering the trade as minors, but on probing and calculating their ages backwards, the figures were alarming. 61 per cent entered the trade when they were under twenty-one years of age. There is a strong need for protection of commercial sex workers in terms of working conditions and their rights, including occupational health and safety provisions, particularly so, in the context of HIV/AIDS and other sexually transmitted diseases.

Sita was alarmed by the marked absence of any standard guideline for law enforcement in the intervention or prevention of trafficking. She read an NHRC survey[97] in which data was collected by interviewing 852 police officials (117 senior officials and 735 middle/junior rank officials), which presented the following scenario:

- Awareness – There is a lack of proper delivery of justice to the victims of trafficking since 38.7 per cent of the police officials were not even aware of the issues relating to trafficking.
- Training - Only 6.6 per cent of the police officials had received training on matters related to women and children, which includes certain issues related to trafficking.
- Priority in law enforcement - 54.8 per cent of police officers give no priority at all to trafficking, 25.3 give it low priority, 12.2 per cent consider it to be a medium priority issue, and only 7.7 per cent considered it a high priority issue.
- Registration of crime - Reporting on trafficking appears to be only 40 per cent. As stated by the police officers themselves, 60 per cent of the cases go unreported.
- Pattern of chargesheeting and conviction - Sex-disaggregated data shows that approximately 93 per cent of the persons charged with sex-related trafficking cases are females. So it is not surprising that almost 90 per cent of the persons convicted under the Immoral Traffic (Prevention) Act (ITPA)[98] are women.

What unnerved Sita was that most of the girls who had been trafficked and exploited belonged to the most vulnerable sections of society, i.e.the scheduled castes/scheduled tribes. They came from areas which are relatively inaccessible and deprived. In addition, they were at risk of unsafe migration due to their relative isolation being disturbed because of planned development—dams, mines, industries, and roads. Sita felt that the prevention of trafficking required not only examining the factors that contributed to the problem but also, providing awareness among potential victims in order to reduce their vulnerability.

Abetment to Suicide

Sita never realized that her threats to end her life would unfortunately become trend setting. Cultural contexts are one of the determinants that regulate a person's mood and mind and, especially in India, influence the female psyche significantly. Suicide is so integrated into the culture of Indian society that even minor girls have been reported to die of starvation to earn good luck for their family.[99] It is ironic that the girl belonged to a religion that advocates non-violence and does not allow for accidental killing, even of small insects and microbes. Community members, in fact, wear masks so that they don't accidentally inhale small organisms in the air. In India, depression-related suicide among women is largely related to the feudalistic attitude of males towards females, and the lack of alternative shelter and finances for woman. According to a WHO report, '350 million people suffer from depressive disorders and often start at a young age and manifest with different depressive characters as they grow, and the pattern of depressive characters keeps on changing.'[100]

Sita had threatened to commit suicide a number of times. The first time was as a young girl in the throes of love, defying all logic. She revealed to Ram that had he not succeeded in lifting Shiva's bow, and had her father not allowed her to marry him, then she would have terminated her life rather than continue living. The second time was as a devoted wife in her passion to accompany her husband into exile to the forest. On seeing Ram remaining unconvinced by any of her arguments, she threatened to resort to poison, fire, or water to kill herself if he was not willing to take her. Again, upon being abducted, she is stated to have preferred death rather than surrender. She warned Ravan that the purpose for which he was carrying her off would never be fulfilled, for, being away from her god-like husband, she may not survive.

The different means by which Sita threatened to end her life included consuming poison, hanging, plunging into the river, and self-immolation. They are the methods still employed by women today to commit suicide. A married woman often is so tortured and harassed in her matrimonial home that she is driven to the brink of suicide. The ordeal makes the young woman hit rock bottom emotionally, and when she is all alone she finds an opportunity to end her life. One longs for death only when torture or grief becomes unbearable. Sita remembered the time when she herself considered suicide.

Sita, the enlightened and knowledgeable soul. A staunch believer in God. How could she do something so unbearable, go against nature and give up her life? Or was this also a part of God's plan? Sita, in defiance of her faith, wisdom, and love for God, was overcome by utter hopelessness. Feeling defeated and helpless, she wanted to die, because she thought Ram may not be able to locate her. Just as Ram felt that life was meaningless without Sita, she also felt there could be no happiness for her without Ram. If she had to suffer unhappiness only, and could not be reunited with Ram, then why not court death? Trembling, she approached a tree in bloom, and surveyed various methods to carry through her plan.

As she seized the branch with the intention of hanging herself, at the same moment, a propitious omen never seen before appeared on her person. Her left eye, left shoulder, and left thigh quivered, due to which her clothing glided down a little bit. Sensing the omens, Sita's consciousness was awakened with exaltation. Suddenly she felt relieved. Free from the sorrow which had been pressing down on her. Her weariness disappeared and. And the weight on her mind lifted. The enlivened Sita looked handsome as her lovely face beamed with happiness after what seemed like centuries, like night shining bright in the light of the moon.[101]

Nowadays women do not have long braids such as the one Sita had, and instead use their dupattas or saris and tie themselves to a fan to escape what is often the torture inflicted on them by their husband and matrimonial family. This has even led to ingenious marketing by ceiling fan entrepreneurs, who have started selling suicide-proof fans,[102] as well as fans with siren sensors and a spring device that will lower the fans if anyone tries to hang themselves on it.[103]

Based on the law of public policy, an act of abetting suicide is punishable under the law.[104] To be considered abetment, the intention of the accused to aid, instigate, or abet the deceased to commit suicide is necessary. Courts have held that there should be an intention to provoke, incite or encourage the doing of an act by the latter. The NCRB 2016 statistics reveal an increase in the total cases of abetment of suicides of women, with the maximum number of such cases registered in Maharashtra, followed by Madhya Pradesh and Telangana.[105] The charge of abetment of suicide is usually accompanied by a charge under section 498A of the IPC, if the woman was treated cruelly by her husband or his relatives, or where a woman has died within seven years of her marriage. While the legal recognition of such a crime is heartening, one cannot help but point out how many cases of abetment go unpunished, especially given the heavy burden of proof required in a court of law and the absence of advocacy for the deceased.

Abandonment

Feeling awful, Sita brooded over her own story of abandonment, and the tendency to put the blame on the woman irrespective of who was at fault. Although Sita was not present at the time, she could well imagine what had transpired when Ram took the life-changing decision where she turned from a queen into an abandoned pauper.

On hearing about the circulating rumours from his friends, Ram summoned his brothers, Bharata, Laxman and Shatrughana, and addressed them with tears in his eyes. He told them about the rumours and said,

> *O Laxmana! You know how to prove her innocence and purity, Sita entered the blazing fire. Then the Sun God himself appeared and the Wind God himself declared her free from any taint. In the presence of the gods and sages, the Sun and Moon Gods declared Sita absolutely free of any sin and innocent and pure. My innermost soul also knows she is pure in body and mind. That is why I brought her to Ayodhya. But now these rumours are greatly distressing me.*

His obsession with dharma made him continue, 'For the fear of any scandal besmirching my reputation, I can forsake my life even, let alone Sita. You all can see at this moment I am sinking in the ocean of slander. No one can be more sorrowful than I am.'

Then Ram did the unthinkable. He ordered Laxman to take Sita in the chariot and abandon her in the forest near the hermitage of Maharishi Valmiki. Laxman, not to be silenced, retorted back before he left, 'But let me say this, my Lord; if gossip can drive you to this resolve, it will in turn generate more gossip, no less idle and vicious.'[106]

Ram did not have the courage to confront Sita and reject her. Was it because as a husband, he felt uncomfortable to address her as the King of Ayodhya? Possibly he feared that having a mind of her own, Sita would assert herself as she had when he had asked her to stay behind with the queen mothers and she had, contrary to his wishes, insisted on accompanying him into exile. When he tried to set her free from all obligations of marriage after killing Ravan, she had insisted on walking through fire to prove her chastity. Ram may have apprehended that if he told her about the rumours, she would argue and question him, and he would have had no answer. It was perhaps for the same reasons that Ram had precluded even his brothers from any discussion.

The next day dawned as usual. Laxman, with a darkened face came to Sumantra, the royal charioteer, and instructed him to get the chariot ready. Then he went to Sita, and told her that the king, granting her wish, had directed him to take her to the forest to see the hermitages. Delighted, Sita instantly agreed to go. Taking along expensive clothes and a variety of gems to be donated to the sages, she gleefully mounted the chariot. She was completely unaware of the fact that she was going to be abandoned in a clandestine manner, with no one there to bid her adieu.

After having spent the night on the banks of the River Gomti in a hermitage, the next day in the afternoon they reached the banks of the River Ganga. On seeing the flowing waters of the river, Laxman, who loved Sita like a mother, was unable to control himself, and burst into tears. On reaching the other side of the river, Laxman, with eyes full of tears, with folded hands, and in a choked voice said, 'O Videh kumari! The noble king has deputed me to execute a cruel plan, for which I will always be condemned by generations to come. It would have been better had I died before committing such a heinous act, but I am trapped in a web.' Saying this, Laxman fell at Sita's feet.

Sita was highly distressed to see Laxman behaving in such an unbecoming manner, and a cold hand gripped her heart. She said, 'I do not understand what you are muttering. Say what you want to clearly. From your behavior it seems it has something to do with Ram, I hope he is fine? I command you to reveal the cause of your sorrow.'

Laxman, unable to hide the deceit anymore, with his head bent and voice faltering, spoke about the rumours to Sita. He tried to be brief, not wishing to distress her with details, and said, 'To summarise, the king has abandoned you. But in my eyes you will always remain pure, and even the king has expressed his view on your purity before me; but he fears public censure.'

Sita, on these hearing such harsh and cruel words from Laxman, was stunned and fell unconscious on the earth. Recovering her senses, she got up and with tears in her eyes said, 'God has created me so that I suffer only sorrow in my life. I wonder what sins I have committed in my previous life … What reply will I give to the sages on their asking, when I have committed no sin?' Sita in a frenzy, wanting to show Laxman the signs of her pregnancy, taunted him and said, 'And before you leave, look at me, I have missed several cycles!'[107]

Society always takes its pound of flesh from a woman, who is expected to be pure of body, pure of mind, and pure in reputation. Sita, hemmed in on all sides and betrayed even by Laxman—who left her in the forest on false pretenses, boldly goes to the extent of giving her sons a matrilineal heritage. To be fair to Laxman, he was in great pain at having to obey and carry out such an unjust command by his king and elder brother. However, he did not dare unmask the true intent of their trip to the forest and, squirming with shame, left Sita on a false pretense. When Ram asks Kush and Luv about their teacher and parents, the children introduce themselves as 'Sita's children'. This introduction is meaningful as Kush and Luv have only seen Sita as a parent, who was probably the first-known single mother in history.

Sumantra told Laxman not to be sorrowful over Sita's predicament. Her rejection and banishment was preordained, and had been revealed to King Dashrath by the Brahmins.

Society devalued women, treated them shamefully, and blamed it all on fate! In order to justify the action of Ram deserting her when she was five months pregnant, various stories started circulating. According to one such story,[108] one day during her childhood Sita was playing with her friends, when she saw a couple of parrots.

The parrots talking to each other, said, 'On the earth, charming Rama will be the king. His wife will be (a woman) by name Sita. The intelligent, powerful king, vanquishing (his enemies), will rule (over the earth) along with her for eleven thousand years.' Sita, curious on hearing her name, asked her friends to catch the birds and bring them to her. Sita asked them a number of questions about her future to which they replied. Finally, Sita revealing her identity, said, 'I am that Janaki, the daughter of Janaka, whom you mentioned. I shall truly release you when that very charming Rama comes to me; not otherwise …' The parrots protested that they were birds who lived on trees and freely wandered about. How could they be happy in her house? The female parrot cried, 'I am pregnant. Having gone to my place and having given birth to sons (i.e. young ones) I shall come (back).' Sita refused to free them. The male parrot repeatedly requested her to free them. Sita told him to fly away leaving his wife there. Then the female parrot cursed Sita and said, 'As you are separating me from my husband, in the same way you will be, when pregnant, separated from Rama.' She died with sorrow of separation from her husband. After the death of his wife, the male parrot said, 'In Rama's city, full of people, I will be born as (a sudra so) that due to my words she will be dejected, and extremely unhappy due to separation (from her husband).'

Sita was lucky to find shelter in Valmiki's ashram, where she gave birth to two healthy children, who were looked after with care and affection, and where their proper growth and development was ensured—unlike many women she saw lying on the pavements, who were abandoned by their husbands, or those who opted to be on the streets rather than in an abusive marriage. Sita tried to talk to them and share their sorrow, but they were not willing to engage with her, preferring to stay withdrawn and aloof. Perhaps life on the roadside had made them withdraw into shells where they saw no light; they seemed to be 'living but their souls were lost'.

Sita was dedicated to Ram, and had insisted on being with him and sharing his misfortune during his exile. Despite being a princess, she lived in the wilderness with her husband and Laxman. This time it was different! She had returned to the forest as an abandoned queen. She was compelled to undergo the shame of rejection, the pain of losing a soulmate through betrayal and deceit, and the toll of having to start life all over again. She was all alone! There was no Ram, no Laxman. The mothers-in-law who loved her so dearly also did not come to Sita's aid. They only moaned:

> *'Oh God why have you given us such a pure daughter-in-law, on whom you are determined to pile difficulty after difficulty. My daughter-in-law is carrying the child of my son, why are you determined to pelt her with disrepute? There can be no comparion between the loose talk of some corrupted astray minds and this daughter of the earth and daughter-in-law of mine'*[109]

But it was too late. There was no one to pay attention to the words of the old women. Abandoned and forlorn, Sita was totally dependent on the sages for sustaining herself. Caring for her and counselling her, they helped heal her broken heart. Never once during these adverse conditions did she consider taking her own life. Life was growing within her womb, and she did not want her unborn child to suffer any adversity. The miracle of life within her became the focus of her life. She felt the flutter of a sensation like no other. It is believed that according to the rules of the hermitage everyone had to work. In view of her condition, she was given the task of making floral garlands for the gods. She even made her own clothes and tilled the soil with her tender hands.[110] Motivated by making her own little heaven in the forest and putting the pieces of her life back together, she went about her daily routine, focusing on the life growing within her. It is said that forgiving the offender helps expedite the healing process, and soon resentment against the king began to fade away. Not once did Sita blame Ram, and remained devoted to him—in body, soul and spirit.

Instead of fixating on her own pain, she focused on her unborn child. According to Hindu belief, the soul enters the foetus 22 days after conception. Emotions develop after four months, and the mind begins to function during the fifth month, as the foetus wakes from the sleep of subconscious existence. The intellect develops in the sixth month. Each movement of the baby gave Sita a thrill. Every flutter and kick made her radiant with joy. Her appetite increased, and she smiled more often now. Repeatedly, her hand would go to her belly as if protecting her unborn child. Her body swelled freely, and the moment of birth was approaching. Like any parent to be she looked forward to the birth of her child. Although Ram was not there to support her, she had the support of Valmiki and the ashram mates. Sita thought her situation was much better than a lot of modern India's mothers, who had come for hospital deliveries with their unsympathetic or abusive husbands. The road as a single mother was not easy for her, but she had the right people with her as a birth team, and she and her twin baby boys got through childbirth just as well as she would have with Ram.

Sita's eyes glistened as a shooting star burned its way though the full moon night of Sravan Poornima. At midnight two little miracles were sent from above. Two adorable babies to cuddle and love. Her babies before her, she swept them into the safety of her warm bosom and hugged them, silently promising them unconditional love and protection. She bowed her head listening to them chuckle and cry, and all her sorrows dissipated. They reminded her of Ram, who remained eternally in her heart.

She had done wisely, she felt; she had fought despair and spurned the death wish when her wedded life had crashed on the rocks and she was a castaway. Ah, the bliss of fulfillment in motherhood! The cry of the just-born babe. And so Maithili, tired but contented, rested in peace for a while, and now refreshed and happy, was ready for the tasks of motherhood.[111]

Sita, abandoned in the forest, survived her pregnancy centuries ago, and as a single mother, brought up Kush and Luv in ignorance of their royal lineage and identity. Their childhood was secure and happy, but bereft of the luxuries of the court and comforts of life. They may have had less, but there was an abundance of love both in their home and in their lives. Like their mother, who was dearly loved by the queen mothers and was the apple of their eye, the twins were similarly dearly cherished by the ashram inmates and were the light of their lives. Their affection was the twins' only lifeline. It is only later that they would grow up to find out that their father was so bound to the concept of dharma, that he spurned their pure and devoted mother in her pregnant state. Sita remembered how she did not yearn for palace life, being content with her children, their upbringing, and their education.

She was taken aback to find out that today in India 55,000 women die annually from preventable pregnancy-related causes. In most cases, infections and disease are compounded by chronic hunger, malnutrition, and a lack of access to affordable pre-birth healthcare services because of corruption or caste bias.[112] Maternal death rates remained the highest in the populous states of Assam, Bihar (land of Sita), Madhya Pradesh, Odisha,

Rajasthan, and Uttar Pradesh. Activists have been quoted as stating that caste plays a role in the exclusion of certain women from health services. For example, marginalised tribes like the Saharias[113] lose out nutritionally, socially, and economically.

Maternal deaths also adversely affect the health of the surving newborn children, who are trapped in a vicious cycle of malnutrition, stunting, and poor health outcomes. Women in the lowest socio-economic sections in India are two-and-a-half times more likely to die of childbirth, largely because they don't get the medical support they need to deliver a healthy baby.

The question then arises—what makes a man abandon his wife? Ram deserted his wife to uphold his so-called dharma, giving weight to the suspicious minds of the public. If dharma or duty is going to be defined by popular choice, then only adharma or unethical decisions will be made. In today's democratic system, elected representatives are unlikely to have the courage and integrity to go against popular public opinion and take a decision for the general good of the people, tending instead to curry favour with the intention to be re-elected. A sound leader should respond to the needs of its citizens and have the temerity and integrity to resist the temptation to selfishly echo the preferences of the loudest voices.

Some brides are abandoned on the wedding night itself without the marriage being consummated, some after a brief honeymoon when the woman is pregnant, and some after a few years on some bogus pretext. On asking the man why he got married in the first place when he had no intention to fulfill his marital commitments, the usual answer is to make his parents happy. It is incredulous how the parents can be 'made happy' because, after abandoning the bride, the man usually disappears and his parents have to bear the burden of social stigma and legal cases, if any.

The problem is aggravated when the spouse is an overseas citizen, with women isolated in an alien country facing the constraints of communication and a lack of information about the local criminal justice system. The extent of the problem is so severe that, based on the recommendation of the Parliamentary Committee on Empowerment of Woman (14th Lok Sabha) on the subject 'Plight of Indian woman deserted by NRI husbands', the Ministry of Overseas Indian Affairs[114] nominated The National Commission for Woman as the coordinating agency for dealing with issues pertaining to NRI marriages. The Ministry also has a scheme for legal and financial assistance for women deserted by their overseas Indian spouses. The states most affected include Punjab, Gujarat, and Kerala, among others.[115]

Sita followed a debate raging in the country about triple talaq and the need for its abolition, following petitions by Muslim women in the Supreme Court. A bold Muslim woman had approached the Supreme Court[116] to assail the divorce pronounced by her husband, wherein he affirmed:

> …in the presence of witnesses saying that I gave 'talaq, talaq, talaq', hence like this I divorce from you from my wife. From this date there is no relation of husband and wife. From today I am '*haraam*', and I have become '*naamharram*'. In future you are free for using your life …

She had sought a declaration that the '*talaq-e-biddat*' pronounced by her husband be declared as void ab initio, and had also contended that such a divorce—which abruptly, unilaterally and irrevocably terminates the ties of matrimony under the Muslim Personal Law (Shariat) Application Act, 1937, be declared unconstitutional. *Talaq-e-biddat*, an Islamic practice in India which permitted men to instantly divorce their wives, rendered Muslim women homeless overnight, and left them destitute. Their marriages were dissolved with the word 'talaq' or divorce being pronounced three times. In many cases, the women were not even present when the husband uttered talaq thrice. But what astonished Sita was that Islamic seminaries[117] in Deoband decided that triple talaq could be pronounced through emails and messages too.

The Supreme Court opined that the Hanafi school of Shariat law, recognizing this form of divorce, specifically states that though lawful, it is sinful in that it incurs the wrath of God. Referred to was the case of Shamim Ara[118] where, after referring to a number of authorities including certain recent High Court judgments, it was held that the correct law of talaq, as ordained by the Holy Quran, is that talaq must be for a reasonable cause and must be preceded by attempts at reconciliation between the husband and the wife by two arbiters—one from the wife's family and the other from the husband's. If the attempts fail, talaq may be effected. Finally, the Supreme Court held that given the fact that triple talaq is instant and irrevocable, it is obvious that any attempt at reconciliation between the husband and wife by two arbiters from their families, which is essential to save their marital ties, cannot ever take place. It is also clear that this form of talaq is manifestly arbitrary in the sense that the marital ties can be broken capriciously and whimsically by a Muslim man without any attempt at reconciliation to save it. This form of talaq, therefore, is violative of the fundamental right contained under Article 14 of the Constitution of India.

This landmark judgement was hailed by Muslim women all over India, especially poor and illiterate women who constantly lived under pressure and fear of being given talaq for any petty reason. Despite this, Sita felt that most people had missed the central issue—which was the inability of society and the law to protect women after divorce, while patriarchy and power, masquerading as religion, continued to take centre stage. The government had proposed The Muslim Women (Protection of Rights on Marriage) Bill which criminalised *talaq-e-biddat* and proposed a jail term for a Muslim man who divorced his wife in this way. Interestingly, the Ministry of Women and Child Development (WCD) questioned the need for separate legislation, arguing that divorce by triple talaq amounted to cruelty and hence, fell within the purview of Section 498A of the Indian Penal Code which provided for punitive action against a husband or his relatives.[119] The WCD Ministry also flagged the issues of payment of maintenance, and the custody of children. The proposed Bill provides for maintenance to be paid to the wife through a magistrate, and for her to get custody of the couple's child. Both of these provisions would legitimise the talaq, the WCD Ministry argued. Sita found it incredible that the WCD Ministry was not a part of the inter-ministerial group that was set up to draft the Bill after the Supreme Court 'set aside' the practice of instant triple talaq. The group was headed by the Home Minister and included the External Affairs Minister, Finance Minister, and Law Minister among others. Sita also felt that Muslim women did not need another unenforceable legislation; instead they needed more awareness about their rights within the community, and access to legal representation to avail their entitlements. Sita was gratified to know that young girls rebelling against repressive systems were raising their voices. One such bold voice[120] was of a sixteen-year-old girl from rural Bengal, who gave triple talaq to her husband when he opposed her wish to continue her studies.

Defiling Mother Earth

Sita had returned to earth to ruminate about womanhood in modern India, but now she was feeling overwrought. Her eyes, that once shone with laughter, were now dulled with tears. Her melodious voice that rose in song, soothing many, was now harsh and discordant from protesting. Tired and embittered by unfulfilled promises, she wanted to escape to nature. She calmed herself by splashing the clear pure water of River Ganga on her face. Little did she know that the sacred river, in spite of being declared a living entity by the courts, was dying due to the dumping of toxic waste; and that the waters of most of the rivers were being depleted by a combination of drought and over-consumption. Sita regained her presence of mind by picturing the forest, daydreaming of the feel of sand under her feet, and envisioning wide open spaces.

Sita, the daughter of Mother Earth, always had an innate sense of love for nature and, as a child, found it to be a place to escape for creative inspiration. Her special connection with the earth prompted her to play, explore, and interact with the natural world freely. She climbed on fallen logs, leaped over tiny streams, and wandered through the tall grasses. She could identify birds from their songs, felt exhilarated on spotting butterflies, and followed the pug marks of animals. Sita took delight in the flowers, the animals, and the mountains. She nodded at them, and they to her. Nature activated her senses and expanded her awareness, opening up a new world. The natural beauty of forest life delighted Sita, where she remained cheerful and content, often preferring it to the complexities of palace life. Her love for nature also proved to be a misgiving, for she was deceitfully abandoned on the pretext of being taken to enjoy the calm of the sages' hermitage in the forest.

Sita was welcomed by nature with the same enthusiasm and love she had for it. During their exile, wherever she went, the forests blossomed with her presence each step of the way. Conversing with earth's creations and sharing her joys and sorrows, she walked through the woods, tenderly touching the vegetation in her path, and pushing it aside to make way. When Ravan abducted Sita and forcibly flew off with her, she desperately called out to the trees, the river, the birds and animals, to help her and inform Ram of her abduction. Nature was tormented by her plea. Even the cruelest of animals respond with compassion, but only if humans being are compassionate towards them. Neither had Sita done anything to scare the animals, nor was any animal scared of Sita. Feeling helpless, the trees shed tears in the form of sap, and the lions, deer, and elephants were heartbroken.

When Mother Nature was being violated, did her creatures silently watch the abduction of their mother? Were they convinced of the approaching destruction? Did they not respond? Yes, they did, but in their own way.

Ravan's flight created a gust of upheaval, and nature responded to it in its own unique way. The trees swayed and bent with the wind. When the trees are swaying, will not the birds perched on it chirp and chatter? So, the birds started twittering and the trees swaying, as if gesturing with raised hands and consoling her not to fear. Nature itself was assuring Sita, the earth-born one and kindred of trees, to not be afraid. All the animals, gathered in herds from all over and ran rancorously, pursuing the shadow of Sita.

A mountain cannot fly up to confront Ravan like an eagle, nor can it express it's anguish like a swaying tree or a chirping bird, nor can it doggedly run like other animals. So the mountains appeared to be wailing, shedding tears through their waterfalls. Their peaks seemed like upraised arms, expressing their anguish while Sita was being abducted.[121]

So it was but natural in this woeful moment that Sita, having a special relationship with nature, felt a desire to connect with it. But another horror awaited her, for this safe haven had also been devastated by human beings. The gushing rivers tore their embankments and overflowed, destroying human habitations. It was a forewarning, for man wanted to discover the unknown mysteries of the earth and sky, but failed to value what there was right under his feet. 'The earth lay defiled by its inhabitants, for they transgressed the laws, violated the statutes, and had broken the everlasting covenant.'[122] Plundered, Mother Earth was mourning and withering away, and her people were languishing. Centuries ago, Sita had been aware of human influence on climate change through their behavior. Would people learn to emulate Sita by making simple changes in their habits to help reduce waste and save the planet for future generations? Or would they continue on this path, accustomed to throwaway lifestyles, ever-changing fashions, and fast foods?

Earlier, during her days in Valmiki's ashram, Sita reviewed the course of human growth—the adventure of civilization and the flowering of cultures. She felt that the India of today belied its traditional philosophy that the cosmos was eternal and had neither a beginning nor an end, because today human beings were headed towards the annihilation of their own planet. Did growth in the influence of human civilization over nature have to be equated only to destruction? There seemed to be no end to the sacrilege. Sita could almost hear Mother Earth moan, '*These witless ones, these restless improvident children, are destroying my terrestrial balance. I've bequeathed to them easy conditions of living and surviving as a race leading millions of others and essaying harmony.*'[123]

In this 'concrete jungle' with its busy traffic, massive crowds, and restless nights, where could Sita feel fresh oxygen in her lungs or get some fresh air to feel invigorated?

While searching for Sita, Ram found flowers strewn on the ground, followed by her footprints, as well as the heavy footprints of some male rakshasa. In desperation, he threatened to destroy the three worlds. It was Laxman's reasoning which won over Ram. He tried to dissuade Ram against taking any drastic action, which may have long-term repercussions, in a fit of anger, leading to the annihilation of the world. Now, not anger but man's selfishness and wanton destruction would cause catastrophic devastation.

Laxman cautioned his elder brother that it would be unapt of him to vandalize the world, wreaking havoc merely for an individual's wrong doing. At the spot they could see traces of a terrible struggle, but not footprints of many soldiers. Even the debris of a lone chariot made it apparent that only one culprit had been involvement.

Expounding on the most fundamental questions of life, Laxman told Ram that mishaps happened even to the best of men. It was the law of karma. However if he, Ram, a highly elevated soul, was unable to cope with anguish, then how would an ordinary person, with limited means and nerve, be able to manage? Laxman reminded him of accomplished persons who, due to their impiety, had been reduced to dust. Laxman elucidated that even Mother Earth, who was venerated by animate, inanimate, and even celestial beings, was afflicted with tremors and earthquakes. Even the gods did not remain unscathed by agony and ecstasy, whether it was Indra, the lord of the gods or any other. Laxman adduced that the past, present, and future were a web of delicately woven threads of complex inter-relationships, from which there is no escape. Hence, it was unapt of Ram to fret like that.

Laxman argued that the severity of a punishment should be proportionate to the gravity of the offence. The punishment may be performing a salutary educational function as a deterrent, but it should be imposed only on the offender, and not on the population as a whole, who are innocent of any crime. Won over by Laxman's reasoning, Ram contained his anger.[124]

Sita wondered where the Laxmans of today's world were, as she saw the planet's natural ecosystems and regenerating bio-capacity being severely degraded, compromising the ability of Mother Earth to sustain life. Sita was a mute spectator to the forests, fisheries, oceans, freshwater systems—whether lakes, wetlands, or rivers, and other natural ecosystems—being threatened due to man's greed. What outraged her most was that species were dying out faster than their natural rate of extinction. Forest reserves and wildlife were being depleted by random deforestation, poaching, shifting cultivation, and habitat disturbances. The traditional forest dwellers or the rakshasa,[125] who protected the forests, had been thrown out to satisfy the commercial designs of transnational corporations. Ordinary people no longer spent time sitting around in bonhomie under the winter sun—talking, laughing, singing or simply lazing, and enjoying the cold crisp air against their flushed faces.

Sita was intimidated to read a report, published in The Lancet Journal,[126] which stated that in 2015, pollution was the reason behind nine million deaths worldwide (about one in six), and India accounted for 2.5 million of those deaths. She was horrified to know that pollution was killing more people every year than smoking, hunger, and natural disasters. It even killed more people than AIDS, tuberculosis, and malaria put together. Remembering the battle ground at Lanka made her blood run cold when she was informed that pollution caused 15 times more deaths than wars and other forms of violence. Most of these deaths were due to non-communicable diseases caused by pollution such as heart disease, strokes, lung cancer, and chronic obstructive pulmonary disease (COPD). Of the nine million deaths, air pollution was the biggest contributor, linked to 6.5 million of them, while water pollution was responsible for 1.8 million. Work place-related pollution was the reason behind 0.8

million deaths. Causes for air pollution-linked deaths included ambient air pollution, i.e. outdoor air pollution comprising gases and particulate matter, household air pollution—which results from the burning of wood, charcoal, coal, dung, or crop wastes indoors, as well asambient ozone. Water pollution included unsafe sanitation and polluted water sources. Deaths due to lead pollution were a result of diseases such as high blood pressure, renal failure, and cardiovascular diseases, the study stated.

Sita was consoled to know that some people were trying to find solutions to rejuvenate India's rivers, reduce floods, drought and soil loss, and increase farmers' incomes. Sadhguru of the Isha Foundation himself drove from Kanyakumari to Himalayas to create awareness of the need to rally for rivers.[127] If we do not act now, the legacy we hand over to the next generation will be one of conflict and deprivation. These rivers have nurtured and nourished us for thousands of years. It is time we nurture and nourish them back to health.

The problem of air and water pollution had reached such alarming proportions, causing immense harm to the peace, well-being, and health (both physical and mental) of India's citizens, that the Supreme Court of India was forced to intervene.[128] According to reports, the air quality standards in the National Capital Region of Delhi were the worst in the world and that the Particulate Matter (PM) 2.5 levels recorded were beyond scale values. Sita was aghast to know that on the morning after Diwali the citizens of citizens woke up to an average PM 2.5 level of over 700 $\mu g/m^3$—some of the highest levels recorded the world over, and 29 times above WHO standards. She felt ashamed that a festival to commemorate Ram and her return after 14 years of exile was being celebrated in such a destructive way that the lives of citizens had been brought to a virtual standstill, not to mention the plight of the diverse flora and fauna. Schools had been declared shut, denizens of the city were advised to stay indoors, construction activities were stopped, power stations were shut, and a ban was imposed on the burning of garbage and agricultural waste. The adverse effects of these extreme levels of air pollution spare no one—the young, the old, the infirm, and even future generations.

A study of the data of the Global Health Depository of the World Health Organization revealed that India has the world's highest death rate from chronic respiratory diseases, and that about 1.5 million people in India die annually due to indoor and outdoor pollution. The Kolkata-based Chittaranjan National Cancer Institute (CNCI), in a study commissioned and handed over to the Central Pollution Control Board, found that key indicators of respiratory health, from lung function and palpitation, to vision and blood pressure, of children in Delhi, between four and seventeen years of age, were worse off than their counterparts elsewhere.[129] It also found that more than 40 per cent of school children suffer from lung damage. In addition, nascent studies suggested that pollution can lower children's I.Q., hurt their test scores, and increase the risks of autism, epilepsy, diabetes, and adult-onset diseases like multiple sclerosis. Other health-related issues like allergies and temporary deafness are also on the rise. Various experts have pointed towards the multiple adverse effects of air pollution on human health like premature deaths, rise in mortality rates, palpitations, loss of vision, arthritis, heart ailments, cancer, etc. UNICEF had urged countries to take immediate action to reduce air pollution amid emerging evidence on how toxic air can affect brain development in young children. Almost 17 million babies under the age of one live in areas where air pollution is at least six times higher than international limits, causing them to breathe toxic air, and thus potentially putting their brain development at risk, according to a new UNICEF paper.[130]

The paper shows that air pollution, like inadequate nutrition and stimulation, as well as exposure to violence during the critical first 1,000 days of life, can impact children's early childhood development by affecting their growing brains. Ultra-fine pollution particles are so small that they can enter the blood stream, travel to the brain, and damage the blood-brain barrier, causing neuro-inflammation. Some pollution particles, such as ultra-fine magnetite, can enter the body through the olfactory nerve and the gut and, due to their magnetic charge, create oxidative stress—which is known to cause neurodegenerative diseases. Other types of pollution particles, such as polycyclic aromatic hydrocarbons, can damage areas in the brain that are critical in helping neurons communicate, the foundation for children's learning and development. A young child's brain is especially vulnerable because it can be damaged by a smaller dosage of toxic chemicals, as compared to an adult's brain. Children are also highly vulnerable to air pollution because they breathe more rapidly and because their physical defences and immunities are not fully developed. The paper outlines urgent steps to reduce the impact of air pollution on babies' growing brains, including immediate steps parents can take to reduce their children's exposure in the home to harmful fumes produced by tobacco products, cooking stoves, and fires. Sita totally endorsed the view that no child should have to breathe dangerously polluted air—and that no society can afford to ignore air pollution.

When she had returned with Ram and Laxman, people had illuminated their homes and pathways with great enthusiasm, symbolizing the triumph of good over evil. But what she saw now was the opposite, and was conscience-stricken at how dangerous forms of firecrackers were being rampantly exploded in her name. These fireworks released a deadly concoction of fumes into an almost-still winter air and, apart from causing acute air pollution, also caused severe noise pollution. Numerous accidents took place due to the unregulated manufacture, storage, and transport of fireworks, resulting in substantial damage to life and property. Sita's breath revived on hearing that the Supreme Court recognized that the duty to ensure a healthy environment not only falls on the State, according to Article 48-A of the Constitution, but also on all its citizens under Article 51A (g), and considered it inappropriate that explosives, which are used as fireworks, should be available in the market for consumers. Just then Sita heard the Chief Justice of India speaking at a function, where he voiced what was in her mind. He said everyone had the right to breathe fresh air and have pure water, and that the tribunals, courts, and governments had a 'sacrosanct' duty to see that the appropriate standard of environment was maintained. 'Nature tells you every moment and warns you every moment that look whatever you are doing, is being watched. Do not destroy nature. The day has come when you have to care for Mother Nature every day, every hour, every moment.'[131]

Distraught, there was no piece of land where Sita could find peace, no place that had not been subject to air, light, or noise pollution. Sita jumped over mountains of waste and tried to access a water source, but found the water contaminated with human waste, faeces, and even corpses, making it undrinkable. Understandably, people were afflicted with diseases like diarrhea, cholera, typhoid, respiratory infections, and skin and eye infections. Pure water was in short supply, and only a quarter of the total population in India had drinking water on their premises. The responsibility of collecting drinking water fell on women, who often had to walk long distances to fetch water.[132] Sita disapproved of people indulging in mindless wasteful consumption, and emerging signs of an environmental backlash could be seen, which made Sita realise how far nature had receded from human life.

India's growing ambition to become a digital economy was resulting in disastrous consequences for the nation in the form of e-waste generation, which posed a major threat to the environment and to human health. According to the latest report released by the United Nations International Telecommunication Union, The Global E-Waste Monitor 2017, India generated nearly two million tonnes of electronic waste in 2016, out of the 44.7 million tonnes produced globally. The inability of a growing economy like India in not having a sound disposal strategy was not only concerning, but also embarrassing on a global forum. The growing volume of electronic waste, including discarded products with a battery or plug, such as mobile phones, laptops, televisions, refrigerators, and electrical toys, pose a major threat to the environment and human health. In Asia, India is only second to China in e-waste generation, and is plagued by the informal sector that handles a major quantum of e-waste. The informal sector employs nearly one million people who sift through the e-waste with their bare hands, burn it and, in the process, inhale the fumes, causing dangerous carcinogenic damage to their health, and irreversible destruction for the environment. Most of the people working in the informal waste-recycling sector have very low literacy levels and very little awareness of the dangers of the operations. Severe health impacts and environmental damage are widespread in India due to the final step of e-waste processing by the informal sector.[133] Sita was amazed that a country like India could take pride in its economic development, but compromise the environment and health of its citizens.

The laws were in place with the Forest Act, 1927; The Wildlife Protection Act, 1972; The Environment (Protection) Act, 1986; The Air (Prevention & Control of Pollution) Act, 1981; and The Water (Prevention & Control of Pollution) Act, 1974 (as amended in 1988), but where were the law enforcers? Sita tried to advise some people, urging and cajoling them to act, but they responded with anger and irritation on being pressurised to change their behaviour by an oddly-dressed stranger, and that too a woman. Did they not realise that the expanding human populace and a consumption economy were taking its toll on the environment? Sita was learned enough to know that in ancient times, settlements flourished around river valleys. Even cities like New Delhi and Varanasi developed around the banks of rivers, but due to man's short-sightedness, the rich soils were being paved with roads and highways. India, a developing country, was imitating the consumption model of the west, without realizing that the way they were living now was borrowing against the future.

Sita was disappointed that even organisations claiming to be involved in the spread of peace across communities through diverse humanitarian projects—including conflict resolution, disaster relief, sustainable rural development, and environmental sustainability, were actually 'responsible' for 'causing damage and environmental degradation' to the floodplains of the River Yamuna.[134] The National Green Tribunal-appointed expert committee had noted that the rehabilitation of the floodplains would cost over Rs 42.02 crore, and could take up to ten years. The expert committee found that 'approximately 120 hectares (about 300 acres) of floodplains west (right bank) of the Yamuna and about 50 hectares (120 acres) floodplains of the eastern side (left bank) of the river have been adversely impacted ecologically at different magnitudes'. Further, it said that these activities had led to a 'change in topography and habitat diversity, loss of waterbodies and wetlands, loss of floodplain vegetation and biodiversity, changes in substrata—nature of soil, consolidation and compaction, toxic substances and degradation and loss of ecosystem functions'. The tribunal judgment noted that the organisation had caused 'serious pollution on the floodplain of the river' as nearly 35 lakh people had gathered at the site.

> The flood plains are not and cannot be equated to waste lands. They should not be treated as lands lying fallow and utilized in the manner which is unacceptable and would have adverse impacts. It is the duty of the statutory authority, government and the people at large to protect and preserve the flood plains or River Yamuna.

Since the people of India were hell bent on destroying the environment, the responsibility had fallen on statutory bodies to protect it. Sita read some landmark orders passed by the National Green Tribunal, which bolstered the NGT's objective of effective and expeditious disposal of cases relating to environmental protection and the conservation of forests and other natural resources. Devotees, in order to prove their devotion, had started resorting to loud music and chanting. The NGT had directed the devotees to maintain silence while standing in front of the Amarnath Ji Maha Shivling, which is a natural formation in the cave. Due to a hue and cry being raised in the media, which had misinterpreted the order, the NGT clarified that the direction was required to maintain the sanctity and pristine condition of the holy cave on the one hand, and on the other, to ensure that there are no adverse impacts of noise, heat, vibrations etc. upon the Maha Shivling. The Tribunal elucidated that the restriction would not apply to the daily *aarti* that was performed. The bench, meanwhile, also called for a rehabilitation plan for the horses and mules used in the pilgrimage, including the ones at Mata Vaishno Devi, as well as the pollution caused by them. It also stressed on healthcare and the provision of healthcare clinics along the route of the pilgrimage.[135] In another case, the applicants had approached the NGT, seeking a ban on synthetic, glass-coated, and Chinese *manjha* used for kite flying. Earlier, the victims of such threads were mostly birds, and every year there are wide spread reports of thousands of bird casualties due to nylon thread, but now human beings have also come under this threat. One victim died in Moradabad district (UP) while travelling on a motorcycle with his father. He came in contact with the nylon kite thread which, being lethally sharp, slit his throat. Another person had died in Bareilly district (UP) in similar circumstances because of the nylon thread. Sensitive to the issue of public interest, the Tribunal imposed a complete ban on the manufacture, distribution, sale, and use of nylon or any synthetic *manjha*, holding that they were lethal in nature and non-biodegradable.[136]

Sita was reassured to know that the courts and the NGT were as concerned as she was about the state of the Rivers Ganga and Yamuna. A bench of the NGT primarily concerned with the section of the Yamuna which flows in the Delhi, had issued 28 directions to ensure the complete and effective implementation of the recommendations made by the expert committees in their report.

> The State instrumentalities and authorities have failed to discharge their Constitutional and statutory duties, while citizens have failed to discharge their Fundamental Duty to protect the environment, particularly in relation to River Yamuna… The authorities, as well as the people of Delhi

> owe a Fundamental Duty to do everything in their power to ensure restoration of River Yamuna to its natural flow and tranquility. Thus, there is dire need to take stringent and effective steps, with a determined mind, to ensure that none fails in performance of their respective functions, duties and obligations to achieve the ultimate goal of converting 'Maily Yamuna' into 'Nirmal Yamuna' under the project 'Maily Se Nirmal Yamuna' Revitalization Plan, 2017.[137]

The entire issue was divided into two segments—identified by the primary sources of pollution of the Yamuna. The first, pollution resulting from the discharge of industrial and trade effluents; and the second, sewage and domestic discharge and untreated waste entering the Yamuna through different drains. The Bench prescribed a spot fine of Rs 5,000 for anyone spotted throwing waste in the Yamuna. It also levied a fine of Rs 50,000 on the dumping of construction debris in the river. The Yamuna would not need to be cleaned if people themselves were conscious enough not to pollute it in the first place. Or for that matter the River Ganga, which the Tribunal emphasised was not only a sacred river for the people of India, but a lifeline to a large number of cities located on its banks. It expressed concerned that on the one hand, there was a tremendous decrease in the natural flow of the river, while on the other, it was a source of irrigation and drinking water for a large section of the population in cities and villages along the river. Even the Prime Minister of the country considered the cleaning of River Ganga a paramount national project, and provided Rs 20,000 crores towards this task. The Tribunal held that the Constitution of India, and the central and the state governments had to provide a clean and decent environment as well as clean drinking water for the people of India. Since it is evident that the River Ganga is being highly polluted and that the major sources of pollution are the discharge of treated/untreated trade effluent, treated/untreated sewage, and municipal solid waste etc., directly or indirectly into River Ganga, it issued a slew of directives including the banning of all construction activity within 100 metres of the river edge, and prohibited dumping of waste within 500 metres from the river, among others.[138]

Who was she to advise anyone, Sita thought? Did not her love for nature result in her being deceived by her husband and abandoned in the forest? But how could people forget that nature nurtures and provides shelter and sustenance to so many forms of life around it? Was it not an irony that man was destroying nature—the same nature which had given protection to mother Sita.

Sita found India to be a land that remained replete with contradictions. The female force was worshipped in the form of Kali, Durga, Saraswati, and Lakshmi. With recent legislation against cow slaughter, even 'gau mata' or the cow was deified and considered a mother. Nationhood was also personified as female—Bharat Mata. India had had a woman prime minister and president long before many so-called advanced countries, and women had a strong presence across scientific, legal, political, commercial, and creative fields. So how then did these crimes and inequalities persist? What of the rights of the silent majority of daily wage earners that did back-breaking work on construction sites, earning less than their male counterparts, tilling the fields, and surviving human predators in the urban centers? Ram may have forsaken his dharma as a husband, and erred as a king, but Sita would never forsake her dharma. She remained steadfast in her loyalty to Ram and, in spite of his abandoning her surreptitiously, she continued to love him. Revered even by the gods, whenever mankind goes astray, Sita would return to remind us of our dharma and help us find our way, for Sita signified the Absolute Truth—*Satyam.*[139]

Endnotes

1. K.R. Srinivas Iyengar, *Sitayana: Epic of the Earth-born* (Madras: Samata Books, 1987), pp.245–46.
2. Desiraju Hanumanta Rao and K.M.K. Murthy, trans., *Valmiki Ramayana*, 3:9:3, 4a, https://valmikiramayan.net/utf8/aranya/sarga9/aranya_9_frame.htm
3. Chaturvedi Dwarka Prasad Sharma, trans., *Srimad Valmiki Ramayana*, (Allahabad: Ramnarayana Lal Publisher and Bookseller, 1927), 7:26:40.
4. Vishakha Saxena, '10 Sexist Slurs That Show How Ridiculous Indian Politicians Can Be', *India Today,* July 20, 2016, http://indiatoday.intoday.in/story/sexist-indian-politician-comments/1/719939.html
5. In some versions of the *Ramayana*, the decision to mutilate Surpanakha is Laxman's himself and not Ram's. Most poets are uncomfortable attributing the instruction to commit this act to Ram, being aware of its ambiguous effects.
6. The most brutal version of her mutilation is found in the Kamban's Tamil *Ramayana* where there is reference to her breasts being cut off, for it was believed that the power of a woman resided in her breasts.
7. Desiraju Hanumanta Rao and K.M.K. Murthy, trans., *Valmiki Ramayana,* 3:18, http://www.valmikiramayan.net/utf8/aranya/sarga18/aranya_18_frame.htm
8. Sunita Tiwari vs the Union of India and Others, Writ Petition (Civil) No. 286 of 2017 (Public Interest Litigation), https://sabrangindia.in/sites/default/files/pil_on_khatna.pdf?362
9. 'Crime in India: 2016', report published by the National Crime Records Bureau for the Ministry of Home Affairs, 2016, http://ncrb.gov.in/StatPublications/CII/CII2016/pdfs/NEWPDFs/Crime%20in%20India%20-%202016%20Complete%20PDF%20291117.pdf
10. 'Daughter-in-law to be Treated as Family Member, Not Housemaid: Supreme Court', *The Times of India,* May 15, 2013, http://timesofindia.indiatimes.com/india/Daughter-in-law-be-treated-as-family-member-not-housemaid-Supreme-Court/articleshow_b2/20069986.cms?prtpage=1
11. Inserted in 1983, Section 498A IPC deals with a non-bailable offence, which applies to a husband or relative(s) of a husband, of a woman, who is/are subjecting her to cruelty. It is punishable with imprisonment for a term which may extend to three years and shall also be liable to fine. For the purpose of this section, 'cruelty' means—(a)any wilful conduct which is of such a nature as is likely to drive the woman to commit suicide or to cause grave injury or danger to life, limb or health (whether mental or physical) of the woman; or (b) harassment of the woman where such harassment is with a view to coercing her or any person related to her to meet any unlawful demand for any property or valuable

security or is on account of failure by her or any person related to her to meet such demand.

12. National Crime Records Bureau, http://ncrb.gov.in/
13. Bharadvaja Sarma, *Valmiki's Ramayanam* (New Delhi: Supernova Publishers & Distributors Pvt. Ltd, 2015). 7:96, p.544.
14. Rajesh Sharma and Ors. vs the State of UP and Anr, Criminal Appeal No.1265 of 2017, https://barandbench.com/wp-content/uploads/2017/07/6593_2017_Judgement_27-Jul-2017-watermark.pdf
15. The Crime Against Women Cell (CAW) was established in 1983 under Section 19 of the Delhi Police Act.
16. Chaturvedi Dwarka Prasad Sharma, trans., *Srimad Valmiki Ramayana*, (Allahabad: Ramnarayana Lal Publisher and Bookseller, 1927), VR 7.
17. 'Two-Third Married Indian Women Victims of Domestic Violence: UN', *The Indian Express,* October 13, 2005, http://expressindia.indianexpress.com/news/fullstory.php?newsid=56501
18. 'Crime in India:2016', report published by the National Crime Records Bureau and the Ministry of Home Affairs, 2016, http://ncrb.gov.in/StatPublications/CII/CII2016/pdfs/NEWPDFs/Crime%20in%20India%20-%202016%20Complete%20PDF%20291117.pdf
19. Ejaz Khan, 'Top Ten Countries With Maximum Rape Crimes', *Wonderslist.com,* http://www.wonderslist.com/top-10-countries-with-maximum-rape-crimes/
20. Chaturvedi Dwarka Prasad Sharma, trans., *Srimad Valmiki Ramayana*, (Allahabad: Ramnarayana Lal Publisher and Bookseller, 1927), 7:26.
21. Ibid, 7:30:40.
22. K.R. Srinivas Iyengar, *Sitayana: Epic of the Earth-born* (Madras: Samata Books, 1987), Canto 13: Ahalya's Outburst, pp.101–109.
23. Colin Freeman, 'Delhi Bus Rapist Blames His Victim in Prison Interview', The Telegraph, March 1, 2015, https://www.telegraph.co.uk/news/worldnews/asia/india/11443462/Delhi-bus-rapist-blames-his-victim-in-prison-interview.html
24. 'Class 7, 5 Students Gangrape 4-Year-Old Girl in Ludhiana', *Punjabikhurki.com,* January 19, 2018, http://punjabikhurki.com/gangrape/
25. 'No Toilet in School, UP Girl Out to Relieve Herself Gangraped by Seniors', *The Indian Express,* March 28, 2015, http://indianexpress.com/article/india/india-others/no-toilet-in-school-up-girl-out-to-relieve-herself-gangraped-by-seniors/
26. '14-Year-Old Abducted, Raped by Neighbour in Outer Delhi', *The Times of India,* February 27, 2018, https://timesofindia.indiatimes.com/city/delhi/14-year-old-abducted-raped-by-neighbour-in-outer-delhi/articleshow/63086573.cms
27. Priyangi Agarwal, 'Rape Survivor Who Gave Birth Marries Accused Due to Poverty', *The Times of India,* July 31, 2017, http://timesofindia.indiatimes.com/city/bareilly/rape-survivor-who-gave-birth-marries-accused-due-to-poverty/articleshow/59836067.cms

28. Sohaila Abdulali, 'I Was Wounded; My Honour Wasn't', *The New York Times,* January 7, 2013, https://www.nytimes.com/2013/01/08/opinion/after-being-raped-i-was-wounded-my-honor-wasnt.html
29. Charu WaliKhanna, *Women, Silent Victims in Armed Conflict: An Area Study of Jammu & Kashmir, India* (Serials Publications, 2004), pp. 2-3.
30. Human Rights Watch, 'The Killing of Thangjam Manorama Devi' in *These Fellows Must be Eliminated: Relentless Violence and Impunity in Manipur'* (2008), pp.25-37, https://www.hrw.org/reports/2008/india0908/3.htm
31. 'India: Overhaul Abusive, Failing Police System', article published by Human Rights Watch, August 4, 2009, https://www.hrw.org/report/2009/08/04/broken-system/dysfunction-abuse-and-impunity-indian-police
32. Sudeep Mishra, '19-Year-Old Preparing For UPSC Gang-Raped in Bhopal For 3 Hours', *The Times of India,* November 3, 2017, https://timesofindia.indiatimes.com/india/19-year-old-preparing-for-upsc-gang-raped-in-bhopal-for-3-hrs/articleshow/61474704.cms
33. Shruti Tomar, 'Bhopal Gangrape Victim: They Would've Killed Me if I Told Them My Father Was a Cop', *Hindustan Times,* November 5, 2017, http://www.hindustantimes.com/india-news/they-would-ve-killed-me-if-i-told-them-my-father-is-a-cop-bhopal-gang-rape-survivor/story-cRJJ63aG0meIdtv6ABU0xI.html
34. Milind Ghatwari, 'Don't Want to Spend My Life Hearing "Bechari Rape Victim": MP Survivor', *The Indian Express,* November 9, 2017, http://indianexpress.com/article/india/dont-want-to-spend-my-life-hearing-bechari-rape-victim-madhya-pradesh-survivor-4928884/
35. 'MP Govt Responds to Bhopal Gang Rape By Asking Coaching Centres to Close at 8:00 PM', *The Huffington Post,* November 7, 2017, India edition, http://www.huffingtonpost.in/2017/11/07/mp-govt-responds-to-bhopal-gang-rape-by-asking-coaching-centres-to-close-by-8-00-pm_a_23268988/
36. Desiraju Hanumanta Rao and K.M.K. Murthy, trans., *Valmiki Ramayana,* 3:46:19–20, 23a, https://valmikiramayan.net/utf8/aranya/sarga46/aranya_46_frame.htm
37. Ibid, 3:47:3,18b,19a, https://valmikiramayan.net/utf8/aranya/sarga47/aranya_47_frame.htm
38. Aditya Raj Kaul, 'Did We Fail Priyadarshini Mattoo and Make Delhi the Rape Capital?', *The Quint,* January 23, 2018, https://www.thequint.com/voices/blogs/did-fail-priyadarshini-mattoo-make-delhi-rape-capital-criminal-justice-nirbhaya-santosh-singh-cbi-court-murder
39. State (through CBI) vs Santosh Kumar Singh, Criminal Appeal No. 233 of 2000, http://www.ebc-india.com/downloads/santoshsingh_conviction.pdf
40. '"Idiots Are Lined Up at Every Step": An IAS Officer is Harassed During Her Sexual Harassment Trial', *Scroll.in,* August 4, 2015, https://scroll.in/article/746091/idiots-are-lined-up-at-every-step-an-ias-officer-is-harassed-during-her-sexual-harassment-trial
41. Harish Iyer, '"I Am Not the Park Street Rape Victim, I Am Suzette Jordan": Remembering a Survivor's Harrowing Ordeals', *Scroll.in,* March 13, 2015,

https://scroll.in/article/713364/i-am-not-the-park-street-rape-victim-i-am-suzette-jordan-remembering-a-survivors-harrowing-ordeals

42. Mahmood Farooqui vs State (Govt of NCT of Delhi), Criminal Appeal No.944 of 2016, http://lobis.nic.in/ddir/dhc/ASK/judgement/25-09-2017/ASK25092017CRLA9442016.pdf
43. Ibid.
44. Independent Thought vs the Union of India, Writ Petition (Civil) No 382 of 2013.
45. 'Marital Rape', Lok Sabha Unstarred Question No.2872, Ministry of Home Affairs, http://mha1.nic.in/par2013/par2016-pdfs/ls-150316/2872.pdf
46. '"Concept of Marital Rape Can't Be Applied in Indian Context": Maneka Gandhi', *The Indian Express,* March 11, 2016. http://indianexpress.com/article/business/budget/imarital-rape-concept-maneka-gandhi-indian-context/
47. Independent Thought vs Union of India and Another, Writ Petition (Civil) No.382 of 2003, http://supremecourtofindia.nic.in/supremecourt/2013/17790/17790_2013_Judgement_11-Oct-2017.pdf
48. Convention on Consent to Marriage, Minimum Age for Marriage and Registration of Marriages, Article 1.
49. Soni Mishra, 'Marital Rape is Not Just Sexual Violence: Flavia Agnes', *The Week,* September 21, 2017,http://www.theweek.in/content/archival/news/india/dont-criminialise-marital-rape-violence-not-just-forcible-sexual-penetration-flavia-agnes.html
50. The Protection of Women from Domestic Violence Act, 2005.

3. Definition of domestic violence.—For the purposes of this Act, any act, omission or commission or conduct of the respondent shall constitute domestic violence in case it—

(a) harms or injures or endangers the health, safety, life, limb or wellbeing, whether mental or physical, of the aggrieved person or tends to do so and includes causing physical abuse, sexual abuse, verbal and emotional abuse and economic abuse; or physical abuse, sexual abuse, verbal and emotional abuse and economic abuse; or

(b) harasses, harms, injures or endangers the aggrieved person with a view to coerce her or any other person related to her to meet any unlawful demand for any dowry or other property or valuable security; or

(c) has the effect of threatening the aggrieved person or any person related to her by any conduct mentioned in clause (a) or clause (b); or

(d) otherwise injures or causes harm, whether physical or mental, to the aggrieved person. Explanation I.—For the purposes of this section,—

(i) 'physical abuse' means any act or conduct which is of such a nature as to cause bodily pain, harm, or danger to life, limb, or health or impair the health or development of the aggrieved person and includes assault, criminal intimidation and criminal force;

(ii) 'sexual abuse' includes any conduct of a sexual nature that abuses, humiliates, degrades or otherwise violates the dignity of woman.

51. Hardik Anand, 'Roktak: Abortion, Delivery Risky for 10-Yr-Old Rape Victim, Hospital Tells Court', *Hindustan Times,* May 25, 2017, http://www.hindustantimes.com/india-news/abortion-delivery-risky-for-10-year-old-pregnant-rape-victim-decision-left-to-court/story-2MXiQfj9nLklGjWi0oYI2H.html
52. 'Indian Court Rejects Abortion For 10-Year-Old Rape Victim', *BBC News,* July 28, 2017, http://www.bbc.com/news/world-asia-india-40753409
53. Medhavi Arora and Manveena Suri, 'India: Court Grants 10-Year-Old Girl Right to Abortion in Rape Case', *CNN,* May 16, 2017, https://edition.cnn.com/2017/05/16/asia/india-underage-abortion/index.html
54. Tanbir Dhaliwal, '10-Yr-Old Chandigarh Rape Victim Told her C-Section Was Surgery to Remove Stone', *Hindustan Times,* August 17, 2017, https://www.hindustantimes.com/punjab/chandigarh-10-yr-old-rape-victim-delivers-baby-girl-was-told-surgery-removed-stone/story-GnjJK7znbcVoWlimvDVfhK.html
55. Sushil Manav, 'Father, Cousin Booked For Raping Minor', *The Tribune,* November 19, 2017, http://www.tribuneindia.com/news/haryana/father-cousin-booked-for-raping-minor/499812.html
56. 'Mumbai Crime: Father Rapes Minor Daughter For Over a Year', *The Free Press Journal,* November 28, 2017, http://www.freepressjournal.in/mumbai/mumbai-crime-father-rapes-minor-daughter-for-over-a-year/1177785
57. 'Father Held For Raping Minor Girl', *The Hindu,* December 4, 2017, http://www.thehindu.com/news/cities/Delhi/father-held-for-raping-minor-girl/article21256159.ece
58. 'Man Allegedly Raped, Impregnated Minor Daughter Twice; Gets Life in Jail', *NDTV*, February 24, 2018, https://www.ndtv.com/india-news/man-allegedly-raped-impregnated-minor-daughter-twice-gets-life-in-jail-1816737
59. 'Father Held for Raping Minor Girl in Jhalawar', *The Times of India,* December 3, 2017, https://timesofindia.indiatimes.com/city/jaipur/father-held-for-raping-minor-girl-in-jhalawar/articleshow/61899651.cms
60. 'Bhopal School Expels Minor Raped by Father', *The New Indian Express,* January 19, 2018, http://www.newindianexpress.com/nation/2018/jan/19/bhopal-school-expels-minor-raped-by-father-1758219.html
61. 'Snapdeal Abduction Case: Accused Stalked Dipti Sarna "150 Times" Since January 2015', *Firstpost,* February 16, 2016, http://www.firstpost.com/india/snapdeal-abduction-case-accused-stalked-dipti-sarna-150-times-since-january-2015-2628576.html
62. 'Crime in India: 2016', report published by the National Crime Records Bureau and the Ministry of Home Affairs, 2016, http://ncrb.gov.in/StatPublications/CII/CII2016/pdfs/NEWPDFs/Crime%20in%20India%20-%202016%20Complete%20PDF%20291117.pdf
63. Desiraju Hanumanta Rao and K.M.K. Murthy, trans., *Valmiki Ramayana*, 3:47:26–50, https://valmikiramayan.net/utf8/aranya/sarga47/aranya_47_frame.htm
64. Ibid, 3:48, https://valmikiramayan.net/utf8/aranya/sarga48/aranya_48_frame.htm

65. Ibid, 3:49, https://valmikiramayan.net/utf8/aranya/sarga49/aranya_49_frame.htm
66. 'Watch: Two Men Kipnap a Woman in Hyderabad as People Look On', *The Huffington Post,* May 18, 2017, http://www.huffingtonpost.in/2017/05/18/watch-two-men-kidnap-a-woman-in-hyderabad-as-people-look-on_a_22096610/
67. The Indian sari worn by the women of yore had an upper-cloth to hang on the shoulder, covering the woman's bust. Some believe that Sita dropped her whole upper cloth, bundled along with her ornaments.
68. Desiraju Hanumanta Rao and K.M.K. Murthy, trans., *Valmiki Ramayana* 3:54:1-5a, https://valmikiramayan.net/utf8/aranya/sarga54/aranya_54_frame.htm
69. Ibid, 3:58,59
70. Ibid, 3:60, https://valmikiramayan.net/utf8/aranya/sarga60/aranya_60_frame.htm
71. IPC Section 509 provides punishment with imprisonment upto 3 years and a fine.
72. Charu WaliKhanna and Jyotika Kalra, *Sex and Harassment: The Sexual Harassment of Women at Workplace* (New Delhi: Kamal Publishers, 2016), p.130
73. Desiraju Hanumanta Rao and K.M.K. Murthy, trans., *Valmiki Ramayana,* 5:19–20.
74. Kanwar Pal Singh Gill vs. State (Admn., U.T. Chandigarh) thro' Secy. and Anr, Appeal (Crl.) No.1032 of 1998.
75. Desiraju Hanumanta Rao and K.M.K. Murthy, trans., *Valmiki Ramayana* , 6:59–60
76. Lord Brihaspati is the son of Angirasa, one of the *saptarishis* or seven sages, according to the *Shiv Purana.* He has two brothers, Utathya and Samvartana, and has sired children by three women, two of them his wives. His first wife Shuba gave birth to seven daughters—Bhanumathi, Raaka, Archishmathi, Mahaamathi, Mahishmathi, Sinivalli and Havishmathi. His second wife Tara gave birth to seven sons and a daughter. Through his brother Utathya's wife Mamata, he has two sons, Kacha and Bharadwaja.
77. Chaturvedi Dwarka Prasad Sharma, trans., *Srimad Valmiki Ramayana,* (Allahabad: Ramnarayana Lal Publisher and Bookseller, 1927), 7:17:4.
78. Ibid, 3:23:1–2.
79. 'Braid Chopping Panic Grips Mp's Morena', *Nyoooz.com,* August 3, 2017, https://www.nyoooz.com/pdf.php?news_id=885266
80. DNA Correspondent, 'Team of 3 Docs Visits Victim of Braid Chop-off', *DNA,* August 3, 2017, New Delhi edition, https://www.pressreader.com/india/dna-delhi/20170803/281659665124047
81. 'Dalit Woman Suspected of Braid Cutting Lynched in Agra', *The Tribune,* August 3, 2017, http://www.tribuneindia.com/news/nation/dalit-woman-suspected-of-braid-cutting-lynched-in-agra/446577.html
82. 'Minutes of the Meeting of the Statutory Full Commission', minutes published by the Human Rights Commission, February 7, 2012, http://nhrc.nic.in/Documents/MINUTES_STAT_%20FC_07_02_2012.pdfMeeting dated 2012
83. 'Crime in India: 2014', report published by the National Crime Records Bureau and the Ministry of Home Affairs, 2014.

84. Sampad Patnaik, 'Bid to "Disrobe" Women: Odisha Tops National List', *The Indian Express,* December 26, 2017, http://indianexpress.com/article/india/bid-to-disrobe-women-odisha-tops-national-list-crime-molestation-4998746/
85. Amit Kumar, 'Vidisha Teacher Disrobes Girl Students', *India Today,* July 30, 2009, https://www.indiatoday.in/headlines-today-top-stories/story/vidisha-teacher-disrobes-girl-students-53205-2009-07-30
86. Sandhya Nair, 'Woman Disrobed, Assaulted by Six Men in Boisar', *The Times of India,* May 24, 2015, http://timesofindia.indiatimes.com/city/mumbai/Woman-disrobed-assaulted-by-six-men-in-Boisar/articleshow/47406647.cms
87. IPC Section 354C provides punishment with imprisonmentof not less than one year, which may extend to three years, and a fine.
88. 'Voyeurism Case: No Hidden Camera in Trial Room, Says Fabindia', *DNA,* April 4, 2015, http://www.dnaindia.com/india/report-voyeurism-case-no-hidden-camera-in-trial-room-saysfabindia-2074650
89. 'Ahead of Holi, Delhi University Student Says "Semen-Filled" Balloon Was Thrown at Her, Police Trying to Contact Girl', *Firstpost,* February 28, 2018, https://www.firstpost.com/india/ahead-of-holi-delhi-university-student-says-semen-filled-balloon-thrown-at-her-police-trying-to-contact-girl-4370073.html
90. Piyush Rai, 'Sisters Set Ablaze in Sleep, Teen Hints at Stalker Role', *The Times of India,* August 12, 2017.
91. 'Dalit Girl Burnt Alive in UP Village, Police Probing Stalking Angle', *The Indian Express,* February 23, 2018, http://indianexpress.com/article/india/dalit-girl-burnt-alive-in-up-village/
92. IPC Section 354 D provides punishment on the first conviction with imprisonment upto three years, and a fine; and on a second or subsequent conviction with imprisonment upto five years, and a fine.
93. Mateen Hafeez, 'In a First, Mumbai Police Issue "LOC" for Stalker', *The Times of India,* December 18, 2017, https://timesofindia.indiatimes.com/city/mumbai/in-a-first-city-police-issue-loc-for-stalker/articleshow/62111191.cms
94. 'Harassed For Months, Minor Sets Self on Fire', *The Times of India,* April 5, 2015, https://timesofindia.indiatimes.com/city/bhopal/Harassed-for-months-minor-sets-self-on-fire/articleshow/46810935.cms
95. 'India Becoming Hub for Child Prostitution', *The Times of India,* Jan 30, 2010, http://timesofindia.indiatimes.com/india/India-becoming-hub-for-child-prostitution/articleshow/5514551.cms
96. 'Research Study on Human Rights Violations of Victims of Trafficking' conducted by SAFMA on behalf of the National Commission for Women.
97. Sankar Sen and P.M Nair, 'A Report on Trafficking in Women and Children in India 2002–03', report undertaken by the National Human Rights Commision with the aid of the United Nations Development Fund for Women and the Institute of Social Sciences, New Delhi, 2004, http://nhrc.nic.in/Documents/ReportonTrafficking.pdf

98. The Suppression of Immoral Traffic in Women and Girls Act 1956, now Immoral Traffic (Prevention) Act (ITPA), was enacted in pursuance of India's international commitment to ratifying the Convention for the Suppression of the Traffic of Persons and of the Exploitation of the Prostitution of others (signed at New York on 9th May, 1950). The entire focus of ITPA appears to be on eliminating prostitution rather than prevention of trafficking in persons.
99. '13-Year-Old Jain Girl Dies After Observing 68-Day Fast to Bring Good Luck to Family', *The Times of India,* October 8, 2016, http://timesofindia.indiatimes.com/city/hyderabad/13-year-old-Jain-girl-dies-after-observing-68-day-fast-to-bring-good-luck-to-family/articleshow/54750457.cms
100. Chitta Ranjan Chowdhury, 'Mental Depression of Indian Women and High Suicide Rate in South-East Asia is a Big Concern Today: An Anthropological Perspective', *Anthropol 1,* issue 4, 2013, https://www.omicsonline.org/mental-depression-of-indian-women-and-high-suicide-rate-in-south-east-asia-is-a-big-concern-today-an-anthropological-perspective-2332-0915.1000111.php?aid=20712
101 Desiraju Hanumanta Rao and K.M.K. Murthy, trans., *Valmiki Ramayana*, 5:26, 29, https://valmikiramayan.net/utf8/sundara/sarga29/sundara_29_frame.htm
102. 'Worth Just Rs 250, the "Anti-Suicide" Ceiling Fan is Winning Hearts in Kota Hostels', *YourStory,* June 7, 2017, https://yourstory.com/2017/06/anti-suicide-rods-kota-sharad-ashrani/
103. 'Kota: Student Hostels to Get Ceiling Fans With Springs, Censors to Check Suicides', *The Indian Express,* March 30, 2017, http://indianexpress.com/article/india/ceiling-fans-with-springs-sensors-to-check-suicides-in-kota-4592665/
104. IPC section 306 provides punishment for abetment of suicide with imprisonment upto ten years and a fine.
105. 'Crime in India: 2016', report published by the National Crime Records Bureau and the Ministry of Home Affairs, 2016.
106. Chaturvedi Dwarka Prasad Sharma, trans., *Srimad Valmiki Ramayana*, (Allahabad: Ramnarayana Lal Publisher and Bookseller, 1927), 7:45.
107. Ibid, 7:46-4.
108. Shyamasundara Dasa, 'Mysteries of the Ramayana: The Real Reason Sita was Expelled by Rama', 2016, https://shyamasundaradasa.com/jyotish/resources/articles/non-jyotish_articles/sita_exiled.html. This story originally appears in the *Padma Purana*, Canto titled 'Patalakhanda', Chapter 57
109. Revaprasada Dvivedi, *Sitacaritam: A New Sanskrit Epic*, (Varanasi: Manisha Prakashan, 1975), pp.29–30.
110. Ibid, p.86.
111. K.R. Srinivas Iyengar, *Sitayana: Epic of the Earth-born* (Madras: Samata Books, 1987), p.591–92.
112. Sanchita Sharma, 'Burden of Birth: Where a Pregnancy Costs a Mother Her Life', *Hindustan Times,* November 22, 2016, http://www.hindustantimes.com/india-news/burden-of-birth-where-a-pregnancy-cost-a-mother-her-life/story-sCN3g6P12U8Pm7g1kvtj5O.html(Accessed February 2, 2018)

113. The Saharia Tribe is the only primitive tribe residing in Baran district in the state of Rajasthan in India. The name Sahariya is said to be derived from the Arabic word 'Sehara' or 'wilderness'. The Muslim rulers found them residing in the jungle, and gave them their present name 'Sahr' which means 'Jungle'. The Saharia are the only primitive tribal group (PTG) in the state of Rajasthan. They are concentrated in the Shahbad and Kishanganj Panchayat Samities of Baran district. They are called Saharia due to their habitatation in forest areas. Yet another view suggests that the word Saharia is etymologically derived from the Persian word 'sahra', meaning wilderness/desert/jungle. Accordingly, they came to be called 'Saharia', meaning residents of the jungle. In the state of Madhya Pradesh they are spread in and around the Gwalior district.
114. Vide order dated 28th April 2008.
115. 'Abandoned Indian Women Trapped in NRI Marriage: The Way Out', report published by the National Commission for Women, http://ncw.nic.in/PDFFiles/AIWTNME.pdf
116. Shayara Bano vs The Union of India and others, Writ Petition (Civil) No.118 of 2016.
117. Vicky Nanjappa, 'Triple Talaq Goes Tech-Savvy: Now Valid on Email, Phones and Messages', *Oneindia.com,* December 30, 2016, http://www.oneindia.com/india/triple-talaq-goes-tech-savvy-now-valid-on-email-phones-and-messsages-2304135.html
118. Shamim Ara vs State of U.P. and Anr, Appeal (Crl.) No.465 of 1996.
119. Shalini Nair, 'Why is a New Law Needed For Triple Talaq, Asks WCD Ministry', *The Indian Express,* December 17, 2017, http://indianexpress.com/article/india/why-is-a-new-law-needed-for-triple-talaq-asked-wcd-ministry-4986137/
120. Krishna Priya Pallavi, '16-Year-Old Divorces her Husband Via Triple Talaq Because He Wouldn't Let Her Study', *Vagabomb,* June 17, 2017, https://www.vagabomb.com/Girl-in-UP-divorces-Her-Husband-via-Triple-Talaq-because-he-wouldnt-let-her-study/
121. Desiraju Hanumanta Rao and K.M.K. Murthy, trans., *Valmiki Ramayana*, 3:52:34–42, https://valmikiramayan.net/utf8/aranya/sarga52/aranya_52_frame.htm
122. The King James Bible, The Old Testament, Isaiah 24:5, https://www.bible.com/bible/1/ISA.24.kjv
123. K.R. Srinivas Iyengar, *Sitayana: Epic of the Earth-born* (Madras: Samata Books, 1987), p.606.
124. Desiraju Hanumanta Rao and K.M.K. Murthy, trans., *Valmiki Ramayana*, 4:66, https://valmikiramayan.net/utf8/aranya/sarga66/aranya_66_frame.htm
125. The rakshasa, resisting any outside influence or culture, lived in Janasthana, an area unexplored by the then people of Aaryavarta. The word 'raksha' means protection, and they protected their own culture and ethnicity, and if any outsiders wanted to join them, they had to be in a subservient position.
126. Mayank Aggarwal, '2.5 Million Died Due to Pollution in India in 2015, says Lancet Journal', *LiveMint,* October 21, 2017, http://www.livemint.com/Scienc

e/6j9LCCGcUiOVgG0gHCkr0O/25-million-died-due-to-pollution-in-India-in-2015-Lancet-s.html

127. 'Sadhguru Calls For Concerted Action to Save World's Water Bodies', *Economic Times,* March 22, 2018, https://economictimes.indiatimes.com/news/politics-and-nation/sadhguru-calls-for-concerted-action-to-save-worlds-water-bodies/articleshow/63415016.cms
128. Arjun Gopal and Others vs Union of India and Others, Writ Petition (Civil) No.728 of 2015, https://www.ercindia.org/files/orders/dt%2011112016.pdf
129. Ibid.
130. '17 Million Babies Under the Age of 1 Breathe Toxic Air, Majority Live in South Asia—UNICEF', press release published by the United Nations Children's Fund, December 6, 2017, https://www.unicef.org/media/media_101774.html
131. 'Tribunals Should Facilitate Growth, Not Strangulate it: Vice-President Venkaiah Naidu', *The Indian Express,* November 4, 2017, http://indianexpress.com/article/india/tribunals-should-facilitate-growth-not-strangulate-it-venkaiah-naidu-4921697/
132. 'Water, Environment and Sanitation', article published by the United Nations Children's Fund, http://unicef.in/Story/1125/Water--Environment-and-Sanitation#sthash.8SMIhMiI.dpuf
133. Kota Sriraj, 'Poisonous Menace in Our Backyard', *The Pioneer*, December 28, 2017, http://www.dailypioneer.com/columnists/oped/poisonous-menace-in-our-backyard.html
134. Sowmiya Ashok, 'Art of Living Festival Damaged Yamuna Floodplains, Rules NGT', *The Indian Express,* December 8, 2017, http://indianexpress.com/article/india/ngt-holds-sri-sri-ravishankars-aol-responsible-for-yamuna-floodplains-damage-4972339/
135. Gauri Maulekhi vs State of J & K and Others, Original Application No.473 of 2015, before the National Green Tribunal, Principal Bench.
136. Khalid Ashraf and Another vs Union of India and Others, and People for the Ethical Treatment of Animals (PETA) India vs Union of India and Others, Original Appication No.384 of 2016, and Original Application No.442 of 2016, before the National Green Tribunal, Principal Bench.
137. Manoj Mishra vs Union of India and Others, Original Application No.06 of 2012, before the National Green Tribunal, Principal Bench.
138. Indian Council for Enviro-Legal Action vs National Ganga River Basin Authority and Others, and M.C. Mehta vs Union of India and Others, Original Application No. 10 of 2015 and Original Application No. 200 of 2014, http://www.greentribunal.gov.in/Writereaddata/Downloads/200-2014(PB-I-Judg)OA_18-12-2015.pdf
139. The letter '*sa*' indicates immortality, the word '*ta*' mortality, and the syllable '*yam*' conditions and bridges both the above, hence satyam is indicative of spiritedness and non-spiritedness. The word 'satya' also means truth.

EPILOGUE

Sita departed, content that her agnipariksha was not in vain.
She will rise again to uphold dharma, and act with honour for justice to prevail.
Her virtue is her strength. Her sacrifice should not be mistaken for weakness.
Her eternal legacy remains forever merged with the essence of womanhood.

O bastions of power, honour your responsibility to protect the vulnerable
And uphold justice and equality.

Empowered Indian woman!
Rise up, go forth, unlock your potential within.
Breaching earth's mantle and man-made walls of oppression,
Hold your head up high and live without fear.

Subjugated for centuries, this is your finest hour.
Become pillars of support for each other.
Be a sister, daughter, and mother; most importantly be yourself!
Cherish the dreams you hold so dearly, and live life on your own terms.

Speak the truth, without doubt or hesitation. Pick up a pen and untie your bonds.

With devotion, stand by your man when problems arise, but be strong to raise your child on your own, when your man has left you all alone.

Let the inner beauty you emanate truly set you apart.

Stand strong against the misogynists, don't let their sharp tongues tear you apart.

Bow your head in respect, not shame.

Your accomplishments and failures make you who you are.

Spirited woman, the world is waiting for you.

Let your patience, foresight, strength, and skill
Overcome adversity. Soaring unfettered to an exalted existence,
Expand your wings and fly, let loose your indomitable eternal spirit
For life begins and ends with you.

Woman, you are beautiful because you are you,
And I, Sita, am forever with you.

Acknowledgements

I want to express my gratitude towards my father and life coach, who read the rough draft of the manuscript and gave it direction.

I'm also grateful to my sister, Renuka Wali. This book is the result of her passionate participation and input.

A special mention to Ranjan Khanna, my husband, who has always given me the space and freedom to express myself.

Finally, I would like to thank my editor, Jyotika, for working on the book, and my publisher, Niyogi Books, for having faith in an unusual topic, and for publishing my work.

Thanks for all the encouragement.